MEN OF THE SUPREME COURT: Profiles of the Justices

by Catherine A. Barnes

Facts On File, Inc.

119 West 57th Street, New York, N.Y. 10019

49938

MEN OF THE SUPREME COURT: Profiles of the Justices

Copyright, 1978 by Facts on File, Inc.

Library of Congress Cataloging in Publication Data

Barnes, Catherine A
   Men of the Supreme Court.

   Bibliography: p.
   Includes index.
   1. United States. Supreme Court—Biography.
   2. Judges—United States—Biography.
I. Title. KF8744.B34 347'.73'2634[B] 78-11633
ISBN 0-87196-459-7

9 8 7 6 5 4 3 2 1

PRINTED IN THE UNITED STATES OF AMERICA

Photo Credits: Bachrach Studios 100; Wide World
Photos 114, 134, 148; National Archives, 24, 34,
38, 46, 50, 54, 61, 72, 78, 84, 92, 104, 110, 118,
122, 126, 130, 138, 140, 152, 160, 166.

To My Mother and Father

Contents

Preface

The United States Supreme Court is a unique governmental institution, and the individuals who comprise it can significantly influence the nation's political, social and economic life. This book presents biographies of the 26 men who served as justices of the Supreme Court between 1945 and 1976. Each portrait contains information on a justice's educational background and his political, academic or legal work before joining the Court. It then focuses on his judicial career in the period after World War II and describes his judicial philosophy and general approach in different types of cases. The profile discusses the individual's most notable opinions, his position in important lawsuits and his role in any public events or controversies apart from the Court's decisions. Each biography summarizes, where possible, the scholarly assessment of the Justice's contribution to the Court and to the law.

The introductory essay provides an overview of major trends on the Supreme Court since 1945. It is intended not only to chronicle the work of the justices as a collective body but also to supply a background that will put the views and impact of the individual justices into perspective. This volume also includes a chronological table of appointments to the high bench and a list of major Court cases and their holdings. In addition, it offers a detailed bibliography on both the justices and the Court.

This book grew out of the *Political Profiles* series published by Facts on File. However, it does not simply reproduce the judicial profiles found in those volumes. Many of the entries in this book incorporate supplementary research. Many have been considerably revised in order to bring together the information on various aspects of an individual's life and work. All the portraits include citations to the Court cases discussed.

Nelson Lichtenstein, Thomas Harrison and Thomas O'Brien wrote those portions of the Arthur Goldberg and Earl Warren profiles describing the non-judicial careers of these two men, and I thank them for their contributions. I am responsible for the rest of this work, but I owe a great debt to two people. Eleanora Schoenebaum of Facts on File first suggested this project and, throughout its course, made many valuable suggestions and improvements. My husband, Bruce Fox, gave the manuscript a careful and critical reading and, more important, supplied constant support and encouragement.

Introduction

In the years after 1945 the Supreme Court operated in a world of often rapid political, economic and social change. The United States emerged from World War II as a major international power. The nation quickly became enmeshed in an unremitting Cold War with the Soviet Union, and the tensions generated by that struggle contributed to the development of a strong domestic anti-Communist movement. The postwar era brought significant technological changes encompassing atomic power and space flight, television and computers. A desire for rest and consolidation of the many changes made during the New and Fair Deals dominated the nation's political and social life until the 1960s. Then the civil rights movement, which had grown steadily since the 1940s, helped usher in a new period of awareness and activism. Radicals and reformers focused attention on a broad array of issues including poverty, racism, the environment and the Vietnam war. Congress responded with a spate of liberal legislation. At the same time, a variety of social trends coalesced to raise important challenges to established cultural norms and engender enormous controversy over questions of values, morals and lifestyles.

Throughout the era the Supreme Court faced the task of applying a constitution more than 150 years old to many of the problems raised by modern life. Contemporary public issues frequently found their way onto the Court's docket, and the Justices were often strongly influenced in their handling of such matters by current domestic and foreign events. In the period of Cold War and McCarthyism, the Court mirrored the prevailing mood of caution and conservatism. Later, the Court was at the forefront of much liberal reform, not only sanctioning but encouraging activism and change. When reformist impulses declined in the 1970s, the Court kept pace by moderating its decisionmaking. While the Justices were generally responsive to prominent national trends, their rulings also helped set the course of the country's political, social and economic development. Throughout the period the Court and the nation maintained a complex pattern of interaction, each influencing and reacting to the other.

The Court's constitutional decisions manifested this relationship. For the postwar Court, the rights of the individual presented the major constitutional issues. The Court's repeated focus on problems of individual liberty both reflected, and in turn, enhanced a broader public concern for the status of the individual in the face of the large, impersonal institutions of modern society. The specific constitutional questions the justices decided

1

ranged from loyalty-security probes, malapportioned legislatures and police procedures to civil rights, public protest and the free exercise of religion. In all of these areas, however, the Court had the recurring task of defining the scope of personal freedoms and the relationship between government and the individual.

The emphasis on civil liberties first appeared during the New Deal era. Beginning in 1937 the Court abandoned its former role as the guardian of the rights of contract and private property against government infringement. With the support of an ever-increasing number of Roosevelt appointees, among them Hugo Black, Felix Frankfurter and William O. Douglas, the Court sustained a wide array of federal and state legislation regulating the economy and providing for social welfare. The justices deferred to the judgments of the legislature and the executive on economic relations and legitimized the vast expansion of government power that came with the New Deal. But rather than lapse into passivity after resolving the constitutionality of government economic and social regulation, the Court began to find a new role for itself in protecting individual freedoms. The very growth of big government raised new questions about its impact on personal rights. The egalitarianism inherent in much of the New Deal created doubts about the second class status of racial minorities. The rise of totalitarian dictatorships in Europe aroused concern for safeguarding fundamental liberties in the United States. The Court responded to these currents by starting to examine intently government action that curtailed individual and civil rights.

Well into the 1940s this scrutiny resulted in an expansion of individual freedoms, particularly First Amendment rights. The Court had decided during the 1920s that the First Amendment's guarantees of freedom of speech and of the press applied to the states as well as the federal government.[1] Then, after 1938, the justices developed the "preferred freedoms" doctrine which held that First Amendment rights were basic to the preservation of all other liberties and thus merited special judicial protection. Under the preferred freedoms approach, the Court refused to presume that legislation affecting First Amendment liberties was constitutional, and it placed the burden on government to justify such laws. The Court often relied on this doctrine as it overturned a variety of restrictive state statutes. It afforded new constitutional protection to labor union picketing, public meetings, parades and speakers, the distribution of pamphlets and door-to-door canvassing.[2] The Court secured the rights of dissident political minorities and unpopular religious groups such as the Jehovah's Witnesses.[3] Its only major departure from a liberal course guaranteeing personal liberties came during World War II. In rulings made during 1943 and 1944, a majority of the justices sanctioned the government's program of relocating and interning thousands of Japanese Americans.[4]

In the immediate postwar period the Court's liberal trend briefly persisted. Although it refused to interfere with the war crimes trials of

---

1. *Gitlow v. New York*, 268 U.S. 652 (1925); *Whitney v. California*, 274 U.S. 357 (1927).

2. *Thornhill v. Alabama*, 310 U.S. 88 (1940); *Hague v. CIO*, 307 U.S. 496 (1939); *Lovell v. City of Griffin*, 303 U.S. 444 (1938); *Murdock v. Pennsylvania*, 319 U.S. 105 (1943).

3. *DeJonge v. Oregon*, 299 U.S. 353 (1937); *Herndon v. Lowry*, 301 U.S. 242 (1937); *West Virginia State Board of Education v. Barnette*, 319 U.S. 624 (1943).

4. *Hirabayashi v. U.S.*, 320 U.S. 81 (1943); *Korematsu v. U.S.*, 323 U.S. 214 (1944).

Japanese and German leaders,[5] the Court decided in 1946 that the use of military tribunals to try civilians in Hawaii during the war had been illegal.[6] It continued to protect the rights of Jehovah's Witnesses to proselytize, and it upset a congressional rider to an appropriations bill which in effect forced three federal employes considered subversive by a House committee off the government's payroll.[7] In May 1949 the Court sustained the free speech rights of a public speaker whose anti-Semitic statements provoked a disturbance among his listeners.[8]

The vote in that case, however, was very close, and the sharp division in it reflected a shift taking place on the Court. As a conservative trend took over in domestic politics and a Cold War developed in foreign affairs, the Court became increasingly cautious and began to cut back on the broad scope previously given to civil liberties. More and more, it applied the concept of judicial restraint and deference to the legislature to questions of individual freedoms as well as economics. The Court gradually discarded the preferred freedoms doctrine and substituted a balancing philosophy which weighed individual rights against society's desire for order and security. Justice Felix Frankfurter was the intellectual leader in developing these themes on the Court. He found allies in Robert Jackson and Stanley Reed. Not until the four justices named by Harry Truman took the bench, however, did Frankfurter's views dominate the Court. Fred Vinson, Harold Burton, Tom Clark and Sherman Minton were all men who were moderate in their politics and conservative in their judicial philosophy. Their appointment assured majority support for the notion that the Court must play a limited role, respecting legislative discretion and avoiding any policymaking of its own. With the deaths in 1949 of Frank Murphy and Wiley Rutledge, both ardent libertarians, only Hugo Black and William O. Douglas still espoused the preferred freedoms doctrine and a generally expansive approach to individual liberties.

The change on the Court was most marked in loyalty-security cases. The anti-Communist drive in the postwar era raised a host of First Amendment problems, but for the most part, the Court sustained federal and state anti-subversion measures. In May 1950, in the first major case growing out of the internal security crusade, the Court upheld the provision in the Taft-Hartley Act requiring labor union officials to swear that they were not members of the Communist Party and did not believe in the overthrow of the government by force. Speaking for the Court, Chief Justice Fred Vinson rejected arguments that the oath requirement impermissibly restricted the rights of free speech, thought and assembly, and he approved the law as a valid exercise of Congress's power over commerce.[9] A year later, in June 1951, Vinson again delivered the opinion of the Court when it sustained the conviction of 11 American Communist Party leaders under the Smith Act. The defendants had not been charged with conspiring to overthrow the government but only with conspiring to teach this idea and to form groups advocating the government's overthrow. Nonetheless, Vinson sustained the convictions. He declared that the government could outlaw advocacy of revolution, no matter how remote the chances of a successful revolt, if those

---

5. *In re Yamashita,* 327 U.S. 1 (1946).
6. *Duncan v. Kahanamoku,* 327 U.S. 304 (1946).
7. *Marsh v. Alabama,* 326 U.S. 501 (1946); *U.S. v. Lovett,* 328 U.S. 303 (1946).
8. *Terminiello v. Chicago,* 337 U.S. 1 (1949).
9. *American Communications Assn. v. Douds,* 339 U.S. 382 (1950).

promoting the idea intended to overthrow the government as soon as circumstances would permit.[10]

The Vinson Court did nothing to hinder the operation of the federal employe loyalty program, challenged on First and Fifth Amendment grounds. Although five justices voted in April 1951 in favor of three groups challenging their placement on the Attorney General's list of subversive organizations, the opinion of the Court avoided the question of the list's constitutionality and thus allowed its continued use by the government.[11] The Court's rulings afforded no shelter to aliens who were barred from entering the country without a hearing for unspecified reasons of security or deported because of past membership in the Communist Party.[12] The justices avoided altogether suits raising the constitutionality of the methods used by congressional committees investigating Communism. They did deal with state loyalty programs and, with only an occasional exception, they upheld them.[13]

The Court displayed a similar conservatism on other civil liberties issues. It narrowed the constitutional protection the New Deal Court had given to picketing and allowed more state regulation of the practice.[14] The justices were also restrained in ruling on other state legislation affecting expression. In contrast to their earlier decision in 1949, they sustained in January 1951 the disorderly conduct conviction of a public speaker whose inflammatory remarks had threatened to create a disturbance among a hostile audience.[15] Several months later a majority upheld a city ordinance restricting door-to-door solicitations and, the next year, an Illinois law prohibiting group libel.[16] The Court did bring movies within the scope of the First Amendment's guarantees of free speech and free press,[17] but it was cautious in its handling of the controversial matter of state aid to religious education. In its initial ruling on the question in 1947, the Court sanctioned state payments for the transportation of children to parochial schools.[18] The next year it invalidated a program for released-time religious instruction of public school students as a violation of the First Amendment's ban on establishment of religion.[19] Four years later, however, the Court distinguished this decision and found grounds to sustain a very similar released-time program.[20]

The Vinson Court produced few new developments in criminal law, but its justices did set out the main positions in what became one of the most basic doctrinal disputes of recent Court history. In a famed June 1947 dissent, Justice Black argued that the framers of the 14th Amendment had intended it to extend all of the guarantees in the Bill of Rights to the states.

10. *Dennis v. U.S.*, 341 U.S. 494 (1951).

11. *Joint Anti-Fascist Refugee Committee v. McGrath*, 341 U.S. 123 (1951).

12. *U.S. ex rel. Knauff v. Shaughnessy*, 338 U.S. 537 (1950); *Harisiades v. Shaughnessy*, 342 U.S. 580 (1952); *Shaughnessy v. U.S. ex rel. Mezei*, 345 U.S. 206 (1953).

13. *Gerende v. Board of Supervisors*, 341 U.S. 56 (1951); *Garner v. Board of Public Works*, 341 U.S. 716 (1951); *Adler v. Board of Education*, 342 U.S. 485 (1952); *Wieman v. Updegraff*, 344 U.S. 183 (1952).

14. *Hughes v. Superior Court*, 339 U.S. 460 (1950); *International Brotherhood of Teamsters v. Hanke*, 339 U.S. 470 (1950).

15. *Feiner v. New York*, 340 U.S. 315 (1951).

16. *Breard v. Alexandria*, 341 U.S. 622 (1951); *Beauharnais v. Illinois*, 343 U.S. 250 (1952).

17. *Burstyn v. Wilson*, 343 U.S. 495 (1952).

18. *Everson v. Board of Education*, 330 U.S. 1 (1947).

19. *Illinois ex rel. McCollum v. Board of Education*, 333 U.S. 203 (1948).

20. *Zorach v. Clauson*, 343 U.S. 306 (1952).

A five-man majority in that case adhered to the established view that the 14th Amendment's due process clause incorporated only rights that were "implicit in the concept of ordered liberty." It required the states, they asserted, to observe only those principles of justice that could be deemed fundamental.[21] Under this "fundamental fairness" approach, which was identified most prominently with Justice Frankfurter, the Court decided in 1949 that the Fourth Amendment's prohibition on unreasonable searches and seizures was basic to a free society and therefore applicable to state governments. At the same time, however, a majority refused to hold the exclusionary rule, which barred the use of illegally seized evidence in federal courts, fundamental and thus left it to each state to determine how it would enforce Fourth Amendment guarantees.[22]

At the federal level, the Fourth Amendment presented the most troublesome criminal issue for the Vinson Court. In 1948, with Justices Murphy and Rutledge still on the bench, a narrow majority decided that the amendment required law enforcement agents to secure a warrant prior to a search whenever this was reasonably practicable.[23] Two years later, however, a new majority overturned that judgment and established a more lenient standard on searches in keeping with its general pro-government stance. The "reasonableness" of a search, the Court now said, was the determining factor in its legality, not the presence of a warrant. It upheld the right of police to make a broad search without a warrant incident to a lawful arrest.[24]

Only in civil rights cases did the Vinson Court break from its predominantly conservative mold. It invalidated several California statutes discriminating against Japanese aliens,[25] and it carried forward a trend initiated by the Roosevelt Court of granting greater recognition to the rights of black citizens. Even here, the Court moved with some caution. In 1948, for example, it decided that court enforcement of restrictive covenants was illegal, but it refused to hold the covenants themselves unconstitutional.[26] Similarly, the justices declined the chance offered in three 1950 cases to discard the "separate but equal" doctrine, the constitutional mainstay of segregation. But they still managed to rule unanimously in favor of black plaintiffs challenging segregation in graduate and professional schools and in railroad dining cars.[27] However wary in its approach, the Vinson Court steadily curtailed racial discrimination in voting, education, transportation, housing and employment. Its decisions prepared the way for the Court's eventual rejection of the "separate but equal" principle.[28]

The Court finally took that step in 1954 under the leadership of a new Chief Justice, Earl Warren. Formerly the liberal Republican governor of California, Warren joined the Court in October 1953. Two months later he presided over the reargument of five cases questioning the legality of

---

21. *Adamson v. California*, 332 U.S. 46 (1947).

22. *Wolf v. Colorado*, 338 U.S. 25 (1949).

23. *Trupiano v. U.S.*, 334 U.S. 699 (1948).

24. *U.S. v. Rabinowitz*, 339 U.S. 56 (1950).

25. *Oyama v. California*, 332 U.S. 633 (1948); *Takahashi v. Fish and Game Commission*, 334 U.S. 410 (1948).

26. *Shelley v. Kraemer*, 334 U.S. 1 (1948); *Hurd v. Hodge*, 334 U.S. 24 (1948).

27. *Sweatt v. Painter*, 339 U.S. 629 (1950); *McLaurin v. Oklahoma State Regents*, 339 U.S. 637 (1950); *Henderson v. U.S.*, 339 U.S. 816 (1950).

28. In addition to the cases cited above, see *Terry v. Adams*, 345 U.S. 461 (1953); *Sipuel v. Board of Regents*, 332 U.S. 631 (1948); *Morgan v. Virginia*, 328 U.S. 373 (1946); *Barrows v. Jackson*, 346 U.S. 249 (1953); *Brotherhood of Railroad Trainmen v. Howard*, 343 U.S. 768 (1952).

segregation in public elementary and secondary schools. On May 17, 1954, speaking for a unanimous Court in *Brown v. Board of Education,* Warren ruled that school segregation deprived black children of equal educational opportunities and was therefore unconstitutional.[29] He called for further argument on implementation of the decision and, a year later, again with unanimous backing, took a gradualist approach to enforcement. The Chief Justice remanded the five cases to lower courts and required them to devise equitable programs that would give school officials time to work out the various administrative difficulties accompanying integration but still achieve school desegregation "with all deliberate speed."[30]

With *Brown,* civil rights emerged as the first major area of Warren Court activism and controversy. After 1954 the justices overturned state-imposed segregation in a wide array of public facilities and without using the "deliberate speed" formula.[31] Outside the schools, they ordered immediate integration of public services. Although the Court displayed an occasional sign of caution, it refused to retreat from its desegregation decrees. It reaffirmed the basic holding of *Brown* in a September 1958 suit growing out of the Little Rock, Ark., school crisis and gave notice that, despite the white South's "massive resistance" program, public hostility would not be allowed to thwart desegregation.[32] The justices checked the efforts of Southern states to oust the NAACP from the region or to hinder its operation.[33] They also approved Congress's attempts to promote equality in the 1957 and 1960 Civil Rights Acts.[34]

In other fields, the Warren Court fluctuated durings its first nine terms between a conservatism like that of the Vinson Court and a somewhat cautious liberalism. The vacillations resulted partly from the much closer division between liberals and conservatives that developed on the bench in the late 1950s. After initially siding with the conservative majority, Earl Warren changed his stance and by mid-1956, voted regularly with Justices Black and Douglas. William Brennan aligned himself with the libertarians from the outset of his Supreme Court career in October 1956. Potter Stewart was a moderate jurist as was John Marshall Harlan initially. Harlan, however, soon became a leading exponent of judicial conservatism. The last Eisenhower appointee, Charles Whittaker, pursued a largely conservative course throughout his years on the bench. As a result of these personnel changes, the Warren Court had a four-man liberal core after 1956. If only one of the justices near the center of the bench joined them, the liberals could win a close case. The Court was still in the hands of moderately conservative judges who supported a policy of judicial restraint. However this control was now more precarious, and occasionally the balance shifted to the liberals.

The Court's loyalty-security decisions demonstrated how liberal victories were sometimes achieved. In Warren's first term on the bench, the Vinson Court trend in loyalty cases continued, and the justices upheld state and

---

29. 347 U.S. 483 (1954).

30. *Brown v. Board of Education,* 349 U.S. 294 (1955).

31. See, for example, *Mayor and City Council of Baltimore v. Dawson,* 350 U.S. 877 (1955): *Holmes v. City of Atlanta,* 350 U.S. 879 (1955); *Gayle v. Browder,* 352 U.S. 903 (1956); *New Orleans City Park Improvement Assn. v. Detiege,* 358 U.S. 54 (1958).

32. *Cooper v. Aaron,* 358 U.S. 1 (1958).

33. *NAACP v. Alabama,* 357 U.S. 449 (1958); *Bates v. City of Little Rock,* 361 U.S. 516 (1960).

34. *U.S. v. Raines,* 362 U.S. 17 (1960); *U.S. v Thomas,* 362 U.S. 58 (1960); *Alabama v. U.S.,* 371 U.S. 37 (1962).

federal security actions against individual rights claims.[35] During the next two terms, however, a wavering majority often ruled against the government in subversion cases, but on narrow grounds. It invalidated government action for statutory or procedural reasons and avoided any constitutionally based decisions. This tactic allowed the Court to afford some protection to civil liberties, but without placing any absolute barriers in the way of government anti-subversive efforts. Federal and state officials could still use various means to protect national security interests, but their programs had to be more carefully drawn and more procedurally correct.

Thus, in two federal employe loyalty cases in 1955 and 1956, the Court ruled in favor of individuals who challenged their security discharges but without determining the constitutionality of the government's loyalty program. In one instance, the Court held, the Loyalty Review Board exceeded the powers given it by executive order, and in the other, the dismissal was not authorized by federal law.[36] In April 1956 the justices refused to pass judgment on a provision in the 1950 Internal Security Act requiring Communist-action organizations to register with the government. Instead, a majority revoked an order from the Subversive Activities Control Board (SACB) for the Communist Party to register because the board's findings rested in part on allegedly perjured testimony.[37] That same month the Court banned state prosecutions for sedition against the United States on the ground that Congress had pre-empted this field in the 1940 Smith Act.[38]

This new liberal bent culminated in a series of widely publicized rulings in the spring of 1957. In two cases the Court overturned the refusal of state bar associations to admit candidates solely because of actual or alleged Communist backgrounds as a denial of due process.[39] A majority also reversed the perjury conviction of a labor union official for allegedly filing a false non-Communist affidavit and stated that the defense in a federal criminal trial must be allowed to see FBI reports made by individuals who testified as government witnesses.[40] Then, on "Red Monday," as critics called it, the Court nullified the convictions of several secondary leaders of the Communist Party for violation of the Smith Act. Without overruling its earlier Smith Act decision, the majority construed the provisions in the law prohibiting the organization of subversive groups and advocacy of overthrow of the government so narrowly that successful prosecutions under them became virtually impossible.[41] On the same day the Court set aside the contempt convictions of witnesses who failed to answer certain questions during state and congressional anti-Communist probes. Technically, the holdings were narrow and the convictions fell because of procedural defects. But Chief Justice Warren's opinions in the two cases lectured Congress and the states on the limits of legislative investigatory powers and seemed, at first glance, to place substantial restrictions on the activities of legislative committees.[42]

The trend toward greater liberalism in loyalty-security cases proved shortlived, however. The Court's anti-government decisions provoked tremendous controversy, despite their narrow basis. In the face of this

---

35. *Barsky v. Board of Regents*, 347 U.S. 442 (1954); *Galvan v. Press*, 347 U.S. 522 (1954).
36. *Peters v. Hobby*, 349 U.S. 331 (1955); *Cole v. Young*, 351 U.S. 536 (1956).
37. *Communist Party v. SACB*, 351 U.S. 115 (1956).
38. *Pennsylvania v. Nelson*, 350 U.S. 497 (1956).
39. *Schware v. New Mexico*, 353 U.S. 232 (1957); *Konigsberg v. California*, 353 U.S. 252 (1957).
40. *Jencks v. U.S.*, 353 U.S. 657 (1957).
41. *Yates v. U.S.*, 354 U.S. 298 (1957).
42. *Watkins v. U.S.*, 354 U.S. 178 (1957); *Sweezy v. New Hampshire*, 354 U.S. 234 (1957).

heightened criticism, judicial conservatism reasserted itself on the Court. During the next term a majority upheld the dismissal of municipal employes for failure to reply to their superiors' questions about membership in the Communist Party.[43] The Court also sustained a section of the 1940 Nationality Act revoking the citizenship of Americans who voted in foreign elections.[44] A narrow majority did overturn another expatriation provision in the same law, and the Court upset the State Department's policy of denying passports to members of the Communist Party.[45] Nevertheless, the shift back to judicial restraint became predominant in the next few years. In June 1959 the Court approved the contempt convictions of individuals who declined to answer state and congressional committee inquiries about Communism. A five-man majority distinguished the very similar 1957 Court decisions and sanctioned the use of legislative power against First Amendment challenges.[46] In April 1961 the conservatives upheld the refusal of state bar examiners to admit an individual who would not answer questions about Communist Party affiliations.[47] Shortly afterwards the Court found valid a new SACB order requiring the Communist Party to register with the government.[48] By a five-to-four vote the Court also sustained the clause in the Smith Act making knowing membership in an organization advocating violent overthrow of the government a crime. Once again, though, the justices construed the provision so strictly that any future prosecutions under it became extremely difficult.[49]

The Court's liberal members prevailed in only a few cases during this period. In June 1959 a majority invalidated a government industrial security program that denied individuals the right to confront and cross-examine their accusers on the ground that neither Congress nor the President had authorized such procedures.[50] The Court unanimously overturned a Florida loyalty oath law in December 1961 because it was unconstitutionally vague.[51] Such decisions had become exceptional, however; judicial conservatism once more dominated loyalty-security issues.

In criminal cases the Warren Court was moderate in its early years, but there were some portents of things to come. A majority ruled in April 1956 that the states had to supply indigent prisoners with a free trial transcript if it was necessary to appeal a conviction.[52] The Court extended a 1943 precedent in June 1957 to hold that any confession obtained during an unnecessary delay between the arrest and arraignment of a defendant was inadmissible in federal court.[53] It began finding a constitutional dimension to the problem of electronic eavesdropping by ruling that the use of a "bug" that physically intruded into a defendant's home violated the Fourth Amendment.[54] Although it continued to resist incorporation of the Bill of Rights to the states and to decide the constitutional claims of state prisoners on a case-by-case basis, the Court did change its mind about the exclusionary rule. In June 1961 it reversed

---

43. *Beilan v. Board of Education*, 357 U.S. 399 (1958); *Lerner v. Casey*, 357 U.S. 468 (1958).
44. *Perez v. Brownell*, 356 U.S. 44 (1958).
45. *Trop v. Dulles*, 356 U.S. 86 (1958); *Kent v. Dulles*, 357 U.S. 116 (1958).
46. *Uphaus v. Wyman*, 360 U.S. 72 (1959); *Barenblatt v. U.S.*, 360 U.S. 109 (1959).
47. *Konigsberg v. California*, 366 U.S. 36 (1961).
48. *Communist Party v. SACB*, 367 U.S. 1 (1961).
49. *Scales v. U.S.*, 367 U.S. 203 (1961).
50. *Greene v. McElroy*, 360 U.S. 474 (1959).
51. *Cramp v. Board of Public Instruction*, 368 U.S. 278 (1961).
52. *Griffin v. Illinois*, 351 U.S. 12 (1956).
53. *Mallory v. U.S.*, 354 U.S. 449 (1957). The earlier case was *McNabb v. U.S., 318 U.S. 332* (1943).
54. *Silverman v. U.S.*, 365 U.S. 505 (1961).

its 1949 decision and announced that evidence seized in violation of the Fourth Amendment could not be admitted in state courts.[55]

In 1962 the balance on the Warren Court shifted decisively toward the judicial liberals with the addition of new justices. That year Byron White replaced the conservative Charles Whittaker and proved to be a surprisingly unpredictable and moderate jurist. More significantly, Arthur Goldberg, who took over Felix Frankfurter's seat, adopted a libertarian stance. His presence gave the Court a clear five-man liberal majority on most issues. Lyndon Johnson's appointees, Abe Fortas and Thurgood Marshall, maintained the liberals' new dominance.

The personnel changes of the 1960s produced a highly activist Court that showed little regard for a philosophy of judicial restraint or for jurisdictional doctrines that limited the Court's role. They also created a libertarian and egalitarian Court whose rulings had an innovative and reformist thrust. Although a majority never adopted the absolutist views that Justices Black and Douglas had come to advocate, still the Court clearly emphasized individual liberties over the authority of government. As it gave increasing scope to individual rights, the Court also sought to guarantee an equality of rights. This theme had been evident all along in the Warren Court's civil rights decrees. But in the 1960s, egalitarianism pervaded its judgments on criminal justice, reapportionment and civil liberties as well. The Court's experiences with racial discrimination seemed to sensitize it to other forms of inequality and to the mistreatment accorded individuals because of their economic status, political views, social nonconformity or lack of power. The Court also betrayed an awareness that minority status often coincided with poverty and powerlessness. Fueled in part by its concern for civil rights, the Court placed itself at the forefront of a movement for greater freedom and equality.

In its criminal decisions the Warren Court engaged in a two-part reform process. Between 1962 and 1969 it gradually extended most of the criminal safeguards listed in the Bill of Rights to the states. Rather than take the "total incorporation" approach urged by Justice Black in 1947, the Court relied on "selective incorporation" to set nationwide standards of fair criminal procedure. On a case-by-case basis, it applied to the states the Fifth Amendment's guarantees against self-incrimination[56] and double jeopardy,[57] the Sixth Amendment's rights to counsel,[58] to a jury trial,[59] and to other elements of a fair trial,[60] and the Eighth Amendment's ban on cruel and unusual punishment.[61] Eventually so many rights were incorporated that even Justice Black declared himself satisfied with the results.[62]

At the same time the Court progressively broadened its interpretation of the Bill of Rights safeguards. It ruled, for example, that the Constitution afforded the right to counsel to a defendant not only at trial on a felony charge, but also for a first appeal of a conviction and at a hearing on possible revocation of probation.[63] The justices also extended the right to an

---

55. *Mapp v. Ohio*, 367 U.S. 643 (1961).

56. *Malloy v. Hogan*, 378 U.S. 1 (1964).

57. *Benton v. Maryland*, 395 U.S. 784 (1969).

58. *Gideon v. Wainwright*, 372 U.S. 335 (1963).

59. *Duncan v. Louisiana*, 391 U.S. 145 (1968).

60. *Pointer v. Texas*, 380 U.S. 400 (1965); *Klopfer v. North Carolina*, 386 U.S. 213 (1967); *Washington v. Texas*, 388 U.S. 14 (1967).

61. *Robinson v. California*, 370 U.S. 660 (1962).

62. See his concurring opinion in *Duncan v. Louisiana*, 391 U.S. at 162 (1968).

63. *Gideon v. Wainwright*, 372 U.S. 335 (1963); *Douglas v. California*, 372 U.S. 353 (1963); *Mempa v. Rhay*, 389 U.S. 128 (1967).

attorney to pretrial police interrogations and lineups.[64] The Court's decisions enlarged the scope of the privilege against self-incrimination[65] and narrowed the range of the search police could make without a warrant in the course of a lawful arrest.[66] The Court overturned precedent to hold the Fourth Amendment applicable to all electronic eavesdropping.[67] It reversed convictions where media coverage infringed on the right to a fair trial[68] and gave juvenile court defendants many of the procedural guarantees possessed by adults.[69]

In its most controversial decree, the Warren Court put constitutional limits on police questioning of criminal suspects. For some years the justices had reversed convictions based on coerced confessions as a denial of due process. In *Miranda v. Arizona*, however, a five-man majority went beyond a "fundamental fairness" standard and held that the Fifth Amendment's privilege against self-incrimination applied to a suspect in police custody. To prevent violation of this right, Chief Justice Warren announced, the police had to employ certain safeguards. They must tell the accused that he had a right to remain silent and that his statements would be used against him in court, that he had a right to counsel and if indigent, to a court-appointed attorney. A confession obtained without such protections was ruled inadmissible at trial.[70]

In contrast to these decisions advancing the rights of the criminally accused, the Warren Court did make judgments favorable to the prosecution. It allowed the states to make a blood test over a defendant's protest to determine if he was driving while drunk.[71] It validated the government's use of informers and said that the government did not have to reveal an informant's identity before trial.[72] It reversed an old precedent that had barred the police from seizing certain types of evidentiary material,[73] and it made clear that it would sanction the use of electronic devices when adequate Fourth Amendment safeguards were applied.[74] The justices also sustained the authority of police to stop and frisk an individual for weapons on the basis of a reasonable suspicion of criminal activity.[75] Nonetheless, the Warren Court's main thrust in the 1960s was in favor of the defendant, not the prosecution; its primary role lay in securing the rights of the individual accused of crime.

The Court displayed a similar concern for the individual in its apportionment decisions. In 1946 a majority on the Court had deemed legislative apportionment a "political question" that was not a proper subject of judicial scrutiny.[76] By the early 1960s, however, most state legislatures and congressional districts had become grossly malapportioned, and there was little prospect of remedy from other branches of the government. With the

64. *Escobedo v. Illinois*, 378 U.S. 478 (1964); *U.S. v. Wade*, 388 U.S. 218 (1967); *Gilbert v. California*, 388 U.S. 263 (1967).

65. See, for example, *Murphy v. Waterfront Commission of New York Harbor*, 378 U.S. 52 (1964); *Garrity v. New Jersey*, 385 U.S. 493 (1967); *Marchetti v. U.S.*, 390 U.S. 39 (1968).

66. *Chimel v. California*, 395 U.S. 752 (1969).

67. *Berger v. New York*, 388 U.S. 41 (1967); *Katz v. U.S.*, 389 U.S. 347 (1967), overruling *Olmstead v. U.S.*, 277 U.S. 438 (1928) and *Goldman v. U.S.*,, 316 U.S. 129 (1942).

68. *Estes v. Texas*, 381 U.S. 532 (1965); *Sheppard v. Maxwell*, 384 U.S. 333 (1966).

69. *In re Gault*, 387 U.S. 1 (1967).

70. 384 U.S. 436 (1966).

71. *Schmerber v. California*, 384 U.S. 757 (1966).

72. *Hoffa v. U.S.*, 385 U.S. 293 (1966); *McCray v. Illinois*, 386 U.S. 300 (1967).

73. *Warden v. Hayden*, 387 U.S. 294 (1967), overruling *Gouled v. U.S.*, 255 U.S. 298 (1921).

74. *Katz v. U.S.*, 389 U.S. 347 (1967).

75. *Terry v. Ohio*, 392 U.S. 1 (1968).

76. *Colegrove v. Green*, 328 U.S. 549 (1946).

political route to reform seemingly blocked, the Court stepped in to make the legislative process more representative. In March 1962, despite vigorous dissents from Justices Frankfurter and Harlan, a six-man majority overturned precedent and decided that federal courts could hear cases involving legislative apportionment.[77] Two years later the Court laid down new standards for legislative districting. In a February 1964 judgment, Justice Black asserted that the Constitution required congressional districts to be as equal in population as possible.[78] Chief Justice Warren delivered the opinion four months later when the Court set the same standard for state legislative apportionment.[79] In April 1968 the Court extended its holding to local units of government.[80] These "one-man, one-vote" rulings established equal representation as a constitutional principle, brought about redistricting in nearly every state in the union, and caused a significant redistribution of political power.

In the loyalty-security field, the Warren Court in the mid-1960s produced almost uniformly libertarian decisions. Although it often distinguished prior rulings instead of reversing them, its judgments effectively undid many precedents from the 1950s and restored the primacy of First Amendment freedoms over government security interests. The Court, for example, overturned various state loyalty programs after 1962 because they were unconstitutionally vague or infringed on the rights of free speech and association.[81] It found grounds for setting aside virtually all contempt convictions of witnesses who refused to answer state and congressional committee questions.[82] A majority held unconstitutional several provisions in federal law revoking American citizenship for certain actions[83] and finally determined in May 1967 that an individual's citizenship could only be relinquished voluntarily.[84] The Court threw out sections of the Subversive Activities Control Act denying passports to Communists and requiring individual party members to register with the government.[85] Without overruling the 1950 decision sustaining the non-Communist oath provision in the Taft-Hartley Act, a majority upset a similar clause in the Landrum-Griffin Act making it a crime for a Communist to serve as a labor union official.[86] The Court also discarded a McCarran Act provision barring Communists from working in defense facilities.[87] By 1969 Warren Court rulings had virtually nullified the Subversive Activities Control Act and made the Smith Act essentially unenforceable. They had checked legislative investigations into subversion, dismantled much state loyalty apparatus, and made it impossible for Congress to remove citizenship. In a clear and sharp reversal of earlier judicial trends, the Court consistently restricted the scope of permissible government intrusion on civil liberties. It afforded greater freedom to dissident

---

.77. *Baker v. Carr*, 369 U.S. 186 (1962).

78. *Wesberry v. Sanders*, 376 U.S. 1 (1964).

79. *Reynolds v. Sims*, 377 U.S. 533 (1964).

80. *Avery v. Midland County*, 390 U.S. 474 (1968).

81. *Baggett v. Bullitt*, 377 U.S. 360 (1964); *Elfbrandt v. Russell*, 384 U.S. 11 (1966); *Keyishian v. Board of Regents*, 385 U.S. 589 (1967); *Whitehill v. Elkins*, 389 U.S. 54 (1967).

82. *Gibson v. Florida Legislative Investigation Committee*, 372 U.S. 539 (1963); *Yellin v. U.S.*, 374 U.S. 109 (1963); *Gojack v. U.S.*, 384 U.S. 702 (1966); *DeGregory v. Attorney General of New Hampshire*, 383 U.S. 825 (1966).

83. *Kennedy v. Mendoza-Martinez*, 372 U.S. 144 (1963); *Schneider v. Rusk*, 377 U.S. 163 (1964).

84. *Afroyim v. Rusk*, 387 U.S. 253 (1967).

85. *Aptheker v. Secretary of State*, 378 U.S. 500 (1964); *Albertson v. SACB*, 382 U.S. 70 (1965).

86. *U.S. v. Brown*, 381 U.S. 437 (1965).

87. *U.S. v. Robel*, 389 U.S. 258 (1967).

political groups while at the same time broadening the range of individual rights generally.

The Warren Court was equally libertarian on other First Amendment issues. It insisted on strict separation of church and state and declared unconstitutional the use of an official, nondenominational prayer, Bible-reading and the recitation of the Lord's Prayer in public schools.[88] The Court also widened the freedom of the press by granting First Amendment protection to certain libelous utterances. In an unprecedented March 1964 decision, it overturned the libel judgment a Southern city official had won against *The New York Times* and announced that a public official could collect damages for a defamatory falsehood relating to his official conduct only if he proved that it had been made with "actual malice." The statement, in other words, could not be an error made in good faith or even negligently but had to be published with the knowledge that it was false or with reckless disregard of its truth or falsity.[89] The Court extended this holding during the next few years to criminal as well as civil libel prosecutions, to invasion of privacy suits against the media and to a broader range of public officials and figures.[90]

Warren Court rulings also limited government attempts at censorship in the realm of obscenity. In a June 1957 case, the justices had decided that obscenity was outside the scope of the First Amendment, and they then tried to define obscenity in a way that made it clearly distinguishable from constitutionally protected material.[91] They were not very successful in this. Probably no other area of the law fragmented the Court so badly. Still, with the exception of one 1966 case,[92] the Court's efforts produced increasingly narrow definitions of obscenity.[93] At the same time the Court lay down stricter procedural standards for government censorship schemes to ensure that protected materials were not suppressed.[94] In the end the Court's obscenity judgments resulted in much greater freedom of sexual expression.

During the 1960s the Warren Court continued to advance the rights of blacks. The justices faced more difficult issues, however, and the unity they had long displayed on civil rights broke down. One key problem stemmed from precedents that had established that the 14th Amendment barred racial discrimination only by the states, not by private parties.[95] Beginning with the student sit-ins in 1960, the civil rights movement repeatedly forced on the Court the question of where the line between government and private action was to be drawn. The Court never really resolved this dilemma with regard to the sit-ins. It initially demonstrated much sympathy for the student protesters, and it found various narrow grounds on which to reverse their convictions

---

88. *Engel v. Vitale*, 370 U.S. 421 (1962); *School District of Abington Township v. Schempp*, 374 U.S. 203 (1963).

89. *New York Times Co. v. Sullivan*, 376 U.S. 254 (1964).

90. *Garrison v. Louisiana*, 379 U.S. 64 (1964); *Time, Inc. v. Hill*, 385 U.S. 374 (1967); *Rosenblatt v. Baer*, 383 U.S. 75 (1966); *Curtis Publishing Co. v. Butts*, 388 U.S. 130 (1967).

91. *Roth v. U.S.*, 354 U.S. 476 (1957).

92. *Ginzburg v. U.S.*, 383 U.S. 463 (1966).

93. *Manual Enterprises Inc. v. Day*, 370 U.S. 478 (1962); *Jacobellis v. Ohio*, 378 U.S. 184 (1964); *Memoirs v. Massachusetts*, 383 U.S. 413 (1966); *Mishkin v. New York*, 383 U.S. 502 (1966). See also *Stanley v. Georgia*, 394 U.S. 557 (1969).

94. *Marcus v. Search Warrant of Property*, 367 U.S. 717 (1961); *Bantam Books Inc. v. Sullivan*, 372 U.S. 58 (1963); *A Quantity of Books v. Kansas*, 378 U.S. 205 (1964); *Freedman v. Maryland*, 380 U.S. 51 (1965).

95. *U.S. v. Cruikshank*, 92 U.S. 542 (1876); *Civil Rights Cases*, 109 U.S. 3 (1883).

under breach-of-the-peace or similar laws.[96] Gradually, however, some justices began arguing that discrimination by a private restaurant or store owner was permissible under the Constitution and that a state could prosecute demonstrators who entered such property for trespass.[97] By 1964 the Court was badly split on the matter. The Civil Rights Act adopted that year removed a major source of the problem by forbidding racial discrimination in public accommodations, and in December, the Court unanimously sustained the law.[98] At the same time, a five-man majority decided that the Act in effect voided the many prosecutions still pending against demonstrators who had tried to integrate the places of business covered by the new statute.[99]

on the matter. The Civil Rights Act adopted that year removed a major source of the problem by forbidding racial discrimination in public accommodations, and in December, the Court unanimously sustained the law.[98] At the same time, a five-man majority decided that the Act in effect voided the many prosecutions still pending against demonstrators who had tried to integrate the places of business covered by the new statute.[99]

Other black protests continued to divide the Court after 1964, but a majority managed to overturn the convictions resulting from them through the 1965 term.[100] Then, in November 1966, the Court ruled against peaceful civil rights demonstrators for the first time. By a five-to-four vote, the justices sustained the trespass convictions of protesters who had gathered outside a Florida jail where fellow demonstrators were incarcerated and had refused to leave when ordered to do so.[101] Seven months later a five-man majority also upheld the contempt convictions of Martin Luther King, Jr., and seven other black leaders for defying a state court injunction against mass protests during the 1963 Birmingham demonstrations.[102]

Other civil rights issues proved less contentious, and the Court remained more united on them. The justices displayed a clear and growing impatience with the slow pace of Southern school desegregation. They invalidated pupil transfer and freedom of choice plans that failed to achieve any real integration[103] and ruled unconstitutional the closing of public schools in Prince Edward County, Va., to avoid desegration.[104] The Court approved the 1965 Voting Rights Act in decisions that took a broad view of congressional power under the 14th and 15th Amendments.[105] It eliminated the poll tax for state elections[106] and increased the federal government's jurisdiction in cases of murder and other violence directed at civil rights workers.[107] The justices were very activist on the question of housing discrimination. In May 1967 a

---

96. *Garner v. Louisiana,* 368 U.S. 157 (1961); *Taylor v. Louisiana,* 370 U.S. 154 (1962); *Edwards v. South Carolina,* 372 U.S. 229 (1963); *Peterson v. City of Greenville,* 373 U.S. 244 (1963); *Lombard v. Louisiana,* 373 U.S. 267 (1963).

97. See, for example, Justice Black's opinion in *Bell v. Maryland,* 378 U.S. 226, 318 (1964).

98. *Heart of Atlanta Motel v. U.S.,* 379 U.S. 241 (1964); *Katzenbach v. McClung,* 379 U.S. 294 (1964).

99. *Hamm v. City of Rock Hill,* 379 U.S. 306 (1964).

100. *Cox v. Louisiana,* 379 U.S. 536 (1965); *Cox v. Louisiana,* 379 U.S. 559 (1965); *Brown v. Louisiana,* 383 U.S. 131 (1966).

101. *Adderley v. Florida,* 385 U.S. 39 (1966).

102. *Walker v. City of Birmingham,* 388 U.S. 307 (1967).

103. *Goss v. Board of Education,* 373 U.S. 683 (1963); *Green v. County School Board,* 391 U.S. 430 (1968).

104. *Griffin v. County School Board,* 377 U.S. 218 (1964).

105. *South Carolina v. Katzenbach,* 383 U.S. 301 (1966); *Katzenbach v. Morgan,* 384 U.S. 641 (1966).

106. *Harper v. Virginia State Board of Elections,* 383 U.S. 663 (1966).

107. *U.S. v. Guest,* 383 U.S. 745 (1966); *U.S. v. Price,* 383 U.S. 787 (1966).

majority nullified a California constitutional amendment that repealed state and local open housing ordinances and barred the passage of any future ones.[108] A year later the Court asserted that a provision in the 1866 Civil Rights Act barred all racial discrimination, private as well as public, in the sale and rental of housing and other property.[109]

For all its activism, the Warren Court showed restraint in one area by never taking a case challenging the legality of the Vietnam war.[110] It rendered judgments, however, on related matters such as the draft and antiwar protests. The Court broadened the eligibility for conscientious objector status[111] and determined that the Selective Service System lacked authority to reclassify men who turned in their draft cards to protest the war.[112] It concluded that the Georgia House of Representatives could not deny a black civil rights worker his seat in the legislature because of his criticism of the war and the draft.[113] The justices found more difficult cases involving "symbolic speech" in which they had to rule if actions intended to protest government policies were entitled to First Amendment protection or were simply forms of conduct which the government could regulate or prohibit. The Court was often sharply divided on this issue; its rulings set no fixed pattern. In May 1968, for example, it refused to label the burning of a draft card as an expression of opposition to the war symbolic speech, and it sustained a federal law banning the practice.[114] Less than a year later, though, a majority stated that public school students had a First Amendment right to wear black armbands in school as a protest against the war.[115]

In its last years the Warren Court began constructing a "new equal protection" doctrine with significant interventionist potential. Although egalitarian ideals lay behind much of its previous activism, the Court had based its judgments in only a few areas, such as race and reapportionment, explicitly on the 14th Amendment's equal protection clause. In the late 1960s, however, the Court enlarged its use of this provision. Its decisions raised the prospect that it would invalidate a wide variety of legislation on equal protection grounds, either because it affected a "fundamental interest" or because it involved a "suspect classification." In the latter case the Court deemed certain group classifications, such as those based on race, to require strict judicial scrutiny and upheld them only if the government could demonstrate a compelling public need for them. In March 1966 the Court overturned state poll taxes as a denial of equal protection because the assessments restricted the exercise of a fundamental right to vote.[116] The justices in June 1969 threw out as discriminatory state laws limiting voting in special elections to a certain class such as property owners or taxpayers.[117] They relied on equal protection in April 1969 to upset state residency requirements for welfare as an impermissible restriction on the right to

---

108. *Reitman v. Mulkey,* 387 U.S. 369 (1967).

109. *Jones v. Mayer,* 392 U.S. 409 (1968).

110. See, for example, *Mora v. McNamara, cert. denied,* 389 U.S. 934 (1967); *Holmes v. U.S., cert. denied,* 391 U.S. 936 (1968); *Hart v. U.S. , cert. denied,* 391 U.S. 956 (1968).

111. *U.S. v. Seeger,* 380 U.S. 163 (1965).

112. *Oestereich v. Selective Service Board,* 393 U.S. 233 (1968).

113. *Bond v. Floyd,* 385 U.S. 116 (1966).

114. *U.S. v. O'Brien,* 391 U.S. 367 (1968).

115. *Tinker v. Des Moines School District,* 393 U.S. 503 (1969). See also *Street v. New York,* 394 U.S. 576 (1969).

116. *Harper v. Virginia State Board of Elections,* 383 U.S. 663 (1966).

117. *Kramer v. Union Free School District No. 15,* 395 U.S. 621 (1969); *Cipriano v. City of Houma,* 395 U.S. 701 (1969).

interstate travel.[118] Although the Court did not expressly hold illegitimacy a suspect class, it extended the guarantee of equal protection to laws discriminating against illegitimate children in May 1968.[119] Those decisions suggested that the Court might eventually set aside a host of legislative distinctions based on such factors as length of residence, legitimacy, economic status, sex and citizenship.

The same expansiveness appeared in the Court's due process decisions, where the justices began to broaden their definition of the "liberty" and "property" interests protected by the due process clause. In June 1965 the Court nullified a state anti-contraceptive law because it infringed on a constitutional right of privacy. Justice Douglas's opinion for the Court attempted to extract the right from various provisions of the Bill of Rights. However, as several concurring and dissenting justices noted, the Court had in fact read a right to privacy into the liberty guaranteed by the due process clause.[120] A majority also concluded in June 1969 that a wage-earner's income was property safeguarded by due process, and therefore, a debtor's wages could not be garnished without prior notice and a hearing.[121] In both its due process and equal protection rulings, the Warren Court clearly exhibited its reformist tendencies and its desire to recognize and defend the rights asserted by diverse political and social minorities.

The Warren Court's activism over such a broad array of fields inevitably provoked controversy. Political battles were fought over its school prayer, reapportionment and loyalty-security decisions in the 1960s, but in these areas, the disputes were relatively shortlived. Criticism died down fairly quickly, and the Court's rulings won general acceptance. More lasting contests arose over school desegregation and over the Court's obscenity and criminal rights decrees. Some observers complained more generally that the Court had abandoned its traditional role of slowing and confining social change and instead seemed intent on fostering all political and social reform movements.

Scholarly disapproval took a different course. Legal analysts were bothered less by the outcome in particular cases than by the Court's decision-making processes. The justices' opinions, many commentators asserted, too often lacked clarity and craftsmanship and failed to justify sufficiently new departures in the law. The Court's rulings seemed to reflect the justices' own policy preferences rather than a disinterested study of constitutional and legal issues. The Court disregarded the limitations inherent in judicial power and diminished its own prestige and influence by altering too quickly too many areas of law. The Court's activism, according to such observers, was improper for it usurped the policymaking functions belonging to the legislature and the executive. It imperiled the democratic process by shifting the people's reliance from their elected representatives to the courts for bringing about change.

The Court's defenders answered such charges mainly by pointing to the important reforms the justices had achieved. At a time when no other institution of government was prepared to act, the Warren Court had recognized and responded to the need to modernize various fields of law and to keep the Constitution abreast of rapid social changes. Moreover, its decrees were all aimed at bringing the nation's practices into closer accord with its professed ideals of freedom, justice and equality. In addition, these analysts argued, the Court had always been a political, policymaking institution. Under

---

118. *Shapiro v. Thompson*, 394 U.S. 618 (1969).
119. *Levy v. Louisiana*, 391 U.S. 68 (1968).
120. *Griswold v. Connecticut*, 381 U.S. 479 (1965).
121. *Sniadach v. Family Finance Corp.*, 395 U.S. 337 (1969).

Earl Warren it had simply used the judicial process to advance rather than obstruct democratic, libertarian reform.

The election of Richard Nixon in 1968 seemed to portend major changes on the Supreme Court. Nixon had criticized the Warren Court during his presidential campaign and had promised to send "strict constructionists" to the high bench. During his first term he made four judicial appointments. The new Chief Justice, Warren Burger, and Justices Harry Blackmun, Lewis Powell, and William Rehnquist all declared themselves to be judicial conservatives, and their backgrounds tended to reinforce these statements. With their accession to the bench, there was a widespread expectation that the Court would turn sharply to the right. The Burger Court was popularly portrayed as an institution undoing much of the Warren Court's work, retreating from activism and removing judicial safeguards from individual liberties.

In fact, the Burger Court built a much more varied and complex record in its first seven terms. The Court demonstrated its independence of the Nixon Administration in decisions that sustained the use of busing for school desegregation,[122] denied state aid to parochial schools[123] and invalidated warrantless electronic surveillance in domestic security cases.[124] It rejected the government's attempt to suppress publication of the *Pentagon Papers*[125] and ruled against Nixon in the Watergate controversy over executive privilege and the presidential tapes.[126] The Burger Court also engaged in considerable activism of its own. It threw out state laws prohibiting abortions during the first six months of pregnancy,[127] put constitutional limits on imposition of the death penalty[128] and gave new recognition to the rights of women, aliens, prisoners and mental patients.[129]

In contrast to the Warren era, the Court under Chief Justice Burger did emphasize different values and operate under alternate assumptions. It had a greater commitment to the tenets of federalism and separation of powers. It showed more regard for a policy of judicial restraint and greater deference to other branches of government. The Court displayed more confidence and trust in public officials and gave greater weight to government and societal interests when balancing them against individual rights.

These dissimilar attitudes produced important changes in several areas of law. The Burger Court reversed the direction of criminal rights judgments and set up a less restrictive definition of obscenity. It gave new attention to questions of justiciability and jurisdiction and so denied a Court hearing to many litigants raising significant claims. But even in these areas, the Burger Court for the most part avoided outright reversals of Warren Court precedents. It tended instead to refuse to extend earlier holdings any further or to cut back, without overruling, prior decisions.

In other fields the Burger Court followed a moderate course. It made advances in some areas, though usually with far more deliberation than the Warren Court in its heyday. In other realms it maintained existing law. Much

---

122. *Swann v. Charlotte-Mecklenburg Board of Education*, 402 U.S. 1 (1971).

123. See, for example, *Lemon v. Kurtzman*, 403 U.S. 602 (1971).

124. *U.S. v. U.S. District Court*, 407 U.S. 297 (1972).

125. *New York Times Co. v. U.S.*, 403 U.S. 713 (1971).

126. *U.S. v. Nixon*, 418 U.S. 683 (1974).

127. *Roe v. Wade*, 410 U.S. 113 (1973); *Doe v. Bolton*, 410 U.S. 179 (1973).

128. *Furman v. Georgia*, 408 U.S. 238 (1972); *Gregg v. Georgia*, 428 U.S. 153 (1976); *Woodson v. North Carolina*, 428 U.S. 280 (1976).

129. See, for example, *Reed v. Reed*, 404 U.S. 71 (1971); *Graham v. Richardson*, 403 U.S. 365 (1971); *Wolff v. McDonnell*, 418 U.S. 539 (1974); *O'Connor v. Donaldson*, 422 U.S. 563 (1975).

of its work consisted of applying broad Warren Court decrees to new issues and situations, and thus of defining the exact scope of its predecessor's rulings. Here the Burger Court varied, sometimes checking and sometimes widening earlier decisions. Overall, its role seemed to be one of consolidation. After an era of great judicial activism and creativity in the 1960s, the Burger Court took up the task of reaffirming many of the basic concepts laid down then and of refining, modifying and limiting them.

On racial issues the Burger Court went beyond *Brown* in its first school segregation case by abandoning the "all deliberate speed" formula and requiring the desegregation of dual school systems "at once."[130] It sanctioned the use of busing and racial quotas and the rezoning of school districts as tools to achieve desegregation.[131] It also ruled school segregation in the North unconstitutional when it could be shown that school officials had systematically followed separationist policies.[132] Although the justices demonstrated a commitment to ending state-imposed school segregation, they also set boundaries on the extent of court-ordered desegregation. In July 1974, for example, the Court overturned a metropolitan-wide desegregation order for the Detroit area and asserted that an interdistrict remedy, combining urban and suburban school systems, was improper when segregation had been proven only within the central city's schools.[133]

The Burger Court failed to enlarge the concept of state action under the 14th Amendment and, as a result, refused to hold certain instances of racial discrimination unconstitutional.[134] In June 1976 a majority also declared that even government action with a racially disproportionate impact did not violate the Constitution unless it had a discriminatory motive.[135] But counterbalancing this the Court strongly supported legislative measures to end discrimination. It sustained a federal law prohibiting literacy tests for voting[136] and gave a broad interpretation to the equal employment provisions of the 1964 Civil Rights Act.[137] It decided that an 1871 federal statute that outlawed conspiracies to deprive others of their civil rights could be applied to private individuals as well as state officials.[138] The justices also construed the 1866 Civil Rights Act to invalidate racial discrimination in a community recreational club and in private nonsectarian schools.[139] The Court's generally moderate course in racial matters was later exhibited in the widely publicized *Bakke* case. There the Court rejected the use of strict racial quotas in a state medical school's admissions program but decreed that race could be considered as one factor in determining university admissions.[140]

In cases raising "new equal protection" questions, the Burger Court again took the middle ground. It expanded the equal protection doctrine into new fields. At the same time it avoided placing absolute restrictions on government action in these areas and deferred to legislative judgments more than the

---

130. *Alexander v. Holmes County Board of Education*, 396 U.S. 19 (1969).

131. *Swann v. Charlotte-Mecklenburg Board of Education*, 402 U.S. 1 (1971).

132. *Keyes v. School District No. 1, Denver*, 413 U.S. 189 (1973).

133. *Milliken v. Bradley*, 418 U.S. 717 (1974). See also *Pasadena City Board of Education v. Spangler*, 427 U.S. 424 (1976).

134. See, for example, *Moose Lodge No. 107 v. Irvis*, 407 U.S. 163 (1972).

135. *Washington v. Davis*, 426 U.S. 229 (1976).

136. *Oregon v. Mitchell*, 400 U.S. 112 (1970).

137. *Griggs v. Duke Power Co.*, 401 U.S. 424 (1971); *Frank v. Bowman Transportation Co.*, 424 U.S. 747 (1976).

138. *Griffin v. Breckenridge*, 403 U.S. 88 (1971).

139. *Sullivan v. Little Hunting Park, Inc.*, 396 U.S. 229 (1969); *Runyon v. McCrary*, 427 U.S. 160 (1976).

140. *Regents of the University of California v. Bakke*, 46 U.S.L.W. 4896 (1978).

Warren Court had. The Burger Court, for example, applied the guarantee of equal protection to women for the first time and threw out a number of federal and state statutes on grounds of sex discrimination.[141] However, it declined to hold sex a "suspect classification," and it sustained some laws discriminating against women.[142] The Court upset some, but not all, statutes discriminating against aliens[143] and illegitimates.[144] It varied in its acceptance of state residency requirements for voting, free hospital care and divorce.[145] The justices seemed most wary of nullifying laws because of distinctions based on economic status. They upheld against equal protection challenges a statute setting a ceiling on welfare benefits for each family, public school financing based on local property taxes and court charges in bankruptcy and welfare cases.[146] The Court did rely on equal protection, however, to eliminate the practice of imprisoning individuals too poor to pay criminal court fines[147] and high filing fees that kept poor candidates off election ballots.[148]

The Court adopted a similar stance in due process cases. It extended procedural due process rights into new arenas to guard against arbitrary government denial of an individual's liberty or property. But it again refrained from setting absolute rules and employed a case-by-case approach, deciding in each instance whether a particular interest was entitled to due process protection. In this way the Court was able to keep the growth of due process rights within certain bounds and to restrict the degree of judicial intervention in the activities of other government agencies. Thus, the Court found that welfare recipients had a right to notice and a hearing prior to termination of their benefits, but not individuals receiving Social Security disability payments.[149] The justices awarded minimal due process safeguards to prison inmates before loss of their good-time credits but not before transfer to another jail.[150] They judged it a denial of due process to suspend public school students without any hearing[151] but upheld the dismissal without prior hearing of an untenured state college teacher, a federal civil service employe a state policeman.[152] The Court also concluded that a person's reputation was not liberty or property within the meaning of the due process clause and so no constitutional violation occurred when police listed an individual as a

141. *Reed v. Reed*, 404 U.S. 71 (1971); *Frontiero v. Richardson*, 411 U.S. 677 (1973); *Weinberger v. Wiesenfeld*, 420 U.S. 636 (1975); *Stanton v. Stanton*, 421 U.S. 7 (1975). See also *Craig v. Boren*, 429 U.S. 190 (1976).

142. *Frontiero v. Richardson*, 411 U.S. 677 (1973); *Geduldig v. Aiello*, 417 U.S. 484 (1974). See also *Kahn v. Shevin*, 416 U.S. 351 (1974); *General Electric Co. v. Gilbert*, 429 U.S. 125 (1976).

143. *Graham v. Richardson*, 403 U.S. 365 (1971); *Sugarman v. Dougall*, 413 U.S. 634 (1973); *In re Griffiths*, 413 U.S. 717 (1973); *Mathews v. Diaz*, 426 U.S. 67 (1976); *Hampton v. Mow Sun Wong*, 426 U.S. 88 (1976); *Examining Board of Engineers v. Flores de Otero*, 426 U.S. 572 (1976).

144. *Labine v. Vincent*, 401 U.S. 532 (1971); *Weber v. Aetna Casualty & Surety Co.*, 406 U.S. 164 (1972); *Gomez v. Perez*, 409 U.S. 535 (1973); *Jimenez v. Weinberger*, 417 U.S. 628 (1974); *Mathews v. Lucas*, 427 U.S. 495 (1976); *Norton v. Mathews*, 427 U.S. 524 (1976).

145. *Dunn v. Blumstein*, 405 U.S. 330 (1972); *Marston v. Lewis*, 410 U.S. 679 (1973); *Burns v. Fortson*, 410 U.S. 686 (1973); *Memorial Hospital v. Maricopa County*, 415 U.S. 250 (1974); *Sosna v. Iowa*, 419 U.S. 393 (1975).

146. *Dandridge v. Williams*, 397 U.S. 471 (1970); *San Antonio Independent School District v. Rodriguez*, 411 U.S. 1 (1973); *U.S. v. Kras*, 409 U.S. 434 (1973); *Ortwein v. Schwab*, 410 U.S. 656 (1973).

147. *Williams v. Illinois*, 399 U.S. 235 (1970); *Tate v. Short*, 401 U.S. 395 (1971).

148. *Bullock v. Carter*, 405 U.S. 134 (1972); *Lubin v. Panish*, 415 U.S. 709 (1974).

149. *Goldberg v. Kelly*, 397 U.S. 254 (1970); *Mathews v. Eldridge*, 424 U.S. 319 (1976).

150. *Wolff v. McDonnell*, 418 U.S. 539 (1974); *Meachum v. Fano*, 427 U.S. 215 (1976); *Montanye v. Haymes*, 427 U.S. 236 (1976).

151. *Goss v. Lopez*, 419 U.S. 565 (1975).

152. *Board of Regents v. Roth*, 408 U.S. 564 (1972); *Arnett v. Kennedy*, 416 U.S. 134 (1974); *Bishop v. Wood*, 426 U.S. 341 (1976).

shoplifter in a circular distributed to storeowners.[153]

In reapportionment cases, the Burger Court adhered to the one-man, one-vote principle and applied it strictly to congressional districting.[154] At the state and local level, however, it decided that more flexibility was permissible, and it allowed greater variances from an exact equal population standard than the Warren Court had.[155] The justices also maintained continuity on religious issues. They gave a libertarian interpretation to the right of free exercise of religion[156] and enforced strict separation of church and state by overturning most forms of state aid to parochial schools.[157] They retained and broadened the "actual malice" rule in libel suits brought by public figures against the press.[158] However, the Burger Court put some limits on the "public figure" category and determined that private individuals suing for publication of defamatory falsehoods could recover actual, though not punitive, damages if they proved negligence rather than actual malice by the media.[159]

The Burger Court held to the basic doctrine that obscenity was not protected by the First Amendment and could be suppressed by the government. It established a less restrictive definition of the term, however, and thus reversed a judicial trend toward ever narrower controls on pornography. The Court decreed that local community, rather than national, standards should be used to judge the prurience of a work,[160] and it approved city zoning ordinances limiting the location of adult movie theaters.[161] These rulings attested to the Burger Court's desire to abandon the role of national censor and to turn responsibility in this area over to local units of government. They also pointed up the Court's new inclination to give more weight to broad societal interests when balancing government regulations against individual rights of free expression.

The same tendency emerged in other First Amendment cases, but the government did not always win these contests. Although less libertarian than the Warren Court, the Burger Court constructed a generally moderate record on free speech and association issues. It cut back on the use of the "overbreadth" doctrine as a device to upset laws allegedly infringing on First Amendment rights.[162] It set aside a Warren Court precedent subjecting privately owned shopping malls to First Amendment requirements.[163] The justices halted the trend toward invalidation of all loyalty-security measures by sustaining a Massachusetts state loyalty oath.[164] They denied journalists' claims that they had a First Amendment right to refuse to testify before grand juries about information from confidential sources.[165]

In contrast to these decisions, however, the Burger Court threw out numerous convictions for the use of scurrilous or offensive language in

---

153. *Paul v. Davis*, 424 U.S. 693 (1976).

154. See, for example, *White v. Weiser*, 412 U.S. 783 (1973).

155. *Abate v. Mundt*, 403 U.S. 182 (1971); *Mahan v. Howell*, 410 U.S. 315 (1973); *Gaffney v. Cummings*, 412 U.S. 735 (1973); *White v. Regester*, 412 U.S. 755 (1973).

156. *Wisconsin v. Yoder*, 406 U.S. 205 (1972).

157. See, for example, *Lemon v. Kurtzman*, 403 U.S. 602 (1971); *Committee for Public Education v. Nyquist*, 413 U.S. 756 (1973); *Meek v. Pittenger*, 421 U.S. 349 (1975).

158. See, for example, *Rosenbloom v. Metromedia, Inc.*, 403 U.S. 29 (1971).

159. *Gertz v. Robert Welch, Inc.*, 418 U.S. 323 (1974).

160. *Miller v. California*, 413 U.S. 15 (1973).

161. *Young v. American Mini Theatres, Inc.*, 427 U.S. 50 (1976).

162. See, for example, *Broadrick v. Oklahoma*, 413 U.S. 601 (1973).

163. *Hudgens v. NLRB*, 424 U.S. 507 (1976), overruling *Amalgamated Food Employees Union v. Logan Valley Plaza*, 391 U.S. 308 (1968).

164. *Cole v. Richardson*, 405 U.S. 676 (1972).

165. *Branzburg v. Hayes*, 408 U.S. 665 (1972).

public[166] and for allegedly contemptuous or improper displays of the flag.[167] The justices gave First Amendment protection to commercial speech[168] and afforded theater productions the same safeguards against government censorship that applied to movies.[169] The Court increased the First Amendment rights of students[170] and overturned the refusal of state bars to admit candidates who failed to answer all but very narrowly drawn questions about their membership in subversive organizations.[171] The justices rejected the government's plea that they enjoin newspaper publication of the *Pentagon Papers*,[172] and they confined the use of judicial "gag" orders on the media as a means of ensuring fair criminal trials.[173]

Although moderate in many areas, the Burger Court was predominantly conservative on criminal matters. Compared to the Warren Court, it shifted the emphasis away from the individual accused of crime and the defense of his rights to the needs of law enforcement agencies and the efficient operation of the criminal justice system. It exhibited less interest in checking potential police abuses and greater trust of public agencies such as the police, prosecutors and juries. It generally curtailed the growth of the procedural rights of the accused but broadened decisions favorable to the prosecution. The Burger Court tended to look at the guilt or innocence of a defendant and seemed reluctant to reverse the conviction of someone clearly guilty because of government error. The justices did not overrule any of the major, controversial Warren Court precedents. They just refused to extend them further, discovered exceptions to them, or interpreted them narrowly when applying the in new situations. Even this process, however, made clear the Burger Court's greater concern for the public interest in prosecuting crime than for the criminal suspect's rights.

The Burger Court, for example, restricted a Warren Court judgment affording a right to counsel at lineups to lineups held after arraignment or indictment of an accused.[174] It declined to find any right to an attorney when photographs of a suspect were shown to witnesses of a crime.[175] It sanctioned plea bargaining arrangements[176] and legitimized the use of six member juries and nonunanimous jury verdicts in state courts.[177] The Court ended the extension of procedural safeguards to juvenile courts[178] and maintained that entrapment by the government could not constitute a defense if the individual had been predisposed to commit the crime, with the possible exception of cases involving "outrageous" police behavior.[179] The justices retreated from

---

166. See, for example, *Cohen v. California*, 403 U.S. 15 (1971); *Gooding v. Wilson*, 405 U.S. 518 (1972); *Hess v. Indiana*, 414 U.S. 105 (1973); *Lewis v. New Orleans*, 415 U.S. 130 (1974).

167. *Smith v. Goguen*, 415 U.S. 566 (1974); *Spence v. Washington*, 418 U.S. 405 (1974).

168. *Virginia State Board of Pharmacy v. Virginia Citizens Consumer Council, Inc.*, 425 U.S. 748 (1976).

169. *Southeastern Promotions Ltd. v. Conrad*, 420 U.S. 546 (1976).

170. *Healy v. James*, 408 U.S. 169 (1972); *Papish v. Board of Curators of University of Missouri*, 410 U.S. 667 (1973).

171. *Baird v. State Bar of Arizona*, 401 U.S. 1 (1971); *In re Stolar*, 401 U.S. 23 (1971); *Law Students Civil Rights Research Council Inc., v. Wadmond*, 401 U.S. 154 (1971).

172. *New York Times Co. v. U.S.*, 403 U.S. 713 (1971).

173. *Nebraska Press Assn. v. Stuart*, 427 U.S. 539 (1976).

174. *Kirby v. Illinois*, 406 U.S. 682 (1972).

175. *U.S. v. Ash*, 413 U.S. 300 (1973).

176. *Brady v. U.S.*, 397 U.S. 742 (1970); *Parker v. North Carolina*, 397 U.S. 790 (1970).

177. *Williams v. Florida*, 399 U.S. 78 (1970); *Johnson v. Louisiana*, 406 U.S. 356 (1972); *Apodaca v. Oregon*, 406 U.S. 404 (1972).

178. *McKeiver v. Pennsylvania*, 403 U.S. 528 (1971).

179. *Hampton v. U.S.*, 425 U.S. 484 (1976).

rigorous application of Fourth Amendment standards. They approved third party bugging without a warrant,[180] enlarged the scope of a permissible "stop and frisk,"[181] and authorized a full personal search following a legal custodial arrest, even for such a minor infringement as a traffic offense.[182] The Court declared that incriminating statements obtained from a suspect in violation of the *Miranda* ruling were nonetheless admissible at trial for the purpose of impeaching the defendant's credibility on the witness stand.[183] A majority consistently took a narrow view of the First Amendment's privilege against self-incrimination[184] and repeatedly supported broad investigatory powers for grand juries.[185]

On the opposite side of the record, the Burger Court largely accepted the incorporation of the Bill of Rights. Several justices strongly denounced the exclusionary rule,[186] but otherwise, they affirmed the application of the Constitution's criminal guarantees to the states. The Court extended the right to counsel to misdemeanor cases in a decision that made it impossible for anyone to be sent to jail without representation by an attorney.[187] In several cases, the justices attempted to equalize the punishments meted out to rich and poor,[188] and they invalidated general vagrancy ordinances.[189] They granted some recognition to the rights of parolees, probationers and prisoners[190] and restricted the use of the death penalty by placing constitutional limits on the manner in which it could be imposed.[191] The Court denied the government's contention that it could employ electronic surveillance without judicial warrants in domestic national security cases.[192] It insisted that warrants be issued by neutral magistrates,[193] and it set up a civil damages remedy for individuals whose Fourth Amendment rights were breached by federal officials.[194] But like the Warren Court's judgments in favor of the prosecution, these Burger Court rulings were contrary to the main trend. In the 1970s the judicial balance tipped in favor of government and against the accused.

The Burger Court also changed direction on matters of jurisdiction. The Warren Court had frequently ignored jurisdictional constraints that might keep it from dealing with significant questions. In contrast, the Burger Court heeded the various restrictions on its work and made access to the federal courts more difficult. It reversed a trend toward greater federal court intervention in state judicial proceedings,[195] and it narrowed federal habeas

---

180. *U.S. v. White*, 401 U.S. 745 (1971).

181. *Adams v. Williams*, 407 U.S. 143 (1972).

182. *U.S. v. Robinson*, 414 U.S. 218 (1973).

183. *Harris v. New York*, 401 U.S. 222 (1971).

184. See, for example, *California v. Byers*, 402 U.S. 424 (1971); *Kastigar v. U.S.*, 406 U.S. 441 (1972); *Andresen v. Maryland*, 427 U.S. 463 (1976).

185. See, for example, *U.S. v. Dionisio*, 410 U.S. 1 (1973); *U.S. v. Mara*, 410 U.S. 19 (1973); *U.S. v. Calandra*, 414 U.S. 338 (1974).

186. See, for example, the dissenting opinions in *Bivens v. Six Unknown Named Agents*, 403 U.S. 388 (1971); *Coolidge v. New Hampshire*, 403 U.S. 443 (1971).

187. *Argersinger v. Hamlin*, 407 U.S. 25 (1972).

188. *Williams v. Illinois*, 399 U.S. 235 (1970); *Tate v. Short*, 401 U.S. 395 (1971).

189. *Papachristou v. City of Jacksonville*, 405 U.S. 156 (1972).

190. *Morrissey v. Brewer*, 408 U.S. 471 (1972); *Gagnon v. Scarpelli*, 411 U.S. 778 (1973); *Wolff v. McDonnell*, 418 U.S. 539 (1974).

191. *Furman v. Georgia*, 408 U.S. 238 (1972); *Gregg v. Georgia*, 428 U.S. 153 (1976); *Woodson v. North Carolina*, 428 U.S. 280 (1976).

192. *U.S. v. U.S. District Court*, 407 U.S. 297 (1972).

193. *Coolidge v. New Hampshire*, 403 U.S. 443 (1971).

194. *Bivens v. Six Unknown Named Agents*, 403 U.S. 388 (1971).

195. See, for example, *Younger v. Harris*, 401 U.S. 37 (1971).

corpus review of state prisoners' Fourth Amendment claims.[196] After initially relaxing standing requirements in the early 1970s,[197] the Court began tightening them again in the middle of the decade.[198] It increased the cost of class action suits[199] and threatened many public interest lawsuits by declaring that federal courts could not award attorneys' fees on a "private attorney general" theory unless Congress had authorized it.[200]

In one respect, the Burger Court differed little from its predecessor for it too encountered scholarly criticism. The justices, some commentators asserted, were still result-oriented, allowing their personal predilections rather than the law to decide various issues. They displayed poor craftsmanship, many complained, in opinions that too often made bad use of history and precedent and were faulty or unpersuasive in their logic. Public controversy also continued to surround the Court with individual cases and larger judicial trends both sparking debate. In addition, the Nixon Administration made several judicial nominations that aroused major political battles in the Senate where they were ultimately rejected.

By the mid-1970s questions of individual rights still dominated the Supreme Court's constitutional agenda. The exact issues had changed over the years, but the justices still determined the boundaries between individual freedom and government action in cases involving First Amendment liberties, civil rights and criminal safeguards and in newer fields such as privacy rights and government welfare programs. On many of these problems, the Burger Court was fragmented. The substantial unity the Nixon justices had first displayed on the bench showed some signs of disintegrating later in the decade, and Gerald Ford's appointee, John Paul Stevens, defied easy liberal or conservative categorization. Despite its divisions, the Court followed a generally moderate course. If less responsive to libertarian and egalitarian themes then the Warren Court, it still recognized such values, though in a more restrained and cautious way and with more attention to countervailing concerns. Whatever direction it chose, the Court seemed certain to retain a prominent position in American society, adjudicating important public issues and rendering decisions that significantly affected daily life.

---

196. *Stone v. Powell*, 428 U.S. 465 (1976).

197. See, for example, *Assn. of Data Processing Service Organizations v. Camp*, 397 U.S. 150 (1970); *Barlow v. Collins*, 397 U.S. 159 (1970); *U.S. v. SCRAP*, 412 U.S. 669 (1973).

198. See, for example, *U.S. v. Richardson*, 417 U.S. 166 (1974); *Schlesinger v. Reservists Committee to Stop the War*, 417 U.S. 208 (1974); *Warth v. Seldin*, 422 U.S. 490 (1975).

199. *Eisen v. Carlisle & Jacquelin*, 417 U.S. 156 (1974).

200. *Alyeska Pipeline Service Co. v. Wilderness Society*, 421 U.S. 240 (1975).

Profiles

BLACK, HUGO L(A FAYETTE)
b. Feb. 27, 1886; Harlan, Ala.
d. Sept. 25, 1971; Bethesda, Md.
Associate Justice, U.S. Supreme
Court, 1937-71.

Born and raised in rural Clay Co., Ala., Hugo Black graduated from the University of Alabama Law School in 1906. He practiced privately in Birmingham, where he was elected to several local offices and, for a brief period from 1923 to 1925, was a member of the Ku Klux Klan. First elected to the U.S. Senate in 1926, Black proved to be a strong supporter of the New Deal. He promoted wages and hours legislation and conducted well-publicized investigations of merchant marine and airline subsidies and the utility lobbies. President Franklin Roosevelt chose Black as his first Supreme Court nominee on Aug. 12, 1937. The Alabaman took the oath of office a week later. The next month a Pittsburgh newspaper published evidence of Black's former Klan membership. In an Oct. 1 radio address, Black acknowledged his past tie to the organization but said he had long since resigned and had had no further dealings with the Klan.

On the bench Black soon displayed an iconoclastic streak. During his first term, for example, he asserted that, contrary to long-established precedent, he did not believe the "persons" protected by the 14th Amendment included corporations.[1] He voted to sustain New Deal legislation and opposed the view that judges should determine for themselves the "reasonableness" of economic and social welfare legislation. Justice Black gave wide scope to the federal government's power to regulate commerce, but unlike some other Roosevelt Court appointees, he also accorded the states considerable power over commerce. Black had strong antimonopoly views and, throughout his years on the bench, supported the rigorous application and enforcement of antitrust laws.

Although he continued to influence economic, antitrust and labor law, Black became known primarily for his civil libertarian philosophy. It took the Alabaman some time to develop his ideas on individual rights, but he began taking strong libertarian stands early in his judicial career. In February 1940, for example, Black reversed the murder convictions of four black tenant farmers whose confessions he ruled had been coerced.[2] During 1942 he argued in a dissent that the right to counsel should be guaranteed to all state as well as federal defendants accused of serious crimes.[3] Two years later, however, in one of his most heavily criticized opinions, Black spoke for the Court to sustain the government's wartime evacuation and relocation of Japanese-Americans.[4] The Justice never repudiated his stance in this case, but most commentators judged it an aberration.

In the June 1947 *Adamson* case, Black gave his first full expression to a view that became one of the foundations of his judicial philosophy. When a five man majority ruled that the Fifth Amendment's privilege against self-incrimination applied only to the federal government, not the states, Black in dissent argued that the 14th Amendment was intended to extend to the states all the liberties in the Bill of Rights.[5] Under this "total incorporation" doctrine, Black particularly pressed for nationalization of the criminal rights guarantees in the Fifth and Sixth Amendments. A constitutional literalist, he also contended that the provisions of the Bill of Rights were absolutes that could not be infringed upon by government.

During the 1940s Black also gave greater expression to his theory of the First Amendment. He considered the amendment "the heart of our government"[6] and

1. *Connecticut General Life Insurance Co. v. Johnson*, 303 U.S. 77 (1938).
2. *Chambers v. Florida*, 309 U.S. 227 (1940).
3. *Betts v. Brady*, 316 U.S. 455 (1942).
4. *Korematsu v. U.S.*, 323 U.S. 214 (1944).
5. *Adamson v. California*, 332 U.S. 46 (1947).
6. *Milk Wagon Drivers Union v. Meadowmoor Dairies*, 312 U.S. 287, 302 (1941).

believed its guarantees of free speech, press and assembly to be the most fundamental of rights, the ones essential to the maintenance of all other liberties. He argued that the amendment unequivocally barred all government interference with thought and expression. The government might regulate the time and place of an individual's speech, but it could never, Black insisted, control its content. In both his absolutist approach to the Constitution and his views on incorporation, Black was for years the adversary of Justice Felix Frankfurter, the prime exponent on the modern Court of the theory of judicial self-restraint.

Through much of the 1940s Black was regarded as the leader of a four-man liberal bloc on the Court. The deaths of Frank Murphy and Wiley Rutledge in 1949, however, reduced the liberals to Black and Justice William O. Douglas. During the 1950s Black often found himself in the minority on many civil liberties and criminal rights issues. In the increasing number of loyalty-security cases that came before the Court, for example, Black regularly voted against the majority to overturn the various restrictions and penalties imposed on Communists because he regarded them as infringements on freedom of belief and expression. The Justice dissented in May 1950 when the Court upheld the non-Communist oath provision in the Taft-Hartley Act.[1] He again objected in June 1951 when a majority sustained the conviction of 11 Communist Party leaders under the Smith Act. Black argued that the Act's prohibition of a conspiracy to teach and advocate overthrow of the government was unconstitutional.[2] When the Court reconsidered the Smith Act in June 1957 and interpreted it in a manner that gave greater scope to freedom of speech but still did not declare it unconstitutional, Black wrote a

separate opinion, maintaining that the statute violated the First Amendment.[3]

The Justice also opposed legislative investigations into subversion that probed individual beliefs. He repeatedly voted to overturn the contempt convictions of witnesses who refused to answer committee questions about their political ideas and associations.[4] He joined the majority in two June 1957 decisions setting limits on congressional and state investigative powers[5] and dissented when the Court retreated from this position in two June 1959 cases.[6] In a dissenting opinion in one of the latter suits, Black contended that the chief aim of the House Un-American Activities Committee (HUAC) was to expose and try witnesses who were suspected Communists and to punish them by humiliation and public scorn. As a result, the Committee was not only violating individual rights of free association and expression but was also illegally exercising a judicial function the Constitution had assigned to the courts.[7] Justice Black did get to speak for the majority in two May 1957 rulings placing limits on the legal profession's power to regulate admission to its ranks. He overturned the refusal of state bar associations to admit candidates with actual or alleged Communist backgrounds as a denial of due process of law.[8]

Black's absolutist views generally led him to give wide scope to the criminal rights guarantees in the Bill of Rights. He continually insisted that the states as well as the federal government must supply counsel to all indigent criminal defendants. In an April 1956 opinion he ruled that the states must also supply an indigent defendant with a free trial transcript if it was essential to appeal a criminal conviction.[9] Black believed that the Fifth Amendment's privilege against self-incrimination was beyond the reach of

1. *American Communications Assn. v. Douds,* 339 U.S. 382 (1950).

2. *Dennis v. U.S.,* 341 U.S. 494 (1951).

3. *Yates v. U.S.,* 354 U.S. 298 (1957).

4. For example, *Quinn v. U.S.* 349 U.S. 155 (1955); *Emspak v. U.S.,* 349 U.S. 190 (1955).

5. *Watkins v. U.S.,* 354 U.S. 178 (1957); *Sweezy*

v. New Hampshire, 354 U.S. 234 (1957).

6. *Barenblatt v. U.S.,* 360 U.S. 109 (1959); *Uphaus v. Wyman,* 360 U.S. 72 (1959).

7. *Barenblatt v. U.S.,* 360 U.S. at 134 (1959).

8. *Schware v. New Mexico,* 353 U.S. 232 (1957); *Konigsberg v. California,* 353 U.S. 252 (1957).

9. *Griffin v. Illinois,* 351 U.S. 12 (1956).

government. He dissented from a February 1954 Court judgment upholding a state gambling conviction because he thought the defendant's Fifth Amendment rights had been denied.[1] The Justice also wrote the majority opinion in a well-known March 1960 case, *Thompson v. City of Louisville*, which held it a denial of due process to convict an individual of loitering or vagrancy when there was no evidence to support the charge.[2] In contrast to his expansive view of most criminal rights, Black took a restrictive approach to the Fourth Amendment. In May 1947, for example, he was part of a five-man majority that considerably widened the scope of a search law enforcement officials might make incident to a valid arrest.[3]

Under Chief Justice Fred Vinson, the Court was a divided and faction-ridden institution, and Black figured in the most noted episode of discord. On June 10, 1946, Justice Robert Jackson issued a statement attacking Black for having participated in the decision of a May 1945 case which was argued by his former law partner.[4] Black never responded publicly to Jackson's statement, which was in part a product of the many ideological and personal differences among the members of the Court. Black's defenders, however, pointed out that the partnership in question had ended over 17 years earlier when Black entered the Senate and that other justices had heard cases argued by former professional associates.

The Vinson Court decided a series of cases brought under the First Amendment clause barring government establishment of religion. In the initial February 1947 suit challenging state payments for the transportation of children to parochial schools, Black spoke for the majority and set forth the principle that the Amendment prohibited the state and federal governments from passing laws "which aid one religion, aid all religions, or prefer one religion over another." But he then upheld the state payments in this instance on the ground that they constituted a social welfare measure and not an aid to religion.[5] In March of the next year, however, Black again wrote for the majority to overturn a program of released-time religious instruction conducted in public schools.[6] He dissented in April 1952 when the Court upheld another released-time program in which the classes were held outside the public school building.[7] Ten years later, in a controversial June 1962 decision, Black, speaking for the majority, held that the use of an official prayer in New York State's public schools violated the First Amendment.[8]

Black was fully in accord with Court rulings overturning racial segregation and discrimination, and he supported a series of Vinson Court judgments expanding the constitutional rights of minorities.[9] He wrote the opinion in a June 1948 decision invalidating a California law that barred Japanese aliens from commercial fishing.[10] He joined in the Court's May 1954 *Brown* decision holding segregated public schools unconstitutional.[11] Black wrote the majority opinion in a December 1960 case ruling segregation in restaurants at interstate bus terminals a violation of the Interstate Commerce Act.[12]

After years of dissent on First Amendment and criminal rights issues, Black finally saw many of his views prevail during the 1960s. A liberal majority emerged then which, without accepting all of the Justice's doctrines, took up many positions that he had long espoused on

---

1. *Irvine v. California*, 347 U.S. 128 (1954).

2. 362 U.S. 199 (1960).

3. *Harris v. U.S.*, 331 U.S. 145 (1947).

4. The case was *Jewell Ridge Coal Corp. v. Local No. 6167, UMWA*, 325 U.S. 161 (1945).

5. *Everson v. Board of Education*, 330 U.S. 1 (1947).

6. *Illinois ex rel. McCollum v. Board of Education*, 333 U.S. 203 (1948).

7. *Zorach v. Clauson*, 343 U.S. 306 (1952).

8. *Engel v. Vitale*, 370 U.S. 421 (1962).

9. For example, *Shelley v. Kraemer*, 334 U.S. 1 (1948); *Sweatt v. Painter*, 339 U.S. 629 (1950); *McLaurin v. Oklahoma State Regents*, 339 U.S. 637 (1950); *Henderson v. U.S.* 339 U.S. 816 (1950).

10. *Takahashi v. Fish and Game Commission*, 334 U.S. 410 (1948).

11. *Brown v. Board of Education*, 347 U.S. 483 (1954); *Bolling v. Sharpe*, 347 U.S. 497 (1954).

12. *Boynton v. Virginia*, 364 U.S. 454 (1960).

specific questions. A majority never subscribed to Black's view of "total incorporation" of the Bill of Rights, for example, but the Warren Court, on a case-by-case basis, gradually extended the major provisions of the Fourth, Fifth, Sixth and Eighth Amendments to the states.[1] At the same time the Court liberalized its interpretations of the criminal rights guarantees in the Fifth and Sixth Amendments, thus adopting positions close to those advocated by Black as a result of his literalist approach to the Constitution. In *Gideon v. Wainwright* in March 1963, for example, Justice Black, writing for a unanimous Court, overturned the 1942 ruling from which he had dissented and held that the states must supply free counsel to any indigent charged with a felony.[2] He also joined the majority in the June 1966 *Miranda* decision that ruled that the Fifth Amendment placed limits on police interrogation of suspects and that ordered the police to advise suspects of their rights prior to questioning.[3] In one instance, Black himself moved to a more liberal position than in in the past. In June 1949 he had agreed with the majority that the Fourth Amendment did not require the states to exclude illegally seized evidence from their courts.[4] Black was part of the five-man majority that overturned this ruling in June 1961, but in a concurring opinion he explained that he had changed his position only because he now considered the use of such evidence in court a violation of the Fifth Amendment's privilege against self-incrimination.[5]

The Warren Court also adopted Black's long-held views on legislative apportionment. When a majority ruled in June 1946 that apportionment was a political question which the judiciary could not consider, Black vigorously dissented. He argued that the issue was justiciable and said the Constitution required election districts that were approximately equal in population.[6] In March 1962 a six-man majority in *Baker v. Carr* reversed the 1946 decision and held that federal courts could try legislative apportionment cases.[7] In February 1964 Black wrote a majority opinion extending this ruling to congressional districting. He also held that such districts should be as equal in population as possible so that each person's vote in a congressional election would have equal worth.[8]

Black's arguments for an absolutist approach to the First Amendment also helped move the Court to increasingly liberal positions on free speech, free press and obscenity. In loyalty-security matters, he was still in dissent in June 1961, when the majority sustained federal laws that required the Communist Party to register with the government and made it illegal to be an active member of a party advocating violent overthrow of the government.[9] Soon after this, however, the Court began moving toward Black's position, and he concurred in May 1962 when the majority reversed the contempt-of-Congress convictions of witnesses who had refused to answer questions before a HUAC subcommittee.[10] He voted with the majority in June 1964 to nullify a federal law denying passports to members of the Communist Party.[11] He also joined majorities that overturned a federal law making it a crime for a Communist Party member to serve as a labor union official in June 1965 and voided a set of New York State teacher loyalty laws in January 1967.[12]

1. *Mapp v. Ohio,* 367 U.S. 643 (1961); *Robinson v. California,* 370 U.S. 660 (1962); *Gideon v. Wainwright,* 372 U.S. 335 (1963); *Malloy v. Hogan,* 378 U.S. 1 (1964); *Pointer v. Texas,* 380 U.S. 400 (1965); *Klopfer v. North Carolina,* 386 U.S. 213 (1967); *Washington v. Texas,* 388 U.S. 14 (1967); *Duncan v. Louisiana,* 391 U.S. 145 (1968); *Benton v. Maryland,* 395 U.S. 784 (1969).

2. 372 U.S. 335 (1963).

3. *Miranda v. Arizona,* 384 U.S. 436 (1966).

4. *Wolf v. Colorado,* 338 U.S. 25 (1949).

5. *Mapp v. Ohio,* 367 U.S. 643 (1961).

6. *Colegrove v. Green,* 328 U.S. 549 (1946).

7. 369 U.S. 186 (1962).

8. *Wesberry v. Sanders,* 376 U.S. 1 (1964).

9. *Communist Party v. SACB,* 367 U.S. 1 (1961); *Scales v. U.S.,* 367 U.S. 203 (1961).

10. *Russell v. U.S.,* 369 U.S. 749 (1962).

11. *Aptheker v. Secretary of State,* 378 U.S. 500 (1964).

12. *U.S. v. Brown,* 381 U.S. 437 (1965); *Keyishian v. Board of Regents,* 385 U.S. 589 (1967).

Black believed that even utterances considered "libelous" and "obscene" were protected by the First Amendment. Consequently, he opposed all government censorship of allegedly obscene materials and urged the Court to protect even malicious criticism of public officials.[1] The Warren Court never adopted these views, but it increasingly narrowed the definition of obscenity and raised the level of procedural safeguards in censorship systems throughout the 1960s.[2] In a series of cases beginning in March 1964, the Court also expanded freedom of the press by ruling that a public official could not recover damages for a defamatory falsehood relating to his official conduct unless he could prove the statement was made with "actual malice."[3] The First Amendment also protected the right of free association. Black joined the majority in a January 1963 decision to nullify a Virginia law barring solicitation of legal business because it infringed on an organization's rights of free speech and association.[4]

In the 1960s Justice Black continued to show support for the ends sought by the civil rights movement. In a sharply worded majority opinion in May 1964, he held that the closing of public schools to avoid desegregation in Prince Edward County, Va. was unconstitutional.[5] He voted to sustain the 1964 Civil Rights Act and joined the majority in June 1968 in holding that an 1866 federal law barred race discrimination in private sales and rentals of housing and other property.[6]

Just when Black seemed at the height of his influence, he began taking "conservative" positions that surprised many observers. He dissented in June 1965 when the majority voided a Connecticut anti-contraceptive law as an invasion of the right to privacy. Black said he could find no "right of privacy" in the Constitution.[7] In March 1966 he dissented from a decision that invalidated a Virginia poll tax applicable to state elections on the ground that it violated the 14th Amendment's equal protection clause. Although he had voted in 1961 and 1963 to void the convictions of nonviolent civil rights demonstrators, Black dissented in June 1964 when the Court overturned the trespass convictions of protesters who sat-in at a Baltimore restaurant. Over the next two years, he dissented when the Court upset similar convictions growing out of nonviolent civil rights demonstrations. Black finally spoke for a five-man majority in November 1966 to sustain the trespass conviction of demonstrators who had gathered outside a Florida jail to protest the arrest of fellow demonstrators and dered.[11] The Justice rejected the argument that these demonstrations were a form of free speech and assembly protected by the First Amendment. As he explained in one dissent, he believed the First Amendment protected expression in any manner in which it could be "legitimately and validly communicated." But it did not

---

1. See, for example, Black's concurring opinions in *Kingsley International Pictures Corp. v. Board of Regents*, 360 U.S. 684 (1959); *Smith v. California*, 361 U.S. 147 (1959); *New York Times v. Sullivan*, 376 U.S. 254 (1964).

2. See, for example, *Marcus v. Search Warrant of Property*, 367 U.S. 717 (1961); *Bantam Books, Inc. v. Sullivan*, 372 U.S. 58 (1963); *Jacobellis v. Ohio*, 378 U.S. 184 (1964); *Freedman v. Maryland*, 380 U.S. 51 (1965); *Memoirs v. Massachusetts*, 383 U.S. 413 (1966).

3. See, for example, *New York Times v. Sullivan*, 376 U.S. 254 (1964); *Garrison v. Louisiana*, 379 U.S. 64 (1964); *Time, Inc. v. Hill*, 385 U.S. 374 (1967); *Rosenbloom v. Metromedia Inc.*, 403 U.S. 29 (1971).

4. *NAACP v. Button*, 371 U.S. 415 (1963).

5. *Griffin v. County School Board*, 377 U.S. 218 (1964).

6. *Heart of Atlanta Motel v. U.S.*, 379 U.S. 241 (1964); *Katzenbach v. McClung*, 379 U.S. 294 (1964); *Jones v. Mayer*, 392 U.S. 409 (1968).

7. *Griswold v. Connecticut*, 381 U.S. 479 (1965).

8. *Harper v. Virginia State Board of Elections*, 383 U.S. 663 (1966).

9. *Garner v. Louisiana*, 368 U.S. 157 (1961); *Edwards v. South Carolina*, 372 U.S. 229 (1963); *Peterson v. City of Greenville*, 373 U.S. 244 (1963); *Shuttlesworth v. City of Birmingham*, 373 U.S. 262 (1963); *Lombard v. Louisiana*, 373 U.S. 267 (1963); *Wright v. Georgia*, 373 U.S. 284 (1963); *Bell v. Maryland*, 378 U.S. 226 (1964).

10. *Hamm v. City of Rock Hill*, 379 U.S. 306 (1964); *Cox v. Louisiana*, 379 U.S. 559 (1965); *Brown v. Louisiana*, 383 U.S. 131 (1966).

11. *Adderley v. Florida*, 385 U.S. 39 (1966).

give people a "constitutional right to go wherever they want, whenever they please, without regard to the rights of private or public property or to state law."[1]

During his last years on the bench, Black[5] continued in this vein. He dissented in February 1969 when the Court held that public school students had a right to nondisruptive political expression.[2] He also objected to a June 1971 ruling in which the majority overturned the conviction of a demonstrator who had entered a courthouse wearing a jacket inscribed with a vulgarism condemning the draft.[3] In a June 1967 case in which the majority invalidated a conviction based on electronic eavesdropping, the Justice dissented and argued that the language of the Fourth Amendment could not be extended to protect individuals from electronic bugging.[4] Black protested when the Court in June 1969 limited the area that police could search without a warrant incident to a suspect's arrest.[5] In March 1970 his opinion for the Court held that a disruptive defendant could be expelled from the courtroom and could even be bound and gagged, if necessary, to maintain order during a trial.[6]

Justice Black also resisted efforts to expand the rights of debtors and of illegitimate children through the courts.[7] He considered welfare a "gratuity," not an entitlement, and dissented from rulings in April 1969 and March 1970 broadening the rights of welfare recipients.[8] Black also cast the deciding vote in a set of December 1970 cases in which the Court held that Congress could lower the voting age to 18 for federal elections, but not for state and local contests.[9] For a five-man majority in June 1971, the Justice ruled that Jackson, Miss., officials had not violated the Constitution when they closed all public swimming pools rather than desegregate them.[10]

Based on such decisions, some observers charged that Black was backsliding and "going conservative" in his old age. Others, including Black himself, said the Justice had not changed and that his views were consistent with those expressed years before. Black had always maintained, for example, that government could regulate the time and place of speech, though never its content. Thus he believed it could forbid political expression and demonstrations in schools or on other public property. In contrast to his broad approach to most criminal rights guarantees, the Justice had repeatedly taken a narrow view of the Fourth Amendment's prohibition on unreasonable searches and seizures and had frequently voted against expanding the scope of this provision. Similarly Black had long inveighed against policymaking by judges. He had objected when a conservative Court majority in the 1930s read its own economic notions into the Constitution, and he protested late in his life when he thought liberal justices, using the due process and equal protection clauses, were attempting to graft their personal social and political ideas onto the Constitution. Black's literalism, as some commentators pointed out, limited him to the express provisions of the Constitution and kept him from recognizing any new constitutional rights such as a right to privacy. Other analysts remarked that Black's "conservatism" demonstrated simply that the judicial revolution he had started had passed him by. Many of Black's goals had essentially been achieved, and when a younger generation sought to move beyond them, Black tried to confine constitutional change within the bounds he had originally set.

1. Brown v. Louisiana, 383 U.S. at 166 (1966).
2. Tinker v. Des Moines School District, 393 U.S. 503 (1969).
3. Cohen v. California, 403 U.S. 15 (1971).
4. Berger v. New York, 388 U.S. 41 (1967).
5. Chimel v. California, 395 U.S. 752 (1969).
6. Illinois v. Allen, 397 U.S. 337 (1970).
7. Sniadach v. Family Finance Corp., 395 U.S. 337 (1969); Levy v. Louisiana, 391 U.S. 68 (1968); Glona v. American Guarantee & Liability Insurance Co., 391 U.S. 73 (1968); Labine v. Vincent, 401 U.S. 532 (1971).
8. Shapiro v. Thompson, 394 U.S. 618 (1969); Goldberg v. Kelly, 397 U.S. 254 (1970).
9. Oregon v. Mitchell, 400 U.S. 112 (1970).
10. Palmer v. Thompson, 403 U.S. 217 (1971).

For all the talk of Black's alleged conservatism, the Justice remained in the forefront in his defense of certain rights, even in his final years on the bench. In a March 1969 majority opinion, Black held that the *Miranda* ruling applied once a suspect was taken into custody, not just before questioning at a police station.[1] He dissented in February 1971 when a new majority authorized the use of incriminating statements obtained in violation of *Miranda* at trial to impeach a defendant's credibility on the witness stand.[2] Black voted in June 1969 to make the provision against double jeopardy applicable to the states and in June 1970 to extend the right to counsel to preliminary hearings.[3] He objected in June 1971 when the majority ruled that juveniles had no right to trial by jury.[4]

In February 1970 Justice Black's majority opinion extended the one-man, one-vote rule to state and local elections for specialized bodies such as school boards.[5] In June 1969 he upheld a federal district court order requiring the Montgomery, Ala., school board to desegregate faculty and staff according to a specific numerical ratio.[6] In a majority opinion in a January 1970 case, the Justice held that the Selective Service System lacked authority to reclassify a youth with a valid student deferment as punishment for turning in his draft card to protest the Vietnam war. Five months later Black's opinion for the Court ruled that a person was entitled to conscientious objector status when he possessed deeply held moral or ethical beliefs against war, even if his beliefs were not religiously based.[8]

Black adhered to his absolutist views on freedom of speech and of the press. In a May 1970 majority opinion, he overturned as a violation of the First Amendment a federal law making it a crime for an actor to wear a U.S. military uniform in a production critical of the armed forces.[9] In three February 1971 cases he voted to invalidate state requirements that applicants for admission to the bar take a loyalty oath or disclose membership in subversive organizations.[10] On June 30, 1971 Black joined the majority to deny the government's request for an injunction prohibiting newspaper publication of a classified study of U.S. involvement in Vietnam known as the *Pentagon Papers.* In a separate opinion the Justice insisted that freedom of the press, like other First Amendment rights, was unassailable and that no judicial restraint on the press was permissible.[11]

The opinion was Justice Black's last. On Aug. 28, 1971, he entered the hospital, and on Sept. 17, after 34 years on the Court, Black resigned because of ill health. Two days later he suffered a stroke. Within a week, he was dead at the age of 85.

Throughout his life, Black had been a man of enormous energy and drive. Extremely hardworking on the bench, he had largely educated himself through a program of extensive reading begun during his Senate years. He was an aggressive man with a zest for confrontation and argument that was generally devoid of any personal animosity or hostility towards his opponent. "The paradox of Hugo Black," John P. Frank once said, was "steel and softness, the sharp cutting edge balanced with kindliness."

At his death all commentators agreed that Black had been the most influential justice of his day and one of the most

1. *Orozco v. Texas*, 394 U.S. 324 (1969).

2. *Harris v. New York*, 401 U.S. 222 (1971).

3. *Benton v. Maryland*, 395 U.S. 784 (1969); *Coleman v. Alabama*, 399 U.S. 1 (1970).

4. *McKeiver v. Pennsylvania*, 403 U.S. 528 (1971).

5. *Hadley v. Junior College District of Metropolitan Kansas City*, 397 U.S. 50 (1970).

6. *U.S. v. Montgomery County Board of Education*, 395 U.S. 225 (1969).

7. *Breen v. Selective Service Local Board No. 16*, 396 U.S. 460 (1970).

8. *Welsh v. U.S.*, 398 U.S. 333 (1970).

9. *Schacht v. U.S.*, 398 U.S. 58 (1970).

10. *Baird v. State Bar of Arizona*, 401 U.S. 1 (1971); *In re Stolar*, 401 U.S. 23 (1971); *Law Students Civil Rights Research Council, Inc. v. Wadmond*, 401 U.S. 154 (1971).

11. *New York Times Co. v. U.S.*, 403 U.S. 713 (1971).

significant in the history of the Supreme Court. Although he did not get the Court to accept all the tenets of his constitutional philosophy, he helped it reach the goals he had set forth regarding nationalization of the Bill of Rights and individual liberties. Black demonstrated, as Norman Dorsen noted, an "important capacity for lonely and persistent dissent." Despite frequent failures and sometimes considerable criticism, he "again and again marshaled arguments to convince the Court of his views on the First Amendment, reapportionment, due process and other issues. At the end, much of what he professed was accepted, and his profound contribution to constitutional law was assured." Justice Black made such a tremendous impression on the law, wrote constitutional scholar Paul Freund, because he "exhibited to a singular degree an intense moral commitment, concentrated through the focus of an unwavering vision, and brought to bear with immense prowess. One thinks of Justice Brandeis's confident formula for achievement: brains, rectitude, singleness of purpose, and time."

BLACKMUN, HARRY A(NDREW)

b. Nov. 12, 1908; Nashville, Ill.
Judge, U.S. Eighth Circuit Court of
Appeals, 1959-70; Associate Justice,
U.S. Supreme Court, 1970-.

Blackmun grew up in St. Paul, Minn., and graduated from Harvard College, Phi Beta Kappa, in 1929. He received a degree from Harvard Law School in 1932 and then clerked for a year for a judge on the U.S. Eighth Circuit Court of Appeals. From 1934 to 1950 Blackmun practiced with a large Minneapolis law firm, where he specialized in taxation and estate planning and became a general partner in 1943. He also taught part-time at several area law schools. In 1950 he began serving as resident counsel at the Mayo Clinic in Rochester, Minn.

A Republican, Blackmun was named a judge on the Eighth Circuit Court in 1959 by President Dwight D. Eisenhower. On the circuit bench he developed a reputation as a cautious and basically conservative judge who respected precedent and favored a policy of judicial restraint. An expert on taxation, Blackmun was a moderate on civil rights and civil liberties issues and a conservative on criminal rights.[1] He was well-regarded within his circuit and was considered a fair and scholarly jurist of complete integrity who wrote thorough and careful opinions.

On April 14, 1970 President Richard Nixon appointed Blackmun to the Supreme Court seat vacated by Abe Fortas in May 1969. The Senate had rejected Nixon's two previous nominees for the post, Clement Haynsworth and G. Harrold Carswell. However Blackmun's record withstood close scrutiny, and his nomination was well-received. He was confirmed by the Senate, 94 to 0, on May 12, 1970. Blackmun was sworn in on June 9 by Chief Justice Warren Burger, with whom he had been friends since childhood.

As most observers had expected, Justice Blackmun was generally conservative in his interpretation of the Constitution and restrained in the use of judicial power, especially in criminal cases. He voted in favor of the prosecution in almost all Fourth Amendment cases.[2] He also took a very narrow view of the Fifth Amendment's privilege against self-incrimination.[3] In an opinion for the Court in June 1971, Blackmun ruled that juvenile defendants were not guaranteed the right to trial by jury.[4] Two years later the Justice held that a defendant's counsel did not have to be present during a pretrial display of photographs to witnesses for the purpose of identifying the accused.[5] Although personally opposed to capital punishment, Blackmun voted in June 1972 and July 1976 to sustain state death penalty laws against the charge that they violated the constitutional ban on cruel and unusual punishment.[6]

On racial issues Blackmun followed a moderate course. He spoke for the Court in February 1973 when it upset a suburban swim club's policy of excluding all blacks from membership,[7] and he participated in decisions interpreting provisions of the 1964 Civil Rights Act favorably to blacks.[8] However, the Justice also joined in several rulings that limited the scope of remedies for school segregation[9] and in a June 1971 decision allowing a

1. See, for example, *Jones v. Mayer*, 379 F. 2d 33 (8 Cir. 1967), reversed 392 U.S. 409 (1968); *Kemp v. Beasley*, 423 F. 2d 851 (8 Cir. 1970); *Maxwell v. Bishop*, 398 F. 2d 138 (8 Cir. 1968), remanded 398 U.S. 262 (1970); *Ashe v. Swenson*, 399 F.2d 40 (8 Cir. 1968), reversed 397 U.S. 436 (1970).

2. See, for example, *Coolidge v. New Hampshire*, 403 U.S. 443 (1971); *Adams v. Williams*, 407 U.S. 143 (1972); *U.S. v. Robinson*, 414 U.S. 218 (1973).

3. See, for example, *California v. Byers*, 402 U.S. 424 (1971); *Kastigar v. U.S.*, 406 U.S. 441 (1972); *Andresen v. Maryland*, 427 U.S. 463 (1976).

4. *McKeiver v. Pennsylvania*, 403 U.S. 528 (1971).

5. *U.S. v. Ash*, 413 U.S. 300 (1973).

6. *Furman v. Georgia*, 408 U.S. 238 (1972); *Gregg v. Georgia*, 428 U.S. 153 (1976).

7. *Tillman v. Wheaton-Haven Recreation Assn.*, 410 U.S. 431 (1973).

8. *Griggs v. Duke Power Co.*, 401 U.S. 424 (1971); *Franks v. Bowman Transportation Co.*, 424 U.S. 747 (1976).

9. *Milliken v. Bradley*, 418 U.S. 717 (1974); *Pasadena City Board of Education v. Spangler*, 427 U.S. 424 (1976).

city to close its public swimming pools rather than desegregate them.[1]

Blackmun voted to overturn most laws discriminating against women and illegitimate children[2] and to hold most forms of state aid to parochial schools unconstitutional.[3] In other areas, however, he was wary of invalidating federal or state statutes. For a five man majority in April 1971, he upheld a federal law revoking the citizenship of individuals born abroad of one American parent who failed to meet a U.S. residency requirement.[4] Although he joined in a March 1972 decision upsetting a one year state residency requirement for voting, Blackmun supported a 50 day state registration requirement in March 1973 and several laws establishing lengthy registration requirements for voting in party primaries.[5] He backed most state welfare regulations[6] and voted to sustain laws authorizing the seizure of goods or wages from an allegedly delinquent debtor without notice or hearing.[7] In his first few years on the Court, Blackmun almost always voted in favor of the government in First Amendment cases.[8] He dissented in June 1971 when the Court refused to grant an injunction against newspaper publication of the *Pentagon Papers*,[9] and he joined in several June 1973 decisions giving the states greater leeway to suppress allegedly obscene materials.[10]

In January 1973 Blackmun made a notable departure from his policy of judicial restraint and, for a seven-man majority, held laws prohibiting abortions during the first six months of pregnancy an unconstitutional violation of women's right to privacy.[11] During the 1974 and 1975 Court terms, commentators detected in Blackmun signs of greater self-confidence and independence. In March 1975, for example, he spoke for the majority to hold that officials in Chattanooga, Tenn., had violated the First Amendment by denying the use of a municipal theater for a production of the controversial rock musical *Hair*.[12] In June 1975 and May 1976, the Justice overturned on First Amendment grounds Virginia laws prohibiting advertisements for abortion services and of drug prices.[13] As the justice overseeing the Eighth Circuit, Blackmun acted independently in November 1975 to invalidate parts of a Nebraska judge's "gag" order restricting media coverage of a mass murder case.[14] In June 1976 he joined with the rest of the Court to overturn the remaining portions of the order.[15] Blackmun once again spoke for the majority in July 1976 to upset state laws requiring women to get the consent of a spouse or parent before having an abortion.[16] He protested a June 1977 ruling holding that states and municipalities were not constitutionally re-

1. *Palmer v. Thompson*, 403 U.S. 217 (1971).

2. See, for example, *Frontiero v. Richardson*, 411 U.S. 677 (1973); *Weinberger v. Wiesenfeld*, 420 U.S. 636 (1975); *Weber v. Aetna Casualty & Surety Co.*, 406 U.S. 164 (1972); *Gomez v. Perez*, 409 U.S. 535 (1973).

3. See, for example, *Lemon v. Kurtzman*, 403 U.S. 602 (1971); *Committee for Public Education v. Nyquist*, 413 U.S. 756 (1973).

4. *Rogers v. Bellei*, 401 U.S. 815 (1971).

5. *Dunn v. Blumstein*, 405 U.S. 330 (1972); *Burns v. Fortson*, 410 U.S. 686 (1973); *Rosario v. Rockefeller*, 410 U.S. 752 (1973); *Kusper v. Pontikes*, 414 U.S. 51 (1973).

6. See, for example, *Wyman v. James*, 400 U.S. 309 (1971); *Jefferson v. Hackney*, 406 U.S. 535 (1972).

7. See, for example, *Fuentes v. Shevin*, 407 U.S. 67 (1972); *Mitchell v. W.T. Grant Co.*, 416 U.S. 600 (1974).

8. See, for example, *Cohen v. California*, 403 U.S. 15 (1971); *Gooding v. Wilson*, 405 U.S. 518 (1972); *Cole v. Richardson*, 405 U.S. 676 (1972).

9. *New York Times Co. v. U.S.*, 403 U.S. 713 (1971).

10. *Miller v. California*, 413 U.S. 15 (1973); *Paris Adult Theatre I v. Slaton*, 413 U.S. 49 (1973).

11. *Roe v. Wade, 410 U.S. 113 (1973); Doe v. Bolton*, 410 U.S. 179 (1973).

12. *Southeastern Promotions Ltd. v. Conrad*, 420 U.S. 546 (1975).

13. *Bigelow v. Virginia*, 421 U.S. 809 (1975); *Virginia State Board of Pharmacy v. Virginia Citizens Consumer Council, Inc.*, 425 U.S. 748 (1976).

14. *Nebraska Press Assn. v. Stuart*, 423 U.S. 1327 (1975).

15. *Nebraska Press Assn. v. Stuart*, 427 U.S. 539 (1976).

16. *Planned Parenthood of Central Missouri v. Danforth*, 428 U.S. 52 (1976).

quired to fund elective abortions for indigent women.[1]

Despite such rulings, Blackmun remained, overall, a largely conservative jurist who was closely aligned in his votes with the other Nixon appointees on the Court. Personally quiet and reserved, Blackmun was not an outstanding justice or a leader on the Court. His opinions offered detailed, scholarly considerations of all aspects of a case, and he was considered a diligent, conscientious and fair-minded jurist.

---

1. *Beal v. Doe,* 432 U.S. 438 (1977); *Maher v. Roe,* 432 U.S. 467 (1977). *Poelker v. Doe,* 432 U.S. 519 (1977).

BRENNAN, WILLIAM J(OSEPH), JR.

b. April 25, 1906; Newark, N.J.
Associate Justice, U.S. Supreme
Court, 1956 –.

The son of Irish immigrants, Brennan received a B.S. from the Wharton School of Finance of the University of Pennsylvania in 1928. He won a degree from Harvard law school in 1931 and then joined a Newark, N.J., law firm, where he became a partner in 1937 and a labor law specialist. A leader of a group of young attorneys who successfully promoted reform and streamlining of the New Jersey judicial system, Brennan was named a judge on the state Superior Court in 1949. The next year he was appointed to the Appellate Division of the Superior Court and in 1952 to the New Jersey Supreme Court.

President Dwight D. Eisenhower announced Brennan's appointment to the U.S. Supreme Court to replace retiring Justice Sherman Minton on Sept. 29, 1956. Although a Democrat, Brennan had not been politically active, and he had the judicial experience and high standing within the legal profession that Eisenhower said he wanted in a Supreme Court candidate. Brennan began serving on the Court under a recess appointment on Oct. 16. The Senate confirmed his nomination on March 19, 1957. Only Sen. Joseph R. McCarthy (R, Wisc.), whose methods Brennan had criticized in two speeches in the mid-1950s, voted against him.

In his early years on the Supreme Court, Justice Brennan often played the role of a mediator between the Court's liberal and conservative wings, writing narrowly based opinions to assemble a majority. In the process, however, he generally aligned himself with the Court's liberal justices and demonstrated a strong commitment to the protection of individual liberties, especially to First Amendment freedoms, and to procedural fairness. In June 1957, for example, his majority opinion in the highly controversial *Jencks* case ruled that in federal criminal trials the government must let the defense examine relevant reports previously made to the government by prosecution witnesses.[1] On the same day Brennan's opinion for the Court in the *E.I. du Pont de Nemours & Co.* case held that the Clayton Antitrust Act applied to vertical as well as to horizontal mergers. Therefore, du Pont, which manufactured certain automotive products, was in violation of the law by its ownership of a 23% share of General Motors Corp. stock.[2] Later in the month he voted in two important cases to reverse the contempt convictions of witnesses who had refused to answer questions during congressional and state investigations of Communism.[3]

Although he had joined the Court's libertarian wing in his votes, Brennan remained largely independent of it in his judicial philosophy. Unlike Justice Hugo Black, for example, Brennan did not consider First Amendment guarantees absolute but believed that these rights must be balanced against government interests. He insisted, however, that only a real and very substantial government need justified any curtailment of individual rights and thus usually favored the individual in loyalty security cases. Brennan dissented, for example, when the majority in two June 1958 cases upheld the dismissal of municipal employes in Philadelphia and New York because they had refused to answer questions from superiors about their political activities. The Justice declared that the government had not offered in either suit sufficient proof of the individual's disloyalty to justify his firing.[4] Brennan again dissented in two cases, decided a year later, in which the

1. *Jencks v. U.S.*, 353 U.S. 657 (1957).

2. *U.S. v. E. I. du Pont de Nemours & Co.*, 353 U.S. 586 (1957).

3. *Watkins v. U.S.*, 354 U.S. 178 (1957); *Sweezy v. New Hampshire*, 354 U.S. 234 (1957).

4. *Beilan v. Board of Education*, 357 U.S. 399, 417 (1958); *Lerner v. Casey*, 357 U.S. 468 (1958).

majority sustained the contempt conviction of witnesses who had failed to provide information during congressional and state investigations into possible subversion. The record in both cases, he asserted, showed the investigations had no valid legislative purpose but only the impermissible goal of exposure for exposure's sake.[1]

In the realm of obscenity law, Brennan emerged as the primary spokesman for the Court in the June 1957 *Roth* case. His opinion held that since obscene expression was "utterly without redeeming social importance," it was not protected by the First Amendment's guarantees of free speech and free press. He also defined the test of obscenity as whether to the average person, applying contemporary community standards, the dominant theme of the material taken as a whole appealed to prurient interest.[2] In later cases Brennan made it clear he believed strict procedural standards must be followed in determining obscenity. In a June 1961 decision he argued that Missouri's censorship system was unconstitutional because it operated in a manner making it likely that nonobscene literature would be seized and taken out of circulation along with obscene literature.[3] Similarly Brennan's majority opinion in a February 1963 case overturned Rhode Island's quasi-governmental book censorship system because it set up an unconstitutional system of prior restraint.[4]

In criminal rights cases, Brennan generally took a liberal stance. He favored extending the right to counsel in state court criminal cases[5] and joined in the June 1961 ruling in *Mapp v. Ohio* requiring state courts to exclude illegally seized evidence.[6] In March 1963 Brennan wrote the majority opinion in *Fay v. Noia*, holding that a procedural default that precluded state court review of a criminal conviction did not bar federal court review of the conviction in habeas corpus proceedings.[7] He dissented in a May 1963 case in which a government agent, wearing a secret recording device, had recorded a defendant's bribery offer. The majority held this evidence was admissible in court, but Brennan saw a danger to individual liberty in electronic surveillance and insisted that the Fourth and Fifth Amendments afforded a "comprehensive right of personal liberty in the face of governmental intrusion."[8] In a March 1959 case, however, Brennan was part of a majority that decided that an individual could be tried in both federal and state courts for the same offense without any violation of the prohibiton against double jeopardy.[9]

One of Brennan's most notable opinions was handed down in March 1962 in *Baker v. Carr*, a 6-2 decision holding that federal courts had the right and duty to try cases involving state legislative apportionment. Overturning a 1946 decision, Brennan's lengthy majority opinion ruled that malapportionment was a proper subject of judicial consideration and presented a justifiable cause of action.[10] The decision launched an extensive process of reapportionment of state legislative and congressional districts, increasing the representation of cities at the expense of rural areas.[11]

As a solid liberal majority emerged on the Warren Court in the early 1960s, Brennan abandoned the narrow ground of many of his early decisions and became more activist and creative in his opinions. He argued that the judiciary was constitutionally vested with the job of protecting

1. *Uphaus v. Wyman*, 360 U.S. 72, 82 (1959); *Barenblatt v. U.S.*, 360 U.S. 109 (1959).

2. *Roth v. U.S.*, 354 U.S. 476 (1957).

3. *Marcus v. Search Warrant of Property*, 367 U.S. 717 (1961).

4. *Bantam Books Inc. v. Sullivan*, 372 U.S. 58 (1963).

5. See, for example, *McNeal v. Culver*, 365 U.S. 109, 117 (1961); *Gideon v. Wainwright*, 372 U.S. 335 (1963).

6. 367 U.S. 643 (1961).

7. 372 U.S. 391 (1963).

8. *Lopez v. U.S.*, 373 U.S. 427, 446 (1963).

9. *Abbate v. U.S.*, 359 U.S. 187 (1959).

10. 369 U.S. 186 (1962), overruling *Colegrove v. Green*, 328 U.S. 549 (1946).

11. See *Wesberry v. Sanders*, 376 U.S. 1 (1964); *Reynolds v. Sims*, 377 U.S. 533 (1964).

the integrity and privacy of the individual from unnecessary government interference, and he became a leader in expanding individual rights and equality.

Brennan wrote some of his most important First Amendment opinions during these years. Speaking for a unanimous Court in March 1964, he expanded the freedom of the press in *New York Times v. Sullivan,* holding that a public official could not recover damages for a defamatory falsehood relating to his official conduct unless he proved the statement was made with "actual malice."[1] Later that year Brennan extended this ruling to cover cases of criminal as well as civil libel,[2] and in a February 1966 decision he gave a broad definition to the term public official.[3] In *Time Inc. v. Hill,* decided in January 1967, Brennan applied the same principle to invasion of privacy suits against the press by newsworthy persons.[4] Brennan found in the 1965 case *Dombrowski v. Pfister* an exception to the general rule that federal courts will not intervene to enjoin threatened state court criminal proceedings. Federal courts could act, he held, when a defendant's First Amendment rights were endangered by the fact of state prosecutions.[5]

The Justice continued to write the Court's leading opinions in the difficult and divisive area of obscenity law. In June 1964 in *Jacobellis v. Ohio,* Brennan reaffirmed the test of obscenity he had established in *Roth.* He gave greater emphasis, however, to the notion that obscene material was utterly without redeeming social importance and said the community standards of the *Roth* test were national, not local.[6] In three March 1966 cases Brennan constructed a narrower test of obscenity and held that to be judged obscene a work had to meet each of three criteria: its dominant theme must appeal to the prurient interest, it must be patently offensive and it must be utterly without redeeming social value.[7]

In one of these cases, *Ginzburg v. U.S.,* Brennan also ruled that "titillating" advertising and pandering in the sale and publicity of a work could be used to determine obscenity.[8] This finding of offense in the conduct of the seller, even though the work itself might not be obscene, has been considered an anomaly for Brennan who was usually careful to guard against the suppression of any non-obscene materials. In a June 1964 case Brennan's plurality opinion reversed a judgment of obscenity by Kansas courts because the books involved had been seized in a manner that endangered non-obscene literature.[9] Brennan overturned Maryland's film censorship system in March 1965 because it provided inadequate safeguards against the suppression of films protected by the First Amendment, and he set out strict procedural guidelines for film censorship systems.[10]

Brennan supported the Warren Court's rulings expanding the constitutional rights of blacks.[11] He wrote the majority opinion in a January 1963 case nullifying a Virginia law which barred solicitation of legal business because it had resulted in an unconstitutional restriction of the NAACP's rights of free speech and association.[12] Brennan's opinion for the Court in the 1966 case *Katzenbach v.*

1. 376 U.S. 254 (1964).

2. *Garrison v. Louisiana,* 379 U.S. 64 (1964).

3. *Rosenblatt v. Baer,* 383 U.S. 75 (1966).

4. 385 U.S. 374 (1967).

5. 380 U.S. 479 (1965).

6. 378 U.S. 184 (1964).

7. *Memoirs v. Massachusetts,* 383 U.S. 413 (1966); *Ginsburg v. U.S.,* 383 U.S. 463 (1966); *Mishkin v. New York,* 383 U.S. 502 (1966).

8. 383 U.S. 463 (1966).

9. *A Quantity of Books v. Kansas,* 378 U.S. 205 (1964).

10. *Freedman v. Maryland,* 380 U.S. 51 (1965).

11. See, for example, *Gayle v. Browder,* 352 U.S. 903 (1956); *Cooper v. Aaron,* 358 U.S. 1 (1958); *Gomillion v. Lightfoot,* 364 U.S. 339 (1960).

12. *NAACP v. Button,* 371 U.S. 415 (1963).

Morgan upheld a section of the 1965 Voting Rights Act designed to guarantee the right to vote to non-English speaking Puerto Ricans. Brennan sustained the law holding that section five of the 14th Amendment gave Congress independent authority to decide if certain conduct violated the Amendment's equal clause[1] This new and broader interpretation of section five has been judged to hold the potential for a vast expansion of federal power.

Brennan also contributed to the Warren Court's criminal decisions in this period. His majority opinion in a June 1964 case held the Fifth Amendment's privilege against self-incrimination applicable to the states[2] The Justice joined in the June 1966 *Miranda* ruling placing limits on police interrogation of arrested suspects[3] In June 1967, he wrote the plurality opinion in two very controversial cases holding that a defendant had a right to counsel at a lineup. In a June 1966 decision, however, Brennan rejected a claim that a blood test to determine if a defendant was driving while drunk, conducted over the defendant's protest, violated his Fourth and Fifth Amendment rights[5] Writing for an eight-man majority in May 1967, Brennan overruled a 1921 Court decision and extended the right of police to use evidence seized in lawful searches of suspects' homes.[6]

On the Burger Court, Brennan's role changed significantly. He became a frequent and vocal dissenter from the decisions of a new, more conservative Court

majority. In most of the Court's terms after 1970, Brennan ranked second only to Justice William O. Douglas in the number of dissents he entered, and he was identified with Douglas and Thurgood Marshall as part of a liberal trio that protested majority rulings on criminal rights, reapportionment, racial discrimination and free expression. Because of the anti-libertarian trend he perceived on the Supreme Court, Brennan urged litigants in a January 1977 *Harvard Law Review* article to turn to the state courts and state constitutional provisions to secure greater expansion and protection of individual rights.

In criminal cases Brennan opposed Court decisions sanctioning warrantless searches and arrests[7] He spoke out strongly against limitations on the exclusionary rule, which barred the use of illegally obtained evidence in court[8] He dissented from February 1971 and December 1975 decisions cutting back on the 1966 *Miranda* ruling[9] Brennan also protested a May 1972 judgment permitting non-unanimous jury verdicts in state courts,[10] but he did join in June 1970 and June 1973 decisions authorizing juries of less than 12 members[11] In June 1970 Brennan's opinion for the Court extended the right to counsel to preliminary hearings,[12] and he dissented from a June 1972 ruling limiting the right to counsel at police lineups to those conducted after a defendant's indictment or arraignment[13] A strong proponent of equal justice for rich and poor, Brennan's majority opinion in a March 1971 case overturned a Texas law limiting punishment for traffic violations to fines

---

1 384 U.S. 641 (1966).

2. *Malloy v. Hogan,* 378 U.S. 1 (1964).

3. *Miranda v. Arizona,* 384 U.S. 436 (1966).

4. *U.S. v. Wade,* 388 U.S. 218 (1967); *Gilbert v. California,* 388 U.S. 263 (1967).

5. *Schmerber v. California,* 384 U.S. 757 (1966).

6. *Warden v. Hayden,* 387 U.S. 294 (1967), overruling *Gouled v. U.S.,* 255 U.S. 298 (1921).

7. See, for example, *U.S. v. White,* 401 U.S. 745 (1971); *U.S. v. Edwards,* 415 U.S. 800 (1974); *U.S. v. Watson,* 423 U.S. 411 (1976).

8. See, for example, *U.S. v. Calandra,* 414 U.S. 338, 355 (1974); *U.S. v. Peltier,* 422 U.S. 531, 544 (1975).

9. *Harris v. New York,* 401 U.S. 222 (1971); *Michigan v. Mosley,* 423 U.S. 96 (1975).

10. *Johnson v. Louisiana,* 406 U.S. 356 (1972); *Apodaca v. Oregon,* 406 U.S. 404 (1972).

11. *Williams v. Florida,* 399 U.S. 78 (1970); *Colgrove v. Battin,* 413 U.S. 149 (1973).

12. *Coleman v. Alabama,* 399 U.S. 1 (1970).

13. *Kirby v. Illinois,* 406 U.S. 682 (1972).

for those able to pay but allowing imprisonment of those who could not pay. In June 1972 and July 1976 cases, Brennan argued that the death penalty violated the Eighth Amendment's ban on cruel and unusual punishment because, under current moral standards, it did not comport with human dignity.[2]

Justice Brennan took a broad view of the equal protection clause and voted to overturn laws discriminating against the poor and illegitimate children.[3] In an April 1969 majority opinion, he overturned state residency requirements for welfare as a denial of equal protection and an unconstitutional restriction on the right to travel.[4] Brennan urged a strict standard of review in cases alleging sex discrimination. He wrote the opinion of the Court in several cases in the 1970s invalidating distinctions between men and women in military dependency benefits, in social security law and in state laws governing the sale of liquor.[5] In racial discrimination cases, Brennan maintained an activist position. His opinion in a March 1976 case held that under the 1964 Civil Rights Act, an individual denied employment by a company because of race and then later hired by the company may be awarded seniority retroactive to the date of his initial job application.[6]

Brennan insisted that the government use fair procedures in taking away from an individual any benefit or entitlement. In a March 1970 majority opinion, he ruled that welfare recipients were entitled to a hearing before their benefits could be cut off.[7] He also voted to grant hearings to debtors before their wages or property was seized by creditors, to drivers before revocation of their licenses for involvement in an accident, to federal civil service and municipal employes before dismissal and to public school students before a disciplinary suspension.[8]

The Justice supported the one-man, one-vote standard for legislative apportionment and, in an April 1969 majority opinion, ruled that no deviation from that standard, no matter how small, was acceptable in congressional districting without strong justification.[9] He objected to February and June 1973 decisions that held that state legislative apportionment did not have to meet the same exacting degree of compliance.[10]

In First Amendment cases Brennan continued to vote in favor of individual rights. In a plurality opinion in a June 1976 suit, he held patronage firings of public employes a violation of their rights of freedom of belief and association.[11] The Justice further expanded the protection of the press from libel judgments in a June 1971 ruling and objected in June 1974 and March 1976 when the majority narrowed this protection in cases involving

1. *Tate v. Short*, 401 U.S. 395 (1971).

2. *Furman v. Georgia*, 408 U.S. 238, 257 (1972); *Gregg v. Georgia*, 428 U.S. 153, 227 (1976).

3. See, for example, *Boddie v. Connecticut*, 401 U.S. 371 (1971); *James v. Valtierra*, 402 U.S. 137 (1971); *San Antonio Independent School District v. Rodriguez*, 411 U.S. 1 (1973); *Levy v. Louisiana*, 391 U.S. 68 (1968); *Labine v. Vincent*, 401 U.S. 532 (1971).

4. *Shapiro v. Thompson*, 394 U.S. 618 (1969).

5. *Frontiero v. Richardson*, 411 U.S. 677 (1973); *Weinberger v. Wiesenfeld*, 420 U.S. 636 (1975); *Craig v. Boren*, 429 U.S. 190 (1976); *Califano v. Goldfarb*, 430 U.S. 199 (1977).

6. *Franks v. Bowman Transportation Co.*, 424 U.S. 747 (1976). See also *Moose Lodge No. 107 v. Irvis*, 407 U.S. 163 (1972); *Keyes v. School District*

No. 1, Denver, 413 U.S. 189 (1973); *Milliken v. Bradley*, 418 U.S. 717 (1974).

7. *Goldberg v. Kelly*, 397 U.S. 254 (1970).

8. *Sniadach v. Family Finance Corp.*, 395 U.S. 337 (1969); *Bell v. Burson*, 402 U.S. 535 (1971); *Arnett v. Kennedy*, 416 U.S. 134 (1974); *Goss v. Lopez*, 419 U.S. 565 (1975); *Bishop v. Wood*, 426 U.S. 341 (1976).

9. *Kirkpatrick v. Preisler*, 394 U.S. 526 (1969); *Wells v. Rockefeller*, 394 U.S. 542 (1969).

10. *Mahan v. Howell*, 410 U.S. 315 (1973); *Gaffney v. Cummings*, 412 U.S. 735 (1973); *White v. Regester*, 412 U.S. 755 (1973).

11. *Elrod v. Burns*, 427 U.S. 347 (1976). See also, for example, *Cohen v. California*, 403 U.S. 15 (1971); *Lloyd Corp. v. Tanner*, 407 U.S. 551 (1972); *Communist Party of Indiana v. Whitcomb*, 414 U.S. 441 (1974).

private citizens rather than public figures or officials.[1] Brennan also dissented from several June 1973 decisions in which the Court gave the states greater leeway to regulate allegedly obscene material. In a significant departure from his earlier position in such cases, Brennan said that the Court's attempts to establish a clear, workable definition of obscenity had failed. Rejecting his own past opinions, he urged the Court to abandon the effort and to overturn all obscenity laws for willing adult audiences.[2] The only Roman Catholic on the bench, Brennan advocated strict separation of church and state and repeatedly voted against state aid to parochial schools.[3]

After the Abe Fortas affair in 1969, Brennan gave up virtually all off-the-bench activities. He became the senior Justice on the Court following William O. Douglas's retirement in 1975. As a Justice he had a reputation for being extremely hard-working and a painstaking legal technician. He wrote intricate and scholarly opinions that explored all aspects of an issue in detail and was considered much better at explaining and rationalizing his decisions than other liberal members of the Court. During his more than 20 years on the bench, Brennan made a significant contribution by writing key opinions in the fields of reapportionment, First Amendment law and criminal and civil rights. Highly regarded by legal scholars, the Justice was widely recognized as a defender of individual freedoms and, in the words of Paul Freund, as "a redoubtable champion of a free, open and just society."

---

1. *Rosenbloom v. Metromedia, Inc.*, 403 U.S. 29 (1971); *Gertz v. Robert Welch, Inc.*, 418 U.S. 323 (1974); *Time, Inc. v. Firestone*, 424 U.S. 448 (1976).

2. *Miller v. California*, 413 U.S. 15, 47 (1973); *Paris Adult Theatre I v. Slaton*, 413 U.S. 49, 73 (1973).

3. See, for example, *Lemon v. Kurtzman*, 403 U.S. 602 (1971); *Hunt v. McNair*, 413 U.S. 734 (1973); *Committee for Public Education v. Nyquist*, 413 U.S. 756 (1973).

BURGER, WARREN E(ARL)

b. Sept. 17, 1907; St. Paul, Minn.
Judge, U.S. Court of Appeals for the
District of Columbia, 1956-69; Chief
Justice of the United States, 1969-.

Warren Burger worked his way through the St. Paul College of Law, graduating third in his class in 1931. A partner in a St. Paul law firm from 1935 to 1953, he maintained a varied general practice while teaching part-time at his alma mater. Burger, a Republican, worked to elect Harold Stassen governor of Minnesota in 1938. He was floor manager for Stassen's unsuccessful presidential bids at the 1948 and 1952 Republican National conventions and shifted his support to Dwight D. Eisenhower at an important moment during the 1952 gathering. Burger was named assistant attorney general in charge of the Civil Division of the Justice Department in 1953. In June 1955 Eisenhower nominated him to a judgeship on the U.S. Court of Appeals for the District of Columbia. Burger was sworn into office in April 1956.

In his 13 years as a circuit judge, Burger developed a reputation as a conservative, particularly in criminal cases. In often articulate, quotable opinions, he opposed the reversal of convictions for what he considered legal technicalities and was a critic of the *Durham* rule which broadened the definition of criminal insanity.[1] Off the bench Burger challenged various aspects of the American criminal justice system, criticized the Warren Court's approach in criminal rights cases and urged reform of the penal system. Active in the American Bar Association (ABA), he was a leader in efforts to improve the management and efficiency of the courts.

On May 21, 1969 President Richard Nixon nominated Burger as Chief Justice to replace the retiring Earl Warren. Nixon had made the Warren Court's criminal rights rulings a target during his 1968 campaign and had promised to appoint "strict constructionists" to the bench. He selected Burger for the Court largely because the Judge's record demonstrated a philosophy of judicial conservatism, especially on criminal issues. Burger's appointment was confirmed by the Senate on June 9 by a 74-3 vote. He was sworn in on June 23, 1969, at the end of the Court term.

In criminal cases Chief Justice Burger usually took a conservative stance. He voted to uphold searches and arrests made without a warrant[2] and vigorously attacked the exclusionary rule that prohibited the use of illegally seized evidence at trial.[3] He took a narrow view of the Fifth Amendment's privilege against self-incrimination[4] and joined in several decisions limiting the scope of the 1966 *Miranda* ruling.[5] Although he voted to guarantee indigent defendants free counsel in certain misdemeanor cases, Burger opposed extending the right to counsel to preliminary hearings, pre-indictment lineups and displays of photographs of a suspect to witnesses.[6] He supported the use of six-member juries and non-unanimous jury verdicts[7] and voted repeatedly to uphold the death penalty against constitutional challenge.[8] In December 1971, however, Burger ruled that prosecutors

1. See, for example, *Killough v. U.S.*, 315 F.2d 241 (D.C. Cir. 1962); *Frazier v. U.S.*, 419 F.2d 1161 (D.C. Cir. 1969); *Blocker v. U.S.*, 288 F.2d 853 (D.C. Cir. 1961).

2. See, for example, *Vale v. Louisiana*, 399 U.S. 30 (1970); *U.S. v.Watson*, 423 U.S. 411 (1976).

3. See his opinions in *Bivens v. Six Unknown Named Agents*, 403 U.S. 388, 411 (1971); *Stone v. Powell*, 428 U.S. 465, 496 (1976).

4. See, for example, *California v. Byers*, 402 U.S. 424 (1971); *Kastigar v. U.S.*, 406 U.S. 441 (1972).

5. *Harris v. New York*, 401 U.S. 222 (1971); *Michigan v. Mosley*. 423 U.S. 96 (1975).

6. *Argersinger v. Hamlin*, 407 U.S. 25 (1972); *Coleman v. Alabama*, 399 U.S. 1 (1970); *Kirby v. Illinois*, 406 U.S. 682 (1972); *U.S. v. Ash*, 413 U.S. 300 (1973).

7. *Williams v. Florida*, 399 U.S. 78 (1970); *Johnson v. Louisiana*, 406 U.S. 356 (1972); *Apodaca v. Oregon*. 406 U.S. 404 (1972).

8. *McGautha v. California*, 402 U.S. 183 (1971); *Furman v. Georgia*, 408 U.S. 238 (1972); *Gregg v. Georgia*, 428 U.S. 153 (1976).

must adhere to their part of plea bargaining agreements.[1] He joined in several decisions banning the imposition of jail terms on convicts solely because they could not pay fines.[2]

In July 1974 Burger spoke for the Court in the celebrated case of *U.S. v. Nixon*. He ordered the President to surrender the tapes and documents subpoenaed by special prosecutor Leon Jaworski for the pending Watergate cover-up trial of six former presidential aides. Nixon's claim of executive privilege, Burger ruled, had to yield in this case to the demonstrated need for evidence in a pending criminal trial.[3] Conversations recorded on several of the tapes that Nixon surrendered in response to the Court's order led directly to his resignation from office on Aug. 9, 1974.

In free speech cases the Chief Justice generally sustained government action against individual rights claims.[4] For a five-man majority in June 1973, he reversed a 16-year Court trend lowering restrictions on pornography and set new guidelines for obscenity laws that gave the states greater leeway to regulate pornographic materials.[5] He dissented in June 1971 when the Court denied the government's request for an injuction to halt newspaper publication of the *Pentagon Papers*. Burger joined the majority a year later in holding that journalists had no First Amendment right to refuse to testify before grand juries about information obtained from confidential sources.[6] However, he spoke for the Court in June 1974, to invalidate as an infringement on free-

dom of the press, a Florida law requiring newspapers to print replies from political candidates whom they criticized.[7] He also overturned a judicial "gag" order restricting pretrial news coverage of a Nebraska mass murder case in June 1976 as an unjustified prior restraint on the press.[8]

Burger wrote several significant opinions on government and religion. In May 1972 he ruled that the application of a state law for compulsory secondary education to the Amish denied the sect their right to free exercise of religion.[9] His May 1970 majority opinion held that tax exemptions for church property used solely for religious purposes did not violate the First Amendment's ban on government establishment of religion.[10] However, Burger overturned several programs for direct state aid to parochial schools in June 1971, because they would result in excessive government entanglement with religion.[11] In later cases he voted to sustain state aid programs in which the benefits went to the individual parents or children rather than directly to the religious schools.[12]

In a widely publicized April 1971 case, Burger spoke for a unanimous Court to uphold court-ordered busing as one means of eliminating state-imposed school segregation.[13] In July 1974, however, he overturned a plan to remedy segregation in Detroit's school system by merging it with suburban districts. For a five-man majority, Burger held such an interdistrict plan inappropriate when segregation had been established only in one district and there was no evidence show-

1. *Santobello v. New York*, 404 U.S. 257 (1971).

2. *Williams v. Illinois*, 399 U.S. 235 (1970); *Tate v. Short*, 401 U.S. 395 (1971).

3. 418 U.S. 683 (1974).

4. See, for example, *Gooding v. Wilson*, 405 U.S. 518 (1972); *Cole v. Richardson*, 405 U.S. 676 (1972).

5. *Miller v. California*, 413 U.S. 15 (1973); *Paris Adult Theatre I v. Slaton*, 413 U.S. 49 (1973).

6. *New York Times Co. v. U.S.*, 403 U.S. 713 (1971); *Branzburg v. Hayes*, 408 U.S. 665 (1972).

7. *Miami Herald Publishing Co. v. Tornillo*, 418 U.S. 241 (1974).

8. *Nebraska Press Assn. v. Stuart*, 427 U.S. 539 (1976).

9. *Wisconsin v. Yoder*, 406 U.S. 205 (1972).

10. *Walz v. Tax Commission of the City of New York*, 397 U.S. 664 (1970).

11. *Lemon v. Kurtzman*, 403 U.S. 602 (1971).

12. See, for example, *Committee for Public Education v. Nyquist*, 413 U.S. 756 (1973).

13. *Swann v. Charlotte-Mecklenburg Board of Education*, 402 U.S. 1 (1971).

ing that school district lines had been drawn in a discriminatory way.[1] In other racial discrimination cases, Burger followed a moderately conservative course.[2]

The Chief Justice applied the constitutional guarantee of equal protection of the laws to women for the first time in November 1971, when he invalidated an Idaho law favoring men over women in the administration of estates.[3] In later sex discrimination suits and other equal protection cases, however, Burger again took moderate to conservative positions.[4] He concurred in January 1973 when the Court upset state laws prohibiting abortions within the first six months of pregnancy as a denial of due process.[5] However, he was otherwise wary of invalidating government action on due process grounds.[6] Burger usually upheld the states' power to establish voting requirements.[7] Nevertheless for a unanimous Court in March 1974, he ruled that states requiring political candidates to pay a filing fee had to provide some alternative means of access to the ballot for individuals too poor to pay the charge.[8] The Chief Justice joined in numerous rulings limiting the Court's jurisdiction to hear cases. He voted, for example, to set restrictive requirements for bringing federal class action suits, to tighten standing requirements and to limit state prisoners' right of appeal in federal courts in certain instances.[9]

As Chief Justice, Burger took a leading role in promoting administrative efficiency and reform in the courts. He publicized the problems of the courts through annual State of the Judiciary addresses given before the ABA, press interviews and public speeches. He suggested a variety of administrative improvements and successfully urged establishment of state-federal judicial councils, a national center for state courts and an institute to train court managers. Burger devoted special attention to what he considered an excessive workload in all of the federal courts. To remedy it, he urged Congress to remove certain cases from federal jurisdiction and to consider the impact of all new legislation on the courts before passage. He also favored studying the possibility of limiting the right of appeal and of having certain types of cases, such as family law problems or prisoner complaints, settled in some other forum than the courts. Burger appointed a seven man committee in the fall of 1971 to study the Supreme Court's caseload. In a controversial December 1972 report, the committee recommended establishment of a new national appeals court to screen all the petitions for review of cases currently filed in the Supreme Court. Burger also promoted penal reform and proposed special training and certification for trial attorneys.

Assessments of Burger varied, depending in part on commentators' agreement with his judicial views. It was generally accepted, however, that the Chief Justice did not dominate his colleagues on the bench but was an articulate, sometimes pungent, advocate of restraint by the Court. He maintained a high level of agreement with Nixon's other Court appointees and argued that judicial decisions should not play a major role in promoting reform. A hardworking man with a pragmatic mind, Burger may make a more lasting impact, according to some observers, as a judicial administrator rather than as a jurist.

---

1. *Milliken v. Bradley*, 418 U.S. 717 (1974).

2. See, for example, *Griggs v. Duke Power Co.*, 401 U.S. 424 (1971); *Moose Lodge No. 107 v. Irvis*, 407 U.S. 163 (1972); *Washington v. Davis*, 426 U.S. 229 (1976).

3. *Reed v. Reed*, 404 U.S. 71 (1971).

4. See, for example, *Geduldig v. Aiello*, 417 U.S. 484 (1974); *San Antonio Independent School District v. Rodriguez*, 411 U.S. 1 (1973); *In re Griffiths*, 413 U.S. 717 (1973).

5. *Roe v. Wade*, 410 U.S. 113 (1973); *Doe v. Bolton*, 410 U.S. 179 (1973).

6. See, for example, *Goldberg v. Kelly*, 397 U.S. 254 (1970); *Fuentes v. Shevin*, 407 U.S. 67 (1972).

7. See, for example, *Phoenix v. Kolodziejski*, 399 U.S. 204 (1970); *Dunn v. Blumstein*, 405 U.S. 330 (1972).

8. *Lubin v. Panish*, 415 U.S. 709 (1974).

9. See, for example, *Zahn v. International Paper Co.*, 414 U.S. 291 (1973); *Warth v. Seldin*, 422 U.S. 490 (1975); *Stone v. Powell*, 428 U.S. 465 (1976).

BURTON, HAROLD H(ITZ)
b. June 22, 1888; Jamaica Plain, Mass.
d. Oct. 28, 1964; Washington, D.C.
Associate Justice, U.S. Supreme
Court, 1945-58.

Harold H. Burton graduated from Bowdoin College in 1909 and from Harvard Law School in 1912. After Army service in World War I, he practiced law in Cleveland and became a member of the Ohio House of Representatives in 1929. Elected mayor of Cleveland in 1935 as a reform candidate, Burton was twice reelected by wide margins. A Republican, he ran successfully for the U.S. Senate in 1940 despite opposition from the state party leadership. In the Senate Burton was an internationalist in foreign policy and a moderate on domestic issues. He served as a member of the Senate committee, headed by Harry S Truman (D, Mo.), that investigated the defense effort in World War II. President Truman chose Burton as his first Supreme Court nominee in September 1945. The first Republican named to the high bench since the Hoover Administration, Burton took his seat on Oct. 1, 1945.

As a justice, Burton normally followed a policy of judicial restraint and supported the government in individual rights cases. He generally voted to sustain both federal and state loyalty programs. In the two most significant loyalty-security cases of the Truman era, he joined the majority to uphold the non-Communist affidavit provision in the Taft-Hartley Act in May 1950[1] and the conviction of 11 American Communist Party leaders under the Smith Act in June 1951.[2] Burton sometimes voted with his more liberal colleagues in security cases but generally for statutory or procedural, not constitutional, reasons. In April 1951, for example, he ruled, on narrow grounds, in favor of three organizations that had challenged

their placement on the Attorney General's list of subversive organizations.[3] Burton also dissented in March 1952 when the majority decided that alien Communists facing deportation could be held without bail if the Attorney General considered this necessary to national security.[4] He wrote the majority opinion in a June 1953 case setting aside the perjury conviction of labor leader Harry Bridges for allegedly having sworn falsely at his 1945 naturalization hearing that he was not a Communist. The Justice based his decision on the ground that the statute of limitations had run out before Bridges was indicted.[5]

During the Vinson years Burton was usually aligned with Truman's other judicial appointees. From 1949 to 1953 this group, joined by Justice Stanley Reed, dominated the Court. Under Chief Justice Earl Warren, Burton adhered to a pattern of mostly conservative but occasionally liberal votes in loyalty-security cases. However, he was now more often among the dissenters, as alignments among the justices and voting trends began to change in civil liberties cases. Burton dissented, for example, from an April 1956 decision upsetting state sedition laws[6] and from a June 1957 ruling placing limits on state subversion investigations.[7] The Justice also objected to a June 1958 judgment holding the denial of passports to members of the Communist Party illegal.[8] In the same month Burton spoke for a five-man majority that upheld the dismissal of a public school teacher for incompetency after he had refused to tell school authorities whether he had once been an officer in a Communist organization.[9]

However, Burton concurred in a June

---

1. *American Communications Association v. Douds*, 339 U.S. 382 (1950).

2. *Dennis v. U.S.*, 341 U.S. 494 (1951).

3. *Joint Anti-Fascist Refugee Committee v. McGrath*, 341 U.S. 123 (1951).

4. *Carlson v. Landon*, 342 U.S. 524 (1952).

5. *Bridges v. U.S.*, 346 U.S. 209 (1953).

6. *Pennsylvania v. Nelson*, 350 U.S. 497 (1956).

7. *Sweezy v. New Hampshire*, 354 U.S. 234 (1957).

8. *Kent v. Dulles*, 357 U.S. 116 (1958).

9. *Beilan v. Board of Education*, 357 U.S. 399 (1958).

1957 decision overturning the convictions of California Communist Party leaders under the Smith Act, though he disagreed with a portion of the Court's opinion giving a limited interpretation to the term "organize" in the Act.[1] Burton also took the narrow ground in another case that month in which the majority ruled that a federal criminal defendant was entitled to see statements government witnesses made to the FBI before trial. In a separate opinion he said the trial judge should examine the statements before they were turned over to defense counsel and withhold those containing national security information.[2]

Burton displayed a similar conservative bent in other civil liberties cases. He dissented in January 1946 when the Court upheld the right of Jehovah's Witnesses to distribute their literature in a company town[3] and again in June 1948 when the majority overturned a local ordinance which banned the use of sound trucks without a police permit.[4] In criminal cases, Burton usually voted against defendants who claimed their rights had been violated.[5] However, he dissented from an unprecedented January 1947 decision in which the majority ruled that Louisiana could try again to execute a man who had survived a first execution attempt because the electric chair had malfunctioned. Burton's opinion asserted that the second execution attempt would constitute cruel and unusual punishment.[6]

In his first civil rights case in June 1946, Burton dissented alone from a judgment that Virginia's segregation law could not be applied to interstate buses.[7] Thereafter, however, he joined in a Court trend expanding the constitutional rights of blacks. In June 1950 Burton wrote the opinion of the Court in a case holding racial segregation in railroad dining cars illegal under the Interstate Commerce Act.[8] He joined in the Court's May 1954 *Brown* decision which ruled public school segregation unconstitutional.[9]

In economic cases Justice Burton tended to vote against labor unions and for the government.[10] He wrote several important antitrust opinions including a landmark June 1946 ruling against three major tobacco companies in which he established that a combination or conspiracy creating the power to exclude competition or raise prices violated the Sherman Antitrust Act, even if the power had never been exercised.[11] The Justice voted against the Truman Administration, however, in June 1952 to hold the President's seizure of the steel industry illegal.[12] He also wrote the dissenting opinion in an important June 1957 case in which the majority held that the DuPont Co.'s acquisition of General Motors stock in 1917-19 violated the Clayton Antitrust Act.[13]

Burton retired from the Supreme Court in October 1958 because of ill health. He was considered then and later to have been a largely conservative jurist but one with a certain flexibility and independence. A very conscientious and hardworking man, Burton had a reputation both on and off the Court for having a judicial temperament because of his capacity to keep an open mind on issues and to

1. *Yates v. U.S.*, 354 U.S. 298 (1957).

2. *Jencks v. U.S.*, 353 U.S. 657, 672 (1957).

3. *Marsh v. Alabama*, 326 U.S. 501 (1946).

4. *Saia v. New York*, 334 U.S. 558 (1948).

5. See, for example, *Haley v. Ohio*, 332 U.S. 596 (1948); *Bute v. Illinois*, 333 U.S. 640 (1948); *Watts v. Indiana*, 338 U.S. 49 (1949).

6. *Louisiana ex rel. Francis v. Resweber*, 329 U.S. 459 (1947).

7. *Morgan v. Virginia*, 328 U.S. 373 (1946).

8. *Henderson v. U.S.*, 339 U.S. 816 (1950). See also *Shelley v. Kraemer*, 334 U.S. 1 (1948); *Sweatt v. Painter*, 339 U.S. 629 (1950); *McLaurin v. Oklahoma State Regents*, 339 U.S. 637 (1950); *Terry v. Adams*, 345 U.S. 461 (1953); *Barrows v. Jackson*, 346 U.S. 249 (1953).

9. *Brown v. Board of Education*, 347 U.S. 483 (1954); *Bolling v. Sharpe*, 347 U.S. 497 (1954).

10. See, for example, *Anderson v. Mt. Clemens Pottery Co.*, 328 U.S. 680 (1946); *United Construction Workers v. Laburnum Construction Corp.*, 347 U.S. 656 (1954); *Lichter v. U.S.*, 334 U.S. 742 (1948); *Lorain Journal Co. v. U.S.*, 342 U.S. 143 (1951).

11. *American Tobacco Co. v. U.S.*, 328 U.S. 781 (1946).

12. *Youngstown Sheet & Tube Co. v. Sawyer*, 343 U.S. 579 (1952).

13. *U.S. v. E.I. du Pont de Nemours & Co.*, 353 U.S. 586 (1957).

maintain an emotional distance from cases. Nonetheless, most legal scholars have ranked him as, at best, an average justice. Burton did not play a leading role on the Court; he was neither a great scholar nor an original thinker. Although his opinions improved during his years on the Court, they remained rather lackluster and tedious. Burton made a special contribution to the Court, however, particularly during the Truman period, by acting as a unifying influence at a time when the Court was deeply and sometimes bitterly divided. The Justice's "personality, including his calm, quiet, earnest manner, his moderation, and his tendency to find narrow grounds for decisions," according to historian Richard Kirkendall, "enabled him to become one of the most effective promoters of cooperation among men who frequently disagreed with one another on fundamental issues." Burton died in Washington in October 1964.

CLARK, TOM C(AMPBELL)

b. Sept. 23, 1899; Dallas, Tex.
d. June 13, 1977; New York, N.Y.
U.S. Attorney General, 1945–49;
Associate Justice, U.S. Supreme
Court, 1949–67.

Tom Clark received a B.A. in 1921 and a law degree the next year from the University of Texas. He then entered private practice in Dallas. Active in local Democratic politics and a protege of Sen. Tom Connally (D, Tex.) and Rep. Sam Rayburn (D, Tex.), Clark served as civil district attorney of Dallas County from 1927 to 1932 and was named to a Justice Department post in 1937. Over the next six years Clark worked primarily in the Antitrust Division. He coordinated the program under which Japanese-Americans were evacuated from the West Coast and interned during World War II and also led a special unit that investigated war frauds. Clark was appointed head of the Department's Antitrust Division in March 1943 and, five months later, was placed in charge of the Criminal Division.

Clark's war frauds unit cooperated with the Senate committee chaired by Harry S Truman which investigated the defense effort, and the Texan supported Truman for the vice presidential nomination at the 1944 Democratic National Convention. On May 23, 1945 President Truman selected Clark as his Attorney General. Clark was sworn in late the next month. He proved to be energetic and resourceful in his new post and was a Truman loyalist who became a close presidential adviser on domestic issues. Clark started 160 antitrust cases while Attorney General and personally argued a major suit against Paramount Pictures in the Supreme Court.[1] He expanded the Justice Department's role in civil rights by filing an *amicus curiae* brief in a case challenging racially restrictive housing covenants. In May 1948 the Supreme Court adopted the government's position that the covenants were not enforceable in federal or state courts.[2] Clark also initiated in 1946 the litigation

that led to the conviction of John L. Lewis and the United Mine Workers for contempt of court for having disregarded an anti-strike injunction issued at a time when the government had seized the mines. The Attorney General argued the case himself when it was appealed to the Supreme Court. The Justices upheld the government in a March 1947 decision.[3]

Clark also played a key role in the development of the Truman Administration's loyalty program. He believed that even one disloyal government employe posed a threat to the nation's security, and he urged the President to appoint a committee to review existing loyalty procedures for federal employes. The committee was named in November 1946. When a new loyalty program, based on its recommendations, was established in March 1947, Clark successfully argued that the FBI should be chosen as the investigative unit for the program.

Clark also won presidential approval of the use of wiretaps by the FBI in national security cases. In 1948 and 1949 he recommended legislation to make unauthorized disclosure of national defense information a crime, to require Communist Party members to register as foreign agents and to remove the statute of limitations in espionage cases. He drew up the first Attorney General's list of subversive political organizations in 1947 and the next year started proceedings against the leaders of the U.S. Communist Party for violation of the Smith Act. Clark made frequent public statements on the dangers of Communism and the threat of internal subversion, encouraged the adoption of loyalty standards by non-governmental organizations and, in the 1948 presidential campaign, defended Truman against

---

1. *U.S. v. Paramount Pictures, Inc.*, 334 U.S. 131 (1948).
2. *Shelley v. Kraemer*, 334 U.S. 1 (1948); *Hurd v.*
Hodge, 334 U.S. 24 (1948).
3. *U.S. v. United Mine Workers*, 330 U.S. 258 (1947).

charges that he was "soft on Communism."

Clark's anti-Communist efforts were the most controversial aspect of his years as Attorney General. He defended his actions as necessary steps to prevent subversion. His supporters argued that the Truman Administration's loyalty program, unlike McCarthyism, recognized certain constitutional limitations on anti-subversive endeavors. Clark's critics charged, however, that even the Truman program too often disregarded civil liberties and that the Attorney General exaggerated the danger of subversion. Clark's anti-Communist statements and actions, critics asserted, helped legitimize inquiries into individual political beliefs and associations and helped create the atmosphere that made McCarthyism possible.

On July 28, 1949 Truman announced Clark's nomination to the Supreme Court. Despite criticism from some liberals who alleged that he was anti-labor and anti-civil liberties, Clark's appointment was confirmed by the Senate on August 18 by a 73-8 vote. Justice Clark was scrupulous about disqualifying himself from cases that had been handled by the Justice Department while he was Attorney General, and as a result, he did not participate in many important cases during his early years on the bench. When he did join in decisions, Clark regularly voted in accord with Chief Justice Fred Vinson, another Truman appointee. He showed little independence and innovation, dissenting only 15 times in the four terms from 1949 to 1952. His accession to the Court helped create a five-man conservative bloc led by Vinson which generally supported the government in loyalty-security and criminal cases against individual rights claims.

Justice Clark, for example, wrote a majority opinion in June 1951 upholding a Los Angeles ordinance that required city employes to swear that they were not members of the Communist Party and had not advocated overthrow of the government.[1] In March 1952 he voted to sustain a New York State law which barred members of subversive organizations from teaching in public schools.[2] Later the same month he voted to approve the holding of alien Communists facing deportation without bail if the Attorney General considered them security risks.[3]

Clark was not insensitive to all civil liberties claims. In a unanimous May 1952 case, he wrote an opinion holding that movies were entitled to protection under the First Amendment and overturning a state ban on the Italian film, *The Miracle,* because it was allegedly sacrilegious.[4] He also spoke for the Court in December 1952 when it ruled an Oklahoma law requiring loyalty oaths from state employes unconstitutional. Unlike the Los Angeles oath he had upheld, the Oklahoma program made no distinction between innocent and knowing membership in a subversive organization.[5] Clark also joined the majority in two June 1950 decisions which eliminated racial segregation at the University of Texas law school and at the graduate school at the University of Oklahoma.[6]

The one major exception to Clark's alignment with Vinson in this period came in the June 1952 steel seizure decision. Clark agreed with the Chief Justice that the President could act on his own to resolve national emergencies in the absence of any congressional authorization. But here, he concluded, Congress had passed laws establishing procedures to deal with a threatened steel strike, and in such a case, the President was obliged to follow the methods prescribed in the law. Since Truman had not, Clark wrote in a concurring opinion, the steel seizure was invalid.[7]

---

1. *Garner v. Board of Public Works,* 341 U.S. 716 (1951).

2. *Adler v. Board of Education,* 342 U.S. 485 (1952).

3. *Carlson v. Landon,* 342 U.S. 524 (1952).

4. *Burstyn v. Wilson,* 343 U.S. 495 (1952).

5. *Wieman v. Updegraff,* 334 U.S. 183 (1952).

6. *Sweatt v. Painter,* 339 U.S. 629 (1950); *McLaurin v. Oklahoma State Regents,* 339 U.S. 637 (1950).

7. *Youngstown Sheet & Tube Co. v. Sawyer,* 343 U.S. 579, 660 (1952).

On the Warren Court, Clark demonstrated greater self-confidence as a jurist, and he gradually took on a more independent role. In most areas of the law, he became increasingly moderate, and he was often considered a "swing" vote between the Court's liberal and conservative blocs. On loyalty-security questions, however, Clark remained a conservative, and he entered strong objections when the Court began placing limits on government anti-Communist efforts in the mid-1950s. Clark dissented in June 1956 from a decision holding that under federal law a government employe could be summarily dismissed as a security risk only if he held a sensitive job. In his opinion he accused the majority of robbing the government of its most potent weapon in the battle against subversion.[1] He again dissented from a June 1957 ruling that a defendant charged with filing a false non-Communist affidavit under the Taft-Hartley Act had to be allowed to see certain secret FBI documents material to his case.[2] The Justice objected to two other decisions that month placing limits on congressional and state investigations into subversion.[3] He was the sole dissenter in another case in which the Court significantly narrowed the scope of the Smith Act.[4]

In June 1959 Clark finally spoke for the majority to sustain the contempt conviction of a minister who had refused to turn over to New Hampshire's attorney general the guest list of a summer camp suspected of being a Communist meeting place. The Justice ruled that the state's interest in discovering the presence of possible subversives outweighed any individual rights of privacy or association involved.[5] In one of the few exceptions to his usual pattern, Clark wrote the majority opinion in an April 1956 case holding that a teacher at a municipal college could not be fired without notice or hearing solely because he had invoked the Fifth Amendment before a congressional committee.[6]

Loyalty-security issues remained important to Clark in the 1960s. He voted with a five man majority in two 1961 cases upholding the investigative powers of the House Un-American Activities Committee and the contempt-of-Congress convictions of witnesses who had refused to answer committee questions.[7] In two five-to-four decisions in June 1961, Clark voted with the majority to sustain key provisions in the 1940 Smith Act and the 1950 Internal Security Act.[8] In 1964 he dissented in two cases in which the Court invalidated state loyalty laws in Washington and a federal law canceling the citizenship of naturalized Americans who returned to their native land for a period of three years or more.[9] Clark also objected in 1965 when the Court voided a clause in the Landrum-Griffin Act barring Communist Party members from serving as labor union officials.[10]

In criminal rights cases Clark also tended to uphold government power against individual claims. In February 1954, for example, he voted to sustain a state gambling conviction based on illegally seized evidence.[11] He joined the majority in two March 1959 cases ruling that persons tried for the same offense in both federal and state courts had not been subjected to double jeopardy.[12] Clark dissented when the Court held in 1964 that the Fifth Amendment's privilege against self-incrimination applied in state as well as federal court proceedings.[13] The Justice

---

1. *Cole v. Young*, 351 U.S. 536, 565 (1956).
2. *Jencks v. U.S.*, 353 U.S. 657 (1957).
3. *Watkins v. U.S.*, 354 U.S. 178 (1957); *Sweezy v. New Hampshire*, 354 U.S. 234 (1957).
4. *Yates v. U.S.*, 354 U.S. 298 (1957).
5. *Uphaus v. Wyman*, 360 U.S. 72 (1959).
6. *Slochower v. Board of Education*, 350 U.S. 551 (1956).
7. *Wilkinson v. U.S.*, 365 U.S. 399 (1961); *Braden v. U.S.*, 365 U.S. 431 (1961).

8. *Scales v. U.S.*, 367 U.S. 203 (1961); *Communist Party v. Subversive Activities Control Board*, 367 U.S. 1 (1961).
9. *Baggett v. Bullitt*, 377 U.S. 360 (1964); *Schneider v. Rusk*, 377 U.S. 163 (1964).
10. U.S. v. *Brown*, 381 U.S. 437 (1965).
11. *Irvine v. California*, 347 U.S. 128 (1954).
12. *Bartkus v. Illinois*, 359 U.S. 121 (1959); *Abbate v. U.S.* 359 U.S. 187 (1959).
13. *Malloy v. Hogan*, 378 U.S. 1 (1964).

also dissented in the landmark case of *Miranda v. Arizona* (1966), in which a five-man majority defined the constitutional limitations on the power of police to question criminal suspects and set out specific rules for police interrogations.[1]

However, Clark was more flexible in this area than in loyalty-security matters, and he often voted in support of defendants' rights. In April 1956 he was part of a five-man majority which ruled that states must, under certain circumstances, supply indigent defendants with free trial transcripts on appeal.[2] Clark wrote the plurality opinion in one of the Court's most significant criminal rights cases in 1961. Along with four other justices, Clark overturned previous Court rulings and, in *Mapp v. Ohio,* held that illegally obtained evidence was not admissible in state courts.[3] He also wrote the opinion of the Court in a 1967 case which held that the use of electronic devices to record conversations was a search within the meaning of the Fourth Amendment. As a result, Clark upset a state bribery conviction based on electronic eavesdropping that did not meet the constitutional standards for a legal search.[4]

Justice Clark was also sensitive to the possibility of publicity infringing on a defendant's right to a fair trial. He wrote the majority opinion in a 1965 decision overturning the state conviction of Texas financier Billie Sol Estes on swindling charges. Estes's trial had been televised, and Clark ruled that the televising of criminal trials could have a prejudicial effect on the judge, jurors and witnesses.[5] Similarly, Clark was the author of a 1966 decision reversing a defendant's murder

conviction because of the "massive pretrial publicity" and the "carnival atmosphere"[6] that had reigned during the trial. Clark also joined the majority in a 1967 decision extending to children in juvenile court proceedings the procedural guarantees, such as the right to counsel, afforded adults by the Constitution.[7]

Justice Clark took a moderate position on First Amendment and reapportionment issues. He wrote the opinion of the Court in a five-to-four decision in January 1961 upholding a Chicago ordinance that barred the public showing of movies without prior approval of city censors.[8] However, he agreed with a majority of the Court in June 1962 that prayer in the public schools violated the First Amendment.[9] In June 1963 Clark wrote the majority opinion in two controversial cases holding unconstitutional state and local rules requiring recitation of the Lord's Prayer and Bible-reading in public schools. In that decision Clark ruled that the First Amendment committed the state to "a position of neutrality" in the "relationship between man and religion."[10]

Clark concurred in *Baker v. Carr* in March 1962 in which the Court overturned a long-standing precedent and ruled that apportionment of legislative districts was subject to federal court scrutiny.[11] However, he rejected the "one-man, one-vote" standard established by the majority in two 1964 cases.[12] Clark argued that although the Constitution required "rational" apportionment, it did not mandate exact one-man, one-vote districting.[13]

In the realm of civil rights, Clark joined in the major Supreme Court decisions outlawing racial segregation, including

---

1. 384 U.S. 436 (1966).

2. *Griffin v. Illinois,* 351 U.S. 12 (1956).

3. 367 U.S. 643 (1961), overruling *Wolf v. Colorado,* 338 U.S. 25 (1949).

4. *Berger v. New York,* 388 U.S. 41 (1967).

5. *Estes v. Texas,* 381 U.S. 532 (1965).

6. *Sheppard v. Maxwell,* 384 U.S. 333 (1966).

7. *In re Gault,* 387 U.S. 1 (1967).

8. *Times Film Corp. v. Chicago,* 365 U.S. 43 (1961).

9. *Engel v. Vitale,* 370 U.S. 421 (1962).

10. *Abington School District v. Schempp,* and *Murray v. Curlett,* 374 U.S. 203 (1963).

11. 369 U.S. 186 (1962), overruling *Colegrove v. Green,* 328 U.S. (1954).

12. *Wesberry v. Sanders,* 376 U.S. 1 (1964); *Reynolds v. Sims,* 328 U.S. 549 (1946).

13. See Clark's concurring opinions in *Baker v. Carr,* 369 U.S. at 251 (1962), *Wesberry v. Sanders,* 376 U.S. at 18 (1964), and *Reynolds v. Sims,* 377 U.S. at 587 (1964).

the landmark *Brown* ruling of May 1954.[1] In two 1964 cases, Clark delivered the opinion for a unanimous Court upholding the public accommodations section of the 1964 Civil Rights Act.[2] He also voted in 1966 to reinstate federal conspiracy charges against 14 men alleged to have murdered three civil rights workers in Mississippi in 1964 after District Judge W. Harold Cox had dismissed the charges.[3] In 1967 he voted to invalidate anti-miscegenation statutes.[4]

Although Clark usually approved the Court's efforts to expand civil rights, he did not always condone the activities of civil rights demonstrators. He was the sole dissenter in a 1963 case, for example, in which the Court overturned the breach-of-the-peace convictions of nearly 200 blacks who had demonstrated against discriminatory state laws on the state capitol grounds in Columbia, S.C. Though the majority held that the demonstrations were peaceful and had been protected by the First and 14th Amendments, Clark argued that the arrests had been justified because there was evidence that a "dangerous situation" had been developing and that the peace had been threatened.[5]

In a five-to-four decision in 1964, however, Clark wrote the majority opinion holding that the public accommodations section of the 1964 Civil Rights Act barred state prosecution of demonstrators who had previously tried by peaceful means to desegregate the business places covered by the new law.[6] But this proved to be an exceptional decision for Clark. In 1966 he voted against reversing the breach-of-the-peace convictions of five blacks who had tried to integrate a public library in Louisiana.[7] He voted to sustain the trespass convictions of demonstrators who had protested outside a county jail in Florida against the arrest of other civil rights demonstrators.[8] Clark was also part of a five-member majority that in 1967 upheld the contempt-of-court convictions of Martin Luther King and seven other black leaders who had led protest marches during the 1963 Birmingham demonstrations in defiance of a temporary restraining order.[9]

In February 1967 President Lyndon Johnson appointed Clark's son Ramsey Attorney General. Justice Clark announced that he would retire from the Court at the end of that term to avoid any suspicion of conflict of interest. After he retired in June 1967, Clark was generally rated as an able jurist who had grown during his 18 years on the bench and who had become a very productive member of the Court, writing some of its most important opinions. The major criticism leveled against Clark was that he had unduly emphasized the needs of government and society over the rights of defendants and of the individual, particularly in the loyalty-security field. Historian Richard Kirkendall wrote that Clark "brought the fears of the Cold War to the Supreme Court and helped to translate them into the law of the land."

Clark remained active in the law following his retirement from the Supreme Court. He sat as a judge on the lower federal courts, and he kept up the extensive efforts he had begun some years earlier to improve the administration of justice at

---

1. *Brown v. Board of Education*, 347 U.S. 483 (1954); *Bolling v. Sharpe*, 347 U.S. 497 (1954). See also *Mayor and City Council of Baltimore v. Dawson*, 350 U.S. 877 (1955); *Holmes v. City of Atlanta*, 350 U.S. 879 (1955); *Gayle v. Browder*, 352 U.S. 903 (1956); *Cooper v. Aaron*, 358 U.S. 1 (1958).

2. *Heart of Atlanta Motel v. U.S.*, 379 U.S. 241 (1964); *Katzenbach v. McClung*, 379 U.S. 294 (1964).

3. *U.S. v. Price*, 383 U.S. 787 (1966).

4. *Loving v. Virginia*, 388 U.S. 1 (1967).

5. *Edwards v. South Carolina*, 372 U.S. 229, 238 (1963).

6. *Hamm v. City of Rock Hill*, 379 U.S. 306 (1964).

7. *Brown v. Louisiana*, 383 U.S. 131 (1966).

8. *Aderley v. Florida*, 385 U.S. 39 (1966).

9. *Walker v. City of Birmingham*, 388 U.S. 307 (1967).

the state and federal levels. Clark served as head of an advisory committee of the National Commission on Reform of Federal Criminal Laws and from 1968 to 1970 was the director of the Federal Judicial Center, a research and training agency of the federal judiciary. Clark also headed an American Bar Association committee that recommended in 1970 reform of disciplinary procedures for lawyers involved in misconduct. He died in New York City in June 1977.

DOUGLAS, WILLIAM O(RVILLE)
b. Oct. 16, 1898; Maine, Minn.
Associate Justice, U.S. Supreme
Court, 1939–75.

Douglas grew up in an impoverished family in Yakima, Wash., and attended nearby Whitman College on a scholarship. He worked his way through Columbia Law School, graduating second in his class in 1925. After a brief period in private practice, Douglas taught from 1927 to 1934 at Columbia and then Yale law schools where he developed a reputation for his work on corporate law and bankruptcy. From 1934 to 1936 he directed a study of protective and reorganization committees for the Securities and Exchange Commission (SEC). As a member of the SEC in 1936 and its chairman from 1937 to 1939, Douglas secured a reorganization of the stock exchange, promoted securities reforms and helped establish the basic guidelines of federal securities regulations. Part of the New Deal inner circle, Douglas was Franklin Roosevelt's fourth Supreme Court appointee, nominated in March 1939 and easily confirmed the next month.

When named to the Court Douglas was viewed as a financial and corporate law expert. Over the years he wrote important opinions in areas such as ratemaking by public utilities, bankruptcy, patents and securities.[1] He supported New Deal measures expanding government power over the economy and favored rigorous enforcement of antitrust laws.[2] In June 1948, for example, Douglas vigorously dissented when the Court sanctioned the purchase of Consolidated Steel Co., the largest independent steel fabricator on the West Coast, by U.S. Steel.[3] The next June he objected to a majority ruling that he believed would lead oil companies to supplant independent service station opera-

tors with their own stations.[4] In the same month Douglas criticized the long-established rule that the 14th Amendment applied to corporations.[5] He also wrote the majority opinions in two June 1950 cases ruling that the federal government had "paramount rights" to the oil rich lands off the Texas and Louisana coasts.[6]

Despite his record in business law, Justice Douglas ultimately became best known as one of the foremost exponents of individual freedom on the Court. His civil libertarianism developed significantly in the years after World War II as he came to the conclusion that First Amendment freedoms were the cornerstone of an open democratic society. Douglas insisted that government infringement on these rights was justified only when they seriously impaired an important government interest. Under this "clear and present danger" standard, the Justice rarely found government interference with First Amendment rights permissible.

In June 1948, for example, Douglas spoke for a five-man majority to upset a local ordinance banning the use of sound trucks without police permits as an unconstitutional restraint on free speech.[7] For another five-man majority, Douglas, in May 1949, overturned the disorderly conduct conviction of a speaker whose anti-Semitic utterances had nearly caused a riot. In a controversial opinion, he declared that free speech must be guaranteed even to a speaker who "stirs the public to anger, invites dispute, brings about . . . unrest or creates a disturbance."[8]

Douglas's views on freedom of belief and expression also led him to oppose all manner of loyalty-security measures. He

---

1. See, for example, *Case v. Los Angeles Lumber Products Co.*, 308 U.S. 106 (1939); *Cuno Engineering Corp. v. Automatic Devices Corp.*, 314 U.S. 84 (1941); *Federal Power Commission v. Hope Natural Gas Co.*, 320 U.S. 591 (1944); *SEC v. Variable Annuity Life Insurance Co.*, 359 U.S. 65 (1959).

2. See, for example, *Sunshine Anthracite Coal Co. v. Adkins*, 310 U.S. 381 (1940); *U.S. v. Socony-Vacuum Oil Co.*, 310 U.S. 150 (1940).

3. *U.S. v. Columbia Steel Co.*, 334 U.S. 495 (1948).

4. *Standard Oil Co. v. U.S.*, 337 U.S. 293 (1949).

5. *Wheeling Steel Corp. v. Glander*, 337 U.S. 562 (1949).

6. *U.S. v. Louisiana*, 339 U.S. 699 (1950); *U.S. v. Texas*, 339 U.S. 707 (950).

7. *Saia v. New York*, 334 U.S. 558 (1948).

8. *Terminiello v. Chicago*, 337 U.S. 1, 2 (1949).

dissented in June 1951 when the Court upheld the conviction of American Communist Party leaders for violation of the Smith Act. In what some consider his best single opinion, Douglas pointed out that the defendants were not charged with conspiring to overthrow the government or with any overt acts of subversion, but only with conspiring to form groups that would teach and advocate overthrow of the government. In a careful application of the clear and present danger test, Douglas found no evidence of any imminent peril to the government in such activity that justified the denial of free speech rights.[1] Justice Douglas also opposed the deportation of aliens solely because they had once been members of the Communist Party, and he objected to loyalty oaths.[2] In a vivid March 1952 dissent, he attacked a New York law that barred members of subversive organizations from teaching in public schools as a destroyer of free thought and expression in the classroom.[3]

Douglas took a relatively moderate position in church-state cases during the Truman era. He voted in February 1947 to uphold state payments for the transportation of children to parochial schools.[4] In March 1948 he joined in a decision that overturned a program of released-time religious instruction in public schools.[5] However, four years later, he wrote the majority opinion in a case sustaining a similar program in New York City. Because the religious instruction in New York did not take place in the schools or at public expense, Douglas held it was permissible. He declared that the First Amendment required only government neutrality, not government hostility, toward religion.[6]

In criminal cases Douglas generally gave a broad interpretation to the guarantees afforded in the Bill of Rights. Like Justice Hugo Black, the colleague with whom he was most closely aligned on civil liberties questions, Douglas believed these guarantees should extend to state as well as federal defendants.[7] He favored extending the right to counsel to all accused of crime and took a strong stand against denials of the privilege against self-incrimination.[8] Douglas pursued an erratic course on Fourth Amendment issues in the late 1940s,[9] but in June 1949 he voted to extend the Amendment's ban on unreasonable searches and seizures to the states. He dissented when the Court at the same time held the state courts might still use illegally seized evidence.[10]

In February 1946 Douglas turned down President Harry S Truman's offer to name him Secretary of the Interior. Two years later some friends started a presidential boom for the Justice. He eliminated himself from that race on July 10, 1948, but was then asked by Truman to run with him as the Democratic vice-presidential nominee. After several days of considering the proposal, Douglas once again turned down the President, saying that he had decided to make a career of the Supreme Court.

Often a controversial figure, Douglas became a center of conflict in June 1953 when he granted convicted atomic spies Julius and Ethel Rosenberg a stay of execution. Although he had voted several times not to hear an appeal of the Rosenbergs' conviction,[11] Douglas nonetheless granted this stay when new legal arguments were presented on the couple's behalf. Chief Justice Fred Vinson then called the Court into special session. After hearing arguments the Court vacated Douglas's stay on June 19.[12] On June 17

---

1. *Dennis v. U.S.*, 341 U.S. 494, 581 (1951).

2. *Harisiades v. Shaughnessy*, 342 U.S. 580 (1952); *Wieman v. Updegraff*, 344 U.S. 183 (1952).

3. *Adler v. Board of Education*, 342 U.S. 485, 508 (1952).

4. *Everson v. Board of Education*, 330 U.S. 1 (1947).

5. *Illinois ex rel. McCollum v. Board of Education*, 333 U.S. 203 (1948).

6. *Zorach v. Clauson*, 343 U.S. 306 (1952).

7. *Adamson v. California*, 332 U.S. 46 (1947).

8. *Betts v. Brady*, 316 U.S. 455 (1942); *Johnson v. U.S.*, 318 U.S. 189 (1943).

9. See, for example, *Harris v. U.S.*, 331 U.S. 145 (1947) and *Trupiano v. U.S.*, 334 U.S. 699 (1948).

10. *Wolf v. Colorado*, 338 U.S. 25 (1949).

11. *Rosenberg v. U.S.* 344 U.S. 838, 889 (1952).

12. *Rosenberg v. U.S.* 346 U.S. 273 (1953).

Rep. William M. Wheeler (D, Ga.) introduced a resolution to impeach Douglas for his action, but the House Judiciary Committee killed the resolution in July.

During the 1950s Douglas became even more liberal in his constitutional views. In free speech cases, for example, he abandoned the clear and present danger rule and took up the absolutist position that the First Amendment barred all government regulation of expression unless it was tied to illegal action.[1] He also took a stricter view of the Fourth Amendment's prohibition on unreasonable searches and seizures.[2] Underlying such shifts, many commentators believed, was a growing skepticism and distrust of government. Douglas showed an increasing concern for protecting the individual from the power and intrusiveness of big government. Himself something of a rebel and nonconformist, the Justice demonstrated a special interest in safeguarding the rights of dissenters and outcasts, the poor and minority groups.

Throughout this period Douglas maintained his opposition to all loyalty-security programs. In June 1958 he wrote the majority opinion in a decision overturning the State Department's policy of nying passports to members of the Communist Party. Douglas stated that the Department did not have congressional authorization for this practice. In addition, he ruled that the right to travel was protected by the Fifth Amendment's due process clause.[3] That same month Douglas wrote a dissenting opinion in two cases where the Court upheld the dismissal of public employes who had refused to answer questions about possible Communist Party affiliations.[4] Douglas again dissented in two February 1961 cases where the majority upheld the contempt-of-Congress convictions of witnesses who had refused to answer questions before a House Un-American Activities subcommittee.[5] He also objected to two decisions in June 1961 sustaining provisions in federal anti-subversive laws.[6]

Douglas also continued to vote for extension of the right to counsel to all during the 1950s.[7] In March 1956 he wrote a dissenting opinion when the Court upheld a federal law under which the government could force a witness to testify in security cases by promising him immunity from prosecution. Douglas asserted that the Fifth Amendment made it unconstitutional for Congress to compel anyone to confess to a crime, even with an immunity guarantee.[8] His opinion for the Court in a November 1959 case held that mere suspicion that someone had committed a felony was not sufficient grounds for his arrest.[9] A strong supporter of the guarantee of equal protection of the laws, Douglas joined in a Court trend expanding the constitutional rights of blacks.[10] He unhesitatingly voted with his colleagues in May 1954 to hold racial segregation in public schools a violation of the 14th Amendment.[11] He also favored extension of this decision to other public facilities.[12]

After years of expressing many of his views in dissent, Douglas saw a liberal Court majority adopt many of his positions during the 1960s. In criminal cases, for example, the Court overturned in June 1961 the 1949 ruling to which Douglas had objected and held that state courts

---

1. See, for example, his dissenting opinion in *Roth v. U.S.,* 354 U.S. 476, 508 (1957).

2. See, for example, his dissenting opinion in *On Lee v. U.S.,* 343 U.S. 747, 762 (1952), and *Irvine v. California,* 347 U.S. 128, 149 (1954).

3. *Kent v. Dulles,* 357 U.S. 116 (1958).

4. *Beilan v. Board of Education,* 357 U.S. 399 (1958); *Lerner v. Casey,* 357 U.S. 468 (1958).

5. *Wilkinson v. U.S.,* 365 U.S. 399 (1961); *Braden v. U.S.,* 365 U.S. 431 (1961).

6. *Communist Party v. Subversive Activities Control Board,* 367 U.S. 1 (1961); *Scales v. U.S.,* 367 U.S. 203 (1961).

7. See, for example, *Moore v. Michigan,* 355 U.S. 155 (1957); *Cash v. Culver,* 358 U.S. 633 (1959).

8. *Ullman v. U.S.,* 350 U.S. 422, 440 (1956).

9. *Henry v. U.S.,* 361 U.S. 98 (1959).

10. See, for example, *Shelley v. Kraemer,* 334 U.S. 1 (1948); *Sweatt v. Painter,* 339 U.S. 629 (1950); *McLaurin v. Oklahoma State Regents,* 339 U.S. 637 (1950); *Henderson v. U.S.,* 339 U.S. 816 (1950).

11. *Brown v. Board of Education,* 347 U.S. 483 (1954).

12. See, for example, his dissenting opinions in *On Baltimore v. Dawson,* 350 U.S. 877 (1955); *Gayle v. Browder,* 352 U.S. 903 (1956).

must exclude illegally seized evidence.[1] In March 1963 a unanimous Court finally agreed that the right to counsel must be afforded to all state criminal defendants charged with a serious crime.[2] Douglas himself wrote the majority opinion in another March 1963 case requiring the states to supply counsel to an indigent defendant for appeal of a criminal conviction.[3] He also spoke for the majority in an April 1965 case holding it a violation of the Fifth Amendment's privilege against self-incrimination for a state judge or district attorney to comment during a trial on a defendant's refusal to take the stand.[4] The Justice joined in the June 1966 *Miranda* decision in which the Court adopted views he had long urged and ruled that the Fifth Amendment required police to tell a criminal suspect of his rights to remain silent and to counsel during interrogation. Douglas wrote for the majority in January 1967 when it ruled that self-incriminating statements made by public employes who had been threatened with dismissal if they invoked their Fifth Amendment rights were inadmissible at trial.[7]

In March 1962 the Court also overruled a 1946 precedent from which Douglas had dissented and held that federal courts could try legislative apportionment cases.[8] Douglas then wrote the majority opinion in a March 1963 decision that invalidated Georgia's county-unit system of voting and mandated in its place a one-man, one-vote standard of apportionment.[9] He also joined in two 1964 decisions which established a one-man, one-vote standard for both congressional and state legislative districting.[10]

During the 1960s Douglas moved to an absolutist position on freedom of religion and separation of church and state. He dissented from four May 1961 cases upholding state laws for Sunday closings of businesses, contending that the statutes enforced the Christian view of Sunday as a day of rest.[11] Douglas concurred in Court decisions of June 1962 and June 1963 holding prayer and Bible-reading in public schools unconstitutional.[12] In an opinion in one of those cases, the Justice disavowed his acceptance during the 1940s of even limited state aid to parochial school students.[13]

Douglas extended his First Amendment views into new fields in these years. With Justice Black, he had insisted in a June 1957 case that the Amendment prohibited all government regulation of allegedly obscene materials, and the two reaffirmed this view in important obscenity decisions in June 1964 and March 1966.[14] Douglas also joined in concurring opinions in two 1964 cases that urged the Court to hold that there was an absolute right to criticize—even maliciously—the conduct of public officials.[15] Although a majority did not go as far as Douglas wished in obscenity and libel cases, it did join him in the mid-1960s in overturning many federal and state loyalty-security measures.[16] In addition, in May 1964, Douglas wrote the Court's five-man majority opinion overturning a federal law

1. *Mapp v. Ohio,* 367 U.S. 643 (1961).

2. *Gideon v. Wainwright,* 372 U.S. 335 (1963).

3. *Douglas v. California,* 372 U.S. 353 (1963).

4. *Griffin v. California,* 380 U.S. 609 (1965).

5. See, for example, *Crooker v. California,* 357 U.S. 433 (1958); *Reck v. Pate,* 367 U.S. 433 (1961).

6. *Miranda v. Arizona,* 384 U.S. 436 (1966).

7. *Garrity v. New Jersey,* 385 U.S. 493 (1967).

8. *Baker v. Carr,* 369 U.S. 186 (1962), overruling *Colegrove v. Green,* 328 U.S. 549 (1946).

9. *Gray v. Sanders,* 372 U.S. 368 (1963).

10. *Wesberry v. Sanders,* 376 U.S. 1 (1964); *Reynolds v. Sims,* 377 U.S. 533 (1964).

11. *McGowan v. Maryland,* 366 U.S. 420 (1961); *Two Guys from Harrison-Allentown, Inc. v. McGinley,* 366 U.S. 582 (1961); *Braunfeld v. Brown,* 366 U.S. 599 (1961); *Gallagher v. Crown Kosher Super Market,* 366 U.S. 617 (1961).

12. *Engel v. Vitale,* 370 U.S. 421 (1962); *School District of Abington Township v. Schempp,* 374 U.S. 203 (1963).

13. *Engel v. Vitale,* 370 U.S. at 443–444.

14. *Roth v. U.S.,* 354 U.S. 476 (1957); *Jacobellis v. Ohio,* 378 U.S. 184 (1964); *Memoirs v. Massachusetts,* 383 U.S. 413 (1966); *Ginzburg v. U.S.,* 383 U.S. 463 (1966).

15. *New York Times Co. v. Sullivan,* 376 U.S. 254 (1964); *Garrison v. Louisiana,* 379 U.S. 64 (1964).

16. See, for example, *Aptheker v. Secretary of State,* 378 U.S. 500 (1964); *Albertson v. Subversive Activities Control Board,* 382 U.S. 70 (1965); *Keyishian v. Board of Regents,* 385 U.S. 589 (1967).

canceling the citizenship of naturalized Americans who returned to their native land for a three-year period.[1] Dissenting in a 1958 decision, Douglas had expressed the view that Congress could not take away American citizenship;[2] in a May 1967 decision, the Court adopted his position that citizenship could only be relinquished voluntarily.[3]

In the late 1960s Douglas surpassed even his long-time judicial ally, Hugo Black, in his willingness to use the Constitution to safeguard individual freedoms against government interference. Beginning in 1961 Douglas had concurred in decisions overturning the state convictions of civil rights demonstrators.[4] When the Court changed course in November 1966 and, with Black in the majority, upheld the trespass convictions of demonstrators who gathered in protest outside a Florida jail, Douglas wrote the dissenting opinion and asserted that a jail could be a proper place for protest.[5]

Douglas was also willing, unlike Black, to read into the Constitution rights not explicitly guaranteed. In a famed and controversial opinion for the Court in the June 1965 case of *Griswold v. Connecticut,* he overturned an anti-contraceptive law because it invaded a right to marital privacy, which he said was guaranteed by the Constitution. In an expansive reading of the Bill of Rights, Douglas found this right to privacy in the "penumbras, formed by emanations" from the specific guarantees of the First, Third, Fourth, Fifth and Ninth Amendments.[6] Douglas was also a foremost exponent of using the guarantee of equal protection to guard the rights of the poor and other disadvantaged groups as well as racial minorities. His majority opinion in a March 1966 case invalidated a poll tax for state elections on the ground that it was a denial of equal protection to make affluence a qual-

ification for voting.[7] In May 1968 Douglas also overturned a Louisiana law that denied illegitimate children certain rights given to legitimate offspring, insisting[8] upon equal treatment of the two groups. The Justice also took an expansive view of the due process clause in these years[9] and was the sole dissenter from a June 1968 decision upholding the right of police to stop and frisk persons for weapons when the action seemed necessary for the safety of the policeman and others present.[10]

Aside from his constitutional views, Douglas became well-known to the public for his many off-the-bench activities. One of the most colorful justices in the Court's history, Douglas was a vigorous and seemingly tireless man who always disagreed with his colleagues' assertions that the Court's workload was too great. He had become an avid outdoorsman after first taking up hiking in his youth to overcome the effects of polio, and he used his free time to go hiking and mountain climbing and to travel widely. A frequent public speaker and a prolific author, Douglas wrote numerous articles and books on the environment, his travels and international affairs, and he occasionally commented on current events. Douglas also married four times; following his fourth marriage in 1966 to a 23 year old woman, an attempt was made to impeach him for having an allegedly bad moral character.

Outspoken and unconventional, Douglas was by the late 1960s a symbol to many Americans of the liberal judicial activism that characterized the Warren Court. Partly because of that position, he was the target of a third and more serious impeachment attempt in 1970. On April 15, after the Senate had rejected two of President Richard Nixon's nominees for the Court, House Minority Leader Gerald

---

1. *Schneider v. Rusk,* 377 U.S. 163 (1964).

2. *Perez v. Brownell,* 356 U.S. 44, 79 (1958).

3. *Afroyim v. Rusk,* 387 U.S. 253 (1967).

4. See, for example, *Garner v. Louisiana,* 368 U.S. 157 (1961); *Edwards v. South Carolina,* 372 U.S. 229 (1963).

5. *Adderley v. Florida,* 385 U.S. 39 (1966).

6. 381 U.S. 479 (1965).

7. *Harper v. Virginia State Board of Elections,* 383 U.S. 663 (1966).

8. *Levy v. Louisiana,* 391 U.S. 68 (1968).

9. See, for example, *Sniadach v. Family Finance Corp.,* 395 U.S. 337 (1969).

10. *Terry v. Ohio,* 392 U.S. 1 (1968).

R. Ford (R, Mich.) launched a move to impeach Douglas for alleged improprieties in his professional conduct. Ford challenged the Justice's association with the Albert Parvin Foundation prior to 1969 and with the Center for the Study of Democratic Institutions; the views Douglas expressed in his book *Points of Rebellion;* the publication of excerpts from the book in an allegedly pornographic magazine; and, the Justice's participation in several cases in which Ford detected a conflict of interest. A special House Judiciary subcommittee began investigating the charges on April 21. In a report released Dec. 15, the subcommittee cleared Douglas of all the allegations and declared there were no grounds for impeachment.

On the Burger Court Douglas resumed the role he had played earlier in his judicial career of dissenter from the rulings of a more conservative Court majority. Beginning with the 1969 Court term, he entered far more dissents than any other justice, and he staked out a position as the most liberal member of the high bench. Especially notable were Douglas's numerous dissents from Court decisions refusing to hear cases, such as those challenging the legality of the Vietnam war.[1] Douglas favored making the Court an accessible forum where the aggrieved could obtain a remedy for deprivations of their civil and constitutional rights. He urged the Court to take more cases, and he opposed rulings that limited the Court's jurisdiction to decide lawsuits.[2]

Douglas also dissented from many Burger Court criminal decisions. He objected to all rulings that in any way limited the scope of the 1966 *Miranda* decision[3] and to judgments sanctioning warrantless searches and electronic surveillance.[4] In May 1971 and May 1972 dissents, he maintained his position that the Fifth Amendment's privilege against self-incrimination barred the government from compelling anyone to confess to a crime, even with an immunity guarantee. Douglas did join the majority in June 1970 to validate six member juries in state courts, but he opposed a May 1972 decision allowing non-unanimous jury verdicts.[5] He urged the Court to extend the right to a jury to all trials and to juvenile court proceedings.[6] In a June 1972 opinion for the Court, Douglas held that an indigent defendant could not be jailed, even for a misdemeanor, unless given free counsel.[7]

Justice Douglas continued to express his concern for those who were disadvantaged and different from the rest of society. A longtime critic of vagrancy laws, he wrote the majority opinion in a February 1972 case overturning a municipal vagrancy ordinance because it was vague and subject to arbitrary enforcement.[8] The Justice voted to overturn the death penalty in June 1972, largely because under existing laws judges and juries could discriminate against the poor and minorities in imposing the death sentence.[9] Douglas retained a predominantly activist stance in racial discrimination cases[10] and opposed all forms of discrimination against illegitimate children, against the poor and against women.[11] In a June 1969 opinion he overturned state laws permitting garnishment of a debtor's wages prior to any

---

1. See, for example, *Massachusetts v. Laird*, 400 U.S. 886 (1970).

2. See, for example, *O'Shea v. Littleton*, 414 U.S. 488 (1974); *Warth v. Seldin*, 422 U.S. 490 (1975).

3. See, for example, *Harris v. New York*, 401 U.S. 222 (1971); *Michigan v. Tucker*, 417 U.S. 433 (1974).

4. See, for example, *U.S. v. White*, 401 U.S. 745 (1971); *Adams v. Williams*, 407 U.S. 143 (1972); *U.S. v. Robinson*, 414 U.S. 218 (1973).

5. *California v. Byers*, 402 U.S. 424 (1971); *Kastigar v. U.S.*, 406 U.S. 441 (1972).

6. *Williams v. Florida*, 399 U.S. 78 (1970); *Johnson v. Louisiana*, 406 U.S. 356 (1972); *Apodaca v. Oregon*, 406 U.S. 404 (1972).

7. *Baldwin v. New York*, 399 U.S. 66, 74 (1970); *McKeiver v. Pennsylvania*, 403 U.S. 528 (1971).

8. *Argersinger v. Hamlin*, 407 U.S. 25 (1972).

9. *Papachristou v. City of Jacksonville*, 405 U.S. 156 (1972).

10. *Furman v. Georgia*, 408 U.S. 238, 240 (1972).

69. See, for example, *Sullivan v. Little Hunting Park, Inc.*, 396 U.S. 229 (1969); *Moose Lodge No. 107 v. Irvis*, 407 U.S. 163 (1972).

11. See, for example, *Labine v. Vincent*, 401 U.S. 532 (1971); *San Antonio Independent School District v. Rodriguez*, 411 U.S. 1 (1973); *Geduldig v. Aiello*, 417 U.S. 484 (1974).

hearing.[1] In subsequent cases Douglas voted to guarantee hearings to welfare recipients before termination of their benefits, to defendants before revocation of their parole and to public employes prior to dismissal.[2] He favored removing restrictions on the right to vote based on age, residency or status.[3]

In First Amendment cases Douglas adhered to his absolutist position. He opposed all loyalty oath and obscenity laws in these years[4] and favored giving constitutional protection to a wide variety of symbolic forms of expression such as wearing a black armband or putting a peace symbol on the flag to protest the Vietnam war.[5] He believed freedom of the press was unassailable and voted against the government's request for an injunction to halt newspaper publication of the *Pentagon Papers* in June 1971.[6] Douglas also opposed all state aid to parochial education as a violation of the First Amendment[7] and was the lone dissenter in May 1970 when the Court upheld tax exemptions for church property used solely for religious purposes.[8]

A dedicated conservationist and naturalist, Douglas wrote several important environmental law opinions. In an April 1973 case he ruled that the states could establish stiffer penalties for maritime oil spills than the federal government.[9] A year later Douglas sustained a municipal zoning ordinance barring communal living groups as a legitimate land use law aimed at preserving a quiet, uncongested residential area.[10] When the majority ruled in April 1972 that the Sierra Club did not

have the necessary legal interest to challenge the building of a ski resort in Sequoia National Forest, Douglas entered a widely discussed dissent that argued that inanimate objects such as trees and rivers should be accorded legal standing and be allowed to sue in their own name for their preservation.[11]

On Dec. 31, 1974, while vacationing in the Bahamas, Douglas suffered a stroke. He retired from the Court on Nov. 12, 1975, when he found that the after effects of the stroke kept him from performing his share of the Court's work. By the time of his retirement, Douglas had served more than 36 years on the bench, longer than any other justice in the Court's history, and had written over 1,200 opinions.

Assessing that unprecedented career, most commentators praised Douglas for the great range of his legal work and interests and for his growth while on the Court. He broadened, as one observer noted, "from the corporate financial specialist of the New Deal era to a sophisticated expert on important matters ranging from ecology and civil liberties to international relations." Douglas's critics added, however, that he had been too subjective and doctrinaire and too result-oriented in his approach to cases. His opinions, they charged, especially in his later years, showed little regard for history or precedent and were frequently brief, idiosyncratic essays devoid of legal analysis and exposition. The Justice's defenders, however, argued that his decisions reflected a legal realism that attempted to make the law responsive to the new problems and

---

1. *Sniadach v. Family Finance Corp.*, 395 U.S. 337 (1969).

2. *Goldberg v. Kelly*, 397 U.S. 254 (1970); *Morrissey v. Brewer*, 408 U.S. 471 (1972); *Arnett v. Kennedy*, 416 U.S. 134 (1974).

3. See, for example, *Phoenix v. Kolodziejski*, 399 U.S. 204 (1970); *Oregon v. Mitchell*, 400 U.S. 112 (1970); *Dunn v. Blumstein*, 405 U.S. 330 (1972).

4. See, for example, *Cole v. Richardson*, 405 U.S. 676 (1972); *Miller v. California*, 413 U.S. 15 (1973); *Paris Adult Theatre I v. Slaton*, 413 U.S. 49 (1973).

5. *Tinker v. Des Moines School District*, 393 U.S. 503 (1969); *Spence v. Washington*, 418 U.S. 405 (1974).

6. *New York Times Co. v. U.S.*, 403 U.S. 713 (1971).

7. See, for example, *Lemon v. Kurtzman*, 403 U.S. 602 (1971).

8. *Walz v. Tax Commission of the City of New York*, 397 U.S. 664 (1970).

9. *Askew v. American Waterways Operators, Inc.*, 411 U.S. 325 (1973).

10. *Village of Belle Terre v. Boraas*, 416 U.S. 1 (1974).

11. *Sierra Club v. Morton*, 405 U.S. 727, 741 (1972).

needs of a changing society. Douglas, according to law professor Michal Sovern, insisted that "the law must be shaped to bear witness to the moral development of society" and sought "a simple and uncompromising focus on basic values" in Court decisions. As a result, he achieved "an original and profound vision of the role of law in society." All observers recognized Douglas's significant impact in various fields of law and his special devotion to individual freedoms. Douglas's role "in shaping the Constitution into a more effective shield for the rights of individuals," professor William Beany wrote, "and in stressing the Bill of Rights as essential to the maintenance of a free society, will give him a strong claim to a place in the gallery of outstanding American jurists."

FORTAS, ABE

b. June 19, 1920; Memphis, Tenn.
Associate Justice, U.S. Supreme Court,
1965-69.

The son of a Jewish cabinetmaker who had emigrated from England, Fortas worked his way through Southwestern College in Memphis, receiving his B.A. in 1930. Three years later he graduated from Yale Law School, where he had been editor-in-chief of the *Yale Law Journal*. He then taught at the school from 1933 to 1937. During those four years he also worked part-time for the Agricultural Adjustment Administration and the Securities and Exchange Commission (SEC). From 1937 to 1946 Fortas successively held posts in the SEC, the Public Works Administration and the Department of Interior, serving as undersecretary of the interior from 1942 to 1946.

With several other New Dealers, Fortas then entered private practice. The law firm of Arnold, Fortas & Porter soon became one of the most prestigious and prosperous in Washington with a roster of corporate clients that included Coca Cola, Lever Brothers, Philip Morris and Pan American Airways. Fortas was known for his effectiveness in corporate counseling, antitrust litigation, practice before administrative agencies and appellate advocacy. He and his firm also developed a reputation for handling, often without charge, some important civil liberties and individual rights cases. Fortas defended several persons charged with being security risks during the McCarthy era. In 1954, serving as court-appointed counsel, he won a landmark ruling from the District of Columbia Court of Appeals which broadened the criminal insanity rule.[1] Again as court-appointed counsel, Fortas represented Clarence Earl Gideon before the Supreme Court in 1963 and got a unanimous Court to overturn a 1942 decision and rule that the states must supply counsel to an indigent defendant accused of a serious crime.[2]

Fortas successfully represented Lyndon Johnson in legal proceedings following his controversial victory in the 1948 Texas Democratic primary. The incident launched a long, close friendship between the two men, and Fortas became Johnson's confidant and one of his most trusted advisers. Johnson's first phone call following John Kennedy's assassination was to Abe Fortas. He often relied heavily on Fortas's counsel during his presidential years. Fortas helped organized the Warren Commission, which investigated Kennedy's assassination, and advised Johnson on appointments, speeches, legislation and foreign policy. He also participated in strategy conferences during the 1964 presidential campaign. When Walter Jenkins [*q.v.*], a top White House aide, was arrested on a morals charge in the fall of 1964, Fortas attempted to keep the story out of the press and then advised Johnson on how to handle the situation. During the Dominican crisis in the spring of 1965, Fortas acted as an unofficial contact between the U.S. and former Dominican president Juan Bosch.

In 1964 Fortas refused an offer to be named Attorney General, preferring to keep his role as Johnson's unofficial adviser. In July 1965, when Arthur Goldberg [*q.v.*] resigned from the Supreme Court to become ambassador to the U.N., Fortas also turned down a nomination to a Court seat. On July 28, however, when Johnson told Fortas he was going to announce his appointment as Associate Justice that day, Fortas acquiesced. Fortas's nomination was well received, and the Senate confirmed his appointment on Aug. 11.

On the bench Fortas was usually in accord with the liberal, activist justices of the Warren Court. He was part of the five-man majority in the June 1966 *Mi-*

---

1. *Durham v. U.S.*, 214 F.2d 862 (D.C. Cir. 1954)

2. *Gideon v. Wainwright*, 372 U.S. 335 (1963), overruling *Betts v. Brady*, 316 U.S. 455 (1942).

randa decision, which placed limits on police interrogation of criminal suspects.[1] Writing for the Court in the May 1967 case of *In re Gault*, Fortas extended to children in juvenile court proceedings many of the constitutional protections required in adult trials.[2] He also joined the majority in a June 1968 decision which barred the exclusion of individuals from murder trial juries solely because they expressed conscientious or religious scruples against capital punishment.[3] However, later the same month, Fortas was part of a majority which upheld the right of police to stop and frisk persons for weapons under certain circumstances.[4]

Fortas voted repeatedly to sustain civil rights claims. He supported, for example, a March 1966 decision holding unconstitutional a Virginia poll tax for state elections[5] and a June 1968 ruling that an 1866 federal law prohibited racial discrimination in the sale and rental of housing and other property.[6] Fortas's majority opinion in a March 1966 case upheld the federal prosecution, under an 1870 civil rights law, of 17 persons accused of involvement in the murder of three civil rights workers in Mississippi in June 1964.[7] In February 1966 his opinion for the Court overturned the breach-of-the-peace convictions of five blacks who had tried to integrate a public library in Louisiana.[8] Fortas dissented in November 1966 and June 1967 cases in which the majority voted to sustain convictions of civil rights demonstrators.[9]

Fortas's opinion for a unanimous Court in June 1966 reversed the contempt-of-Congress conviction of a former labor union officer who had refused to answer questions before a House Un-American Activities subcommittee.[10] In two 1967 cases Fortas voted to invalidate a Maryland loyalty oath law for public employees[11] and a set of New York State teacher loyalty laws as violations of the First Amendment.[12] He dissented, however, in January 1967 when the Court extended to invasion of privacy suits the rule that erroneous statements had to be made deliberately or recklessly before the press could be held liable.[13] Fortas also voted in favor of a March 1966 ruling that "titillating" advertising could be used to convict a publisher of obscenity, although the materials sold might not in themselves be obscene.[14] As a former corporate attorney, Fortas tended to differ with other liberal justices when they ruled against corporate mergers or altered the judgments of federal regulatory agencies in ways opposed by business.[15]

While on the Court, Fortas remained a close adviser to President Johnson, counseling him on such important and delicate issues as race, urban unrest and the Vietnam War. Reportedly, neither Johnson nor Fortas saw anything wrong in continuing their close, personal relationship, but their friendship became a source of controversy when Fortas was nominated for the chief justiceship.

On June 13, 1968 Chief Justice Earl Warren sent the President a letter of resignation. Announcing Warren's retirement on June 26, Johnson nominated Fortas as Chief Justice and Homer Thornberry, a judge on the U.S. Court of Appeals for the Fifth Circuit and a long -time Johnson as-

---

1. *Miranda v. Arizona*, 384 U.S. 436 (1966).

2. 387 U.S. 1 (1967)

3. *Witherspoon v. Illinois*, 391 U.S. 510 (1968)

4. *Terry v. Ohio*, 392 U.S. 1 (1968)

5. *Harper v. Virginia State Board of Elections*, 383 U.S. 663 (1966)

6. *Jones v. Mayer*, 392 U.S. 409 (1968)

7. *U.S. v. Price*, 383 U.S. 787 (1968)

8. *Brown v. Louisiana*, 383 U.S. 131 (1966)

9. *Adderley v. Florida*, 385 U.S. 39 (1966); *Walker v. City of Birmingham*, 388 U.S. 307 (1967)

10. *Gojack v. U.S.*, 384 U.S. 702 (1966)

11. *Whitehill v. Elkins*, 389 U.S. 54 (1967)

12. *Keyishian v. Board of Regents*, 385 U.S. 589 (1967)

13. *Time, Inc. v. Hill*, 385 U.S. 374 (1967)

14. *Ginzburg v. U.S.*, 383 U.S. 463 (1966)

15. See, for example, Fortas's dissenting opinion in *Baltimore & Ohio Railroad Co. v. U.S.*, 386 U.S. 372 (1967)

sociate, for Fortas's seat. Eighteen Republican senators, led by Robert P. Griffin (R, Mich.) declared shortly afterwards that they would try to block confirmation of the appointments. Aside from the alleged impropriety of Fortas's advisory relationship with Johnson, opponents of the nominations objected to having a "lame-duck" president choose the new Chief Justice and charged Johnson with cronyism in making his selections. In mid-July Fortas made an unprecedented appearance at the Senate Judiciary Committee hearings on his nomination. Unfriendly questioning by several senators, including Strom Thurmond (R, S.C.), made it apparent that hostility to liberal Warren Court decisions and to Fortas's own position on several controversial issues was also a factor in the opposition to his confirmation.

In September it was disclosed that Fortas had received $15,000 for teaching a nine-week course in the summer of 1968 at American University Law School. The money had been raised by one of Fortas's former law partners from five prominent businessmen, one of whom had a son involved in a federal criminal case. The Senate Judiciary Committee reported out Fortas's nomination on Sept. 17, by an 11 to 6 vote, but a coalition of Republicans and conservative Democrats launched a filibuster against the appointment when it came up for Senate consideration late that month. A vote for cloture failed on Oct. 1, and the next day, Fortas asked Johnson to withdraw his nomination. Chief Justice Warren then agreed to stay on until the new president named his successor.

Despite the defeat of his nomination, there was every expectation as the 1968 Court term opened that Fortas would still have a long, productive and influential career as an associate justice. He seemed at ease on the bench and had won respect for his intelligence and legal craftsmanship and for opinions that were thorough and scholarly yet also crisp and colorful in style. During the term Fortas wrote several significant opinions for the Court which advanced the libertarian views he espoused. In November 1968 the Justice held that Arkansas's "monkey law," which forbade the teaching of the Darwinian theory of evolution in public schools, violated the First Amendment's ban on establishment of religion.[1] A week later Fortas ruled that a court order restraining the National States Rights Party from holding a public rally for 10 days was an unconstitutional violation of free speech because the injunction had been granted at a hearing without prior notice to Party representatives.[2] For a seven-man majority in February 1969, Fortas declared that the First Amendment guaranteed public school students the right to peaceful, nondisruptive political expression such as the wearing of black armbands to protest the Vietnam War.[3]

In another February 1969 case involving "jailhouse lawyers," Fortas's majority opinion held that the states could not bar a prisoner from giving legal aid to illiterate or poorly educated fellow inmates when no other provision was made for those inmates to receive legal assistance in appealing their convictions.[4] For a five-man majority Fortas ruled in April 1969 that a lineup identification of a suspect could not be used as evidence at trial when the lineup was arranged so that the defendant stood out as the likely criminal.[5]

Off the bench Justice Fortas and his wife, a top Washington tax attorney, enjoyed a life of comfort and culture. Their Georgetown home contained antique furniture, contemporary works of art and Chinese scrolls and paintings. They drove a Rolls Royce and had a summer house in Connecticut. An accomplished amateur violinist, Fortas played in a string quartet at least once a week.

Fortas's judicial career ended suddenly in May 1969 when he resigned from the

---

1. *Epperson v. Arkansas*, 393 U.S. 97 (1968)
2. *Carroll v. President and Commissioners of Princess Anne*, 393 U.S. 175 (1968)

3. *Tinker v. Des Moines School District*, 393 U.S. 503 (1969).
4. *Johnson v. Avery*, 393 U.S. 483 (1969)
5. *Foster v. California*, 394 U.S. 440 (1969)

Court in the wake of disclosures of questionable financial associations. On May 4 *Life* magazine reported that in January 1966 Fortas had accepted $20,000 from the family foundation of industrialist Louis E. Wolfson. He had returned the money in December 1966 after Wolfson was twice indicted on federal stock charges. Since then, Wolfson had been convicted and imprisoned for selling unregistered securities. On the same day, Fortas issued a statement declaring that he had "not accepted any fee or emolument" from Wolfson or his foundation but then conceding that the foundation had tendered him a fee in 1966 for research and writing services. Fortas said he had returned the fee when he concluded that he could not undertake the assignment. He insisted that he had not intervened in any way in Wolfson's SEC or criminal cases.

Nonetheless, some Congressmen began calling for Fortas's resignation and there was talk of impeachment. The pressure increased when *Newsweek* magazine revealed on May 11 that Attorney General John Mitchell had visited Chief Justice Warren on May 7, reportedly to tell him that the Justice Department had "far more serious" information about Fortas than had already been disclosed. Fortas submitted his resignation on May 14 and made it public the next day along with a letter to Earl Warren explaining his action. In the letter Fortas stated that late in 1965 he had made an agreement with the Wolfson Foundation that gave him $20,000 a year for life in exchange for services to the foundation. He had received the first fee in January 1966 but had canceled the agreement that June because his Court duties were taking more time than anticipated. Fortas had returned the money in December 1966 following Wolfson's indictment. Fortas declared he was resigning for the good of the Court and flatly denied any wrongdoing. On May 20, 1969 the American Bar Association's Committee on Professional Ethics concluded that Fortas's association with Wolfson was "clearly contrary" to the Canons of Judicial Ethics. The Justice Department, which had been conducting its own inquiry, decided that Fortas had done nothing criminal and closed its file on the matter.

The first justice ever to leave the Court under the pressure of public criticism, Fortas made no further public statement about the Wolfson episode and returned quietly to private life. He spent some time writing a book which he later decided not to publish, and he gradually undertook some legal work. By the spring of 1970 Fortas had joined in a small new law firm in Washington.

Although his tenure on the bench was brief, Fortas was well-regarded by legal scholars because of the creativity and craftsmanship of his opinions. Despite their appreciation for the high quality of his work, however, all commentators deplored Fortas's financial indiscretions which damaged the Court's reputation and cut short what had been a most promising judicial career.

FRANKFURTER, FELIX

b. Nov. 15, 1882; Vienna, Austria
d. Feb. 22, 1965; Washington, D.C.
Associate Justice, U.S. Supreme
Court, 1939–62.

Felix Frankfurter emigrated to the United States with his family at the age of 12. He graduated from the City College of New York in 1902 and from Harvard Law School in 1906. During the next eight years he was an assistant U.S. attorney in New York and an aide to Secretary of War Henry Stimson. A faculty member at Harvard Law School from 1914 to 1939, Frankfurter became a noted scholar on the Supreme Court, the Constitution and administrative law. He also maintained a wide range of extracurricular activities that won him a liberal reputation. He served as an adviser to the NAACP and the American Civil Liberties Union, supported labor unions and fought to have the convictions of Italian anarchists Nicola Sacco and Bartolomeo Vanzetti overturned. During the New Deal Frankfurter acted as a counselor to President Franklin Roosevelt, advising him on legislation, appointments and speeches. Roosevelt named him to the Supreme Court in January 1939.

On the Court Justice Frankfurter became the leading advocate of judicial restraint. Legislatures, he contended, were the policymaking bodies in a democratic society, and the Court must defer to their judgments and sustain laws with a constitutional basis, however unwise the justices might think them to be. Frankfurter used this approach not only in the economic arena to uphold New Deal legislation but also in the realm of civil liberties to sustain laws curtailing freedom of belief and expression. Although it meant voting against causes he had earlier championed, Frankfurter insisted that judges must be disinterested and detached and must not read into the Constitution their own notions of good policy. Unlike Justice Hugo Black, Frankfurter did not give First Amendment rights any preferred position over other constitutional guarantees nor did he consider any provisions in the Bill of Rights absolutes. He insisted that the Court must balance the conflicting interests in each case, making its judgments without any doctrinaire presuppositions. When he did vote to overturn government action affecting individual freedoms, Frankfurter usually offered narrow procedural or statutory reasons rather than broad constitutional grounds.

In free speech cases, Justice Frankfurter weighed the rights of the individual against the state's claims of order or security. As a result of such balancing, he voted in February 1947 to uphold the Hatch Act's ban on political activity by federal employes,[1] and in two cases in 1948 and 1949, to sustain local ordinances regulating the use of sound trucks.[2] His majority opinion in an April 1952 case also upheld an Illinois law prohibiting group libel which had been challenged on First Amendment grounds.[3] However, Frankfurter spoke for a unanimous Court in February 1957 to hold unconstitutional a Michigan obscenity law banning all sale of books "inappropriate" for children.[4] In January 1961, though, he voted to sustain a Chicago ordinance barring the public showing of movies without prior approval of city censors.[5]

Frankfurter occupied a center position on the Court on loyalty-security issues. He dissented in January 1950 when a majority held that an alien war bride could be denied entry to the U.S. without a hearing because of accusations that she was a security risk.[6] He also concurred in April 1951 when a majority ordered lower court hearings for three organizations

---

1. *United Public Workers of America v. Mitchell,* 330 U.S. 75 (1947).

2. *Saia v. New York,* 334 U.S. 558 (1948); *Kovacs v. Cooper,* 336 U.S. 77 (1949).

3. *Beauharnais v. Illinois,* 343 U.S. 250 (1952).

4. *Butler v. Michigan,* 352 U.S. 380 (1957).

5. *Times Film Corp. v. Chicago,* 365 U.S. 43 (1961).

6. *U.S. ex rel. Knauff v. Shaughnessy,* 338 U.S. 537 (1950).

which had sued to be taken off the Attorney General's list of subversive organizations. Frankfurter believed the groups' placement on the list without notice or hearing denied the organizations due process.[1] The Justice joined in a June 1957 decision reversing the contempt conviction of an economics professor who had refused to answer a state official's questions about the content of his lectures and his association with the Progressive Party. In a concurring opinion Frankfurter delivered a strong defense of the rights to academic and political freedom.[2] In April 1956 he was part of a six-man majority that overturned a state sedition law because Congress had superseded it in the Smith Act,[3] and he concurred in a June 1957 decision placing limits on congressional investigations of subversion.[4]

But Frankfurter often upheld government security interests against claims of individual freedom. In June 1951 he concurred when the Court upheld the convictions of American Communist Party leaders under the Smith Act. Although his opinion made clear that he considered the act unwise, Frankfurter could not find grounds for declaring it unconstitutional.[5] He joined the majority in two June 1959 cases that sustained the contempt convictions of individuals who refused to answer questions or supply information during congressional and state investigations of Communism.[6] Frankfurter also voted in several cases to uphold the dismissal of municipal and county government employes who had refused to answer question concerning their political views and associations.[7] In June 1961 the Justice wrote the majority opinion in a five-to-four decision upholding the re-

quirement of the 1950 Internal Security Act for Communist organizations to register with the government. Although he recognized that registration and disclosure of membership could infringe on the First Amendment's guarantee of free association in some circumstances, Frankfurter emphasized that this law applied only to U.S. branches of foreign-controlled organizations, and he sustained it as a reasonable legislative action.[8]

Frankfurter was more activist in federal criminal cases where the Supreme Court had special supervisory responsibilities and where relatively specific constitutional clauses were available to guide the justices. He showed a strong concern for procedural fairness and was particularly insistent that the Fourth Amendment's prohibition of unreasonable searches and seizures be strictly observed. In a series of Fourth Amendment cases decided between 1947 and 1950, Frankfurter voted to limit the scope of the search federal officers could make incident to a valid arrest.[9] Building on an opinion he had written in 1943, Frankfurter ruled in the June 1957 *Mallory* case that when there was any unnecessary delay between the arrest and arraignment of a defendant, a confession obtained during that period was inadmissible in federal courts.[10]

The Justice applied less rigid standards to state criminal procedure, however. While Justice Hugo Black argued that all of the Bill of Rights guarantees applied to the states, Frankfurter contended that state proceedings only had to meet certain basic standards of decency and fairness to be constitutional.[11] His opinion for the Court in a June 1949 case held the Fourth Amendment applicable to the states un-

1. *Joint Anti-Fascist Refugee Committee v. McGrath*, 341 U.S. 123 (1951).

2. *Sweezy v. New Hampshire*, 354 U.S. 234, 255 (1957).

3. *Pennsylvania v. Nelson*, 350 U.S. 497 (1956).

4. *Watkins v. U.S.*, 354 U.S. 178 (1957).

5. *Dennis v. U.S.*, 341 U.S. 494, 517 (1951).

6. *Uphaus v. Wyman*, 360 U.S. 72 (1959); *Barenblatt v. U.S.*, 360 U.S. 109 (1959).

7. *Beilan v. Board of Education*, 357 U.S. 399 (1958); *Lerner v. Casey*, 357 U.S. 468 (1958); *Nelson v. Los Angeles*, 362 U.S. 1 (1960).

8. *Communist Party v. Subversive Activities Control Board*, 367 U.S. 1 (1961).

9. *Harris v. U.S.*, 331 U.S. 145 (1947); *Trupiano v. U.S.*, 334 U.S. 699 (1948); *U.S. v. Rabinowitz*, 339 U.S. 56 (1950).

10. *Mallory v. U.S.*, 354 U.S. 449 (1957). The 1943 case was *McNabb v. U.S.*, 318 U.S. 332.

11. See *Adamson v. California*, 332 U.S. 46 (1947).

der this approach, but also declared that state courts did not have to exclude illegally seized evidence the way federal tribunals did.[1] Frankfurter dissented in June 1961 when a majority overturned this decision and held illegally obtained evidence inadmissible in state courts.[2] He delivered the majority opinion in a March 1959 decision holding that a state did not deny due process of law when it tried a person for a crime for which he had already been tried and acquitted in a federal court.[3] The Justice decided state cases involving allegedly coerced confessions or a denial of the right to counsel individually and on the basis of whether events in each instance had resulted in a lack of due process.[4]

In the early 1940s Justice Frankfurter twice voted to sustain compulsory flag-salute laws against charges that they violated freedom of religion. Years later, in May 1961, he concurred when the Court upheld state "blue laws" which prohibited certain types of business on Sundays. The Justice considered the statutes primarily secular rather than religious in character, and he rejected arguments that they violated the First Amendment or the equal protection clause.[6] During the Truman era, however, Frankfurter repeatedly sought to maintain strict separation of church and state in education. In February 1947 he voted against state payments for the transportation of children to parochial schools.[7] In March 1948 and April 1952, Frankfurter objected to released-time programs of religious instruction for public school children.[8]

Throughout his judicial career, Frankfurter voted in support of black Americans' claims for equality under the law.[9] In 1948 he chose a black attorney as his law clerk, the first in the Court's history. There is also considerable evidence that the Justice had a significant part in bringing about the Court's unanimous May 1954 decision in Brown v. Board of Education which held public school segregation unconstitutional.[10] Frankfurter believed a unanimous opinion would be best for the Court and the country, and so he sought to delay a final decision until the Court had reached a consensus. He had one of his clerks research the relevant constitutional history in detail and circulated several memos among the justices on the question of how to implement the decision. The Court's final decree, issued in May 1955, followed the gradualist approach Frankfurter favored and called for school desegregation "with all deliberate speed," a phrase the Justice had used in several other cases and had suggested in one of his memos.[11] When state officials later attempted to forestall school integration in Little Rock, Ark., Frankfurter joined in the Court's September 1958 order mandating the resumption of school desegregation in that city. He also wrote a special concurring opinion affirming the supremacy of the law and condemning defiance and obstruction of its enforcement.[12]

In accord with his commitment to judicial restraint, Frankfurter was very attentive to jurisdictional limits on the Court's work. In June 1946, for a four-man major-

1. Wolf v. Colorado, 338 U.S. 25 (1949).
2. Mapp v. Ohio, 367 U.S. 643 (1961).
3. Bartkus v. Illinois, 359 U.S. 121 (1959).
4. See, for example, Carter v. Illinois, 329 U.S. 173 (1946); Haley v. Ohio, 332 U.S. 596 (1948); Culombe v. Connecticut, 367 U.S. 568 (1961). See also Rochin v. California, 342 U.S. 165 (1952); Irvine v. California, 347 U.S. 128 (1954).
5. Minersville School District v. Gobitis, 310 U.S. 586 (1940); West Virginia State Board of Education v. Barnette, 319 U.S. 624 (1943).
6. McGowan v. Maryland, 366 U.S. 420, 459 (1961).
7. Everson v. Board of Education, 330 U.S. 1 (1947).

8. Illinois ex rel. McCollum v. Board of Education, 333 U.S. 203 (1948); Zorach v. Clauson, 343 U.S. 306 (1952).
9. See, for example, Smith v. Allwright, 321 U.S. 649 (1944); Morgan v. Virginia, 328 U.S. 373 (1946); Shelley v. Kraemer, 334 U.S. 1 (1948); Sweatt v. Painter, 339 U.S. 629 (1950); McLaurin v. Oklahoma State Regents, 339 U.S. 637 (1950); Henderson v. U.S., 339 U.S. 816 (1950).
10. 347 U.S. 483 (1954); Bolling v. Sharpe, 347 U.S. 497 (1954).
11. Brown v. Board of Education, 349 U.S. 294 (1955).
12. Cooper v. Aaron, 358 U.S. 1, 20 (1958).

ity, he ruled that questions of legislative apportionment were outside the Court's domain. The issue was a "peculiarly political" one in which the Court, as a nonpolitical institution, must not become involved, Frankfurter stated.[1] He objected vehemently in March 1962, near the end of his Court tenure, when a majority overruled his 1946 decision and held in *Baker v. Carr* that state legislative apportionment was subject to the constitutional scrutiny of the federal courts.[2] In a 65-page dissent, Frankfurter assailed the majority for reversing a "uniform course of decision" over the years and for violating the precept of self-restraint in political matters. "There is not under our Constitution," he wrote, "a judicial remedy for every political mischief." The proper remedy for malapportionment was an aroused electorate which would act through the legislature, Frankfurter added, warning the Court that its decision would lead it into a "mathematical quagmire."[3]

Frankfurter suffered a stroke while working in his chambers on April 5, 1962 and never recovered his health sufficiently to return to the bench. He resigned from the Court on Aug. 28, 1962 and spent the next few years visiting with friends and carrying on his voluminous correspondence. He died of a heart attack in Washington on Feb. 22, 1965.

Frankfurter was by all accounts personally vivacious and ebullient, a man of considerable wit and charm with a charismatic, captivating personality. An avid and lively conversationalist and correspondent, he numbered among his friends leading figures in law, government, journalism and scholarship. As a Justice, his many questions during oral argument gave evidence of his professorial background, and his scholarly opinions exhibited his concern for craftsmanship and excellence. On his retirement, no commentator doubted that Frankfurter's nearly 50 years at Harvard and on the Court had made a deep impact on American law. Virtually all observers agreed with a *New York Times* editorialist that as "a philosopher and scholar of the law, a judicial craftsman, a master of prose style and a formative influence on a generation of American lawyers and public officials, Felix Frankfurter was a major shaper of the history of his age." His critics felt that he had, nonetheless, missed greatness by taking too narrow a view of the judicial function and that his adherence to a philosophy of judicial restraint in the field of civil liberties "uncoupled him," as Joseph Lash put it, "from the locomotive of history." Frankfurter's defenders, however, argued that he had been an important and necessary stabilizing force on the Court. They agreed with Philip Kurland that the Justice "was the latest of the great keepers of the legend: a legend of a nonpartisan Supreme Court dedicated to the maintenance of a government of laws founded on reason and based on a faith in democracy."

---

1. *Colegrove v. Green*, 328 U.S. 549 (1946).

2. 369 U.S. 186 (1962).
3. *Ibid.*, at 266–330.

GOLDBERG, ARTHUR J(OSEPH)

b. Aug. 8, 1908; Chicago, Ill.
General Counsel, Congress of
Industrial Organizations, 1948–55;
General Counsel, United
Steelworkers of America, 1948-61;
Secretary of Labor, 1961–62;
Associate Justice, U.S. Supreme
Court, 1962–65; Ambassador to the
United Nations, 1965–68.

Goldberg was born the youngest of 11 children of Russian-Jewish parents on Chicago's West Side. After working his way through Northwestern University, he took a law degree in 1930, graduating at the top of his class, and set up his own practice shortly afterwards. Through his activity on behalf of Franklin D. Roosevelt's 1936 presidential campaign, Goldberg came into contact with labor leaders, and he soon represented several important Chicago-based unions. Following service with the Office of Strategic Services during World War II, he was appointed general counsel in 1948 for both the Congress of Industrial Organizations (CIO) and the United Steelworkers of America (USW). Goldberg replaced Lee Pressman, an alleged pro-Communist, in these positions, and in 1949 and 1950 he devised the legal procedures under which such Communist-dominated unions as the United Electrical Workers were expelled from the CIO.

In February 1955 Goldberg sat down with J. Albert Woll, counsel for the American Federation of Labor (AFL), to draft a merger agreement between the AFL and CIO. Both organizations agreed to retain previous organizing jurisdictions for each member union and to recognize the equal legitimacy of both craft and industrial unions. Unity was formally proclaimed at a joint convention in December.

Although he asked for the job of AFL-CIO general counsel, Goldberg did not enjoy the full confidence of the dominant federation leadership and was made special counsel instead. He also served as general counsel for the organization's Industrial Union Department. During the McClellan Committee investigations of 1957 and 1958, spotlighting corruption in the labor movement, Goldberg helped formulate the AFL-CIO's ethical practices code, which led to the expulsion of the Teamsters and several other scandal-ridden member unions. At the same time he worked closely with Sen. John F. Kennedy (D, Mass.) in drawing up moderate labor reform legislation providing for full public disclosure of union finances. He also attempted to forestall the more punitive measures that were ultimately embodied in the Landrum-Griffin Act—measures such as bans on "hot cargo" contracts, under which union members were allowed to refuse to work with non-union materials.

During the Eisenhower Administration Goldberg continued to represent the USW and acted as ex-officio adviser to several other industrial unions as well. Within the USW President David McDonald's interest in extra-union activities increasingly left important decisions in Goldberg's hands. In 1959 and 1960 he conducted USW negotiations during the 116-day steel strike, winning important concessions from the industry on matters of wages and working conditions. Included in the new contract, signed in January 1960, was Goldberg's proposal for a "Human Relations Committee," composed of representatives of the union, the industry and the public, which was aimed at preventing future strikes.

Goldberg was among the earliest labor backers of John F. Kennedy's presidential primary campaign, and in December 1960 the new President chose Goldberg as his Secretary of Labor over five elected union officals nominated by AFL-CIO President George Meany. According to labor historian Thomas R. Brooks, Kennedy chose Goldberg because he needed a Secretary of Labor who could administer the reform provisions of the Landrum-Giffin Act, recently enacted over strong trade union opposition. Goldberg, who was "from the unions but not of them" was the "perfect appointee."

Goldberg was an activist Secretary of Labor. During 1961 he personally intervened to settle a New York tugboat strike in January, a wildcat strike of flight engineers in February, a California agricultural work stoppage in March and a musicians' dispute at New York's Metropolitan Opera in August. In May 1961 Goldberg helped negotiate a no-strike, no-lockout pledge covering construction work at U.S. missile and space bases. President Kennedy then appointed Goldberg to chair an 11-man Missile Sites Labor Commission to handle subsequent labor disputes at the bases.

The principal economic problem facing Goldberg and Kennedy in 1961 was the lingering recession with its continuing 6.8% unemployment rate. At Kennedy's request Goldberg toured areas of high unemployment in five Midwestern states in February and reported that "we are in a full-fledged recession." The Department of Labor announced that "substantial and persistent" labor surpluses existed in 76 of 150 major industrial centers. Adopting the heretofore unsuccessful legislative proposals of Sen. Paul Douglas (D, Ill.) to aid these "depressed areas," the Administration backed a $389-million area redevelopment program in January 1961. Goldberg agreed that the new Redevelopment Agency be administered by the Secretary of Commerce, and he helped win the votes of conservative Southern congressmen by pointing out that federal money would be channeled into depressed areas of the rural South, as well as the high unemployment centers of the industrial North. The bill passed both houses of Congress in April and was signed by the President May 1.

During the spring of 1961 Goldberg also helped secure a 13-week extension of state unemployment benefits and a "pooling"of state tax revenues to spread the burden of increased expenditures among all 50 states. The Administration also won a substantial increase in the minimum wage (from $1 to $1.25 an hour over two years) in early May and extended minimum-wage coverage to an additional 3.6 million workers, the first such extension since 1938. In order to pump more purchasing power into the economy, the Administration won an $800 million increase in Social Security benefits in June. In August 1961 the Senate passed an Administration-sponsored manpower training bill, but the House delayed final passage of the compromise $435-million Manpower Development and Training Act until March 1962. The Act, administered by the Department of Labor, was designed to retrain workers displaced from their jobs by technological change or automation. A notable failure of the Kennedy-Goldberg legislative program came in May 1961 when the House rejected amendments aimed to protecting the wages and jobs of American farm workers. Instead, the lower chamber simply extended the "bracero" program which enabled California and Texas growers to import large numbers of poorly paid Mexican laborers.

Goldberg's term as Secretary of Labor coincided with an important increase in government supervision of peacetime labor-management relations. In the clearest statement of the Administration's labor policy, offered by Goldberg to a Feb. 23, 1962 luncheon of Chicago's Executive Club, the Secretary of Labor announced that the government "must increasingly provide guidelines" to ensure that future wage settlements were in the "public interest." Goldberg linked domestic labor-management peace and non-inflationary settlements directly to the Kennedy Administration's ability to end the nation's balance of payments deficit and conduct a vigorous foreign policy. Despite opposition from the AFL-CIO, Goldberg defended the Administration's determination to hold future wage boosts to 3.2% per year, a figure which the Council of Economic Advisers (CEA) estimated equaled the average annual increase in worker productivity. Goldberg also opposed AFL-CIO efforts to secure the 35-hour week as a means of spreading employment and indirectly raising wages.

The most important application of the Kennedy-Goldberg labor policy came in the negotiations leading up to the 1962 collective bargaining agreement in steel. Goldberg hoped that by persuading the USW to accept a wage package within the 3.2% guideposts the Administration would then be in a position to prevent the industry from raising steel prices after the new contract went into effect on July 1, 1962. To this end Goldberg held several meetings with USW President David J. McDonald and U.S. Steel Chairman Roger Blough in the fall of 1961 and the winter of 1962. Goldberg helped get formal union-management negotiations started in February, several months before the USW contract expired. Urging a wage package based on a CEA analysis, Goldberg met with Blough on March 6 and proposed that the new contract provide for about 10 cents an hour in fringe benefits but no wage increase. Goldberg indicated to Blough that the Administration considered this figure, about 2.5%, well within the capacity of the industry to absorb without a price increase. (According to Kennedy Administration sources, neither Blough nor other steel industry leaders challenged this contention at the time.) Goldberg then urged the same wage package upon McDonald in a private conversation of March 12. McDonald, who had relied heavily upon Goldberg during industry negotiations all during the 1950s, accepted the package, the most modest contract improvement since 1942. Union and company formally ratified the agreement on March 31, and Kennedy praised both parties for their "high industrial statesmanship."

On the afternoon of April 10, Roger Blough met briefly with Kennedy and Goldberg at the White House and unexpectedly announced that U.S. Steel was raising its prices an average of $6 a ton. Kennedy was outraged and Goldberg called the U.S. Steel decision a "double-cross." When five other major steel firms followed suit the next day, Goldberg offered to resign as Secretary of Labor on the grounds that he could no longer preach wage restraint to any union. The President deferred Goldberg's offer and instead stepped up pressure to rescind the industry-wide price increase. Along with CEA Chairman Walter Heller and presidential assistant Theodore Sorensen, Goldberg prepared the sharp verbal attack upon the price increases which Kennedy delivered at a dramatic press conference on April 11. With former Truman adviser Clark Clifford, Goldberg met secretly with U.S. Steel executives during the next two days. Goldberg emphasized that the President could not "restrain the more fiery members of Congress" intent on harsh legislation unless the steel prices were withdrawn. By the afternoon of April 14, after it became clear that some smaller steel makers had decided not to follow Big Steel's price lead, Bethlehem Steel announced it would rescind its price increase. A few hours later U. S. Steel followed suit.

In August 1962 Kennedy nominated Goldberg to fill the the Supreme Court seat held for 23 years by Felix Frankfurter, who had recently suffered a stroke. The appointment, widely hailed in the press, came at a time when Goldberg's warm relationship with organized labor had begun to cool as a result of his vigorous wage restraint policies. The Senate confirmed the nomination in September with but one dissenting vote.

Sworn in on Oct. 1, 1962, Goldberg quickly aligned himself with the more liberal members of the Court. Although generally not an absolutist in his judicial philosophy, Goldberg did take an expansive view of the constitutional provisions guaranteeing individual rights. He believed the Court should rigorously protect personal liberties against government infringement and also displayed a strong commitment to egalitarianism in the law. As a result, Goldberg supported an activist role for the Court in criminal, civil and political rights cases. His appointment established a majority committed to libertarian judicial doctrines on the Court.

In two significant cases, Justice Goldberg voted to extend the right to counsel and the privilege against self-incrimination to the states.[1] He favored equalizing the criminal justice system for rich and poor, and in a March 1963 opinion, ruled that a state could not deny an indigent convict a free trial transcript needed for an appeal because the trial judge thought the appeal "frivolous."[2] In June 1964 for a unanimous Court, Goldberg upset several precedents and held that when an individual was compelled to testify in either a state or federal proceeding under a grant of immunity, the other jurisdiction could not constitutionally use that testimony to prosecute the individual for a crime.[3] The Justice spoke for a five-man majority later the same month to extend the right to counsel to police interrogations of a suspect prior to indictment. In the controversial *Escobedo* decision, he held that incriminating statements obtained from a state criminal defendant who was not told of his right to silence and not allowed to consult his attorney during police questioning were inadmissible at trial because his right to counsel had been violated.[4] Goldberg also unsuccessfully urged the Court in October 1963 to hear argument on the question of whether the death penalty violated the constitutional ban on cruel and unusual punishment.[5]

Goldberg joined in the Court's ruling outlawing racial segregation[6] and voted to protect the efforts of blacks to secure their rights. In a March 1963 opinion for the Court, the Justice reversed the contempt conviction of a Miami NAACP official who had refused to produce the association's membership lists before a state investigating committee.[7] He repeatedly voted to upset the convictions of sit-in demonstrators[8] and, in a June 1964 concurring opinion, expressed his view that the 14th Amendment guaranteed all citizens a right of access to places of public accommodation.[9] In a January 1965 case from Baton Rouge, La., Goldberg's majority opinion ruled that the state could prohibit demonstrations near a courthouse. However, he overturned the conviction of a civil rights protester under such a law in this instance because local officials had given the demonstrators permission to assemble across the street from the courthouse.[10]

The Justice supported Court decisions mandating a one-man, one-vote standard of apportionment in state and congressional districting.[11] He joined in a June 1965 ruling invalidating a state anti-contraceptive law as an invasion of a right to marital privacy. In a concurring opinion, Goldberg argued that the Constitution protected fundamental personal liberties not specifically listed in the Bill of Rights from state infringement.[12] He voted to overturn various federal and state loyalty laws. In a February 1963 majority opinion, he upset a federal statute revoking the citizenship of an American who left the U.S. in time of war to evade the draft as an unconstitutional imposition of punishment without due process.[13] The Justice also spoke for the Court in June 1964 to overturn a law making it a crime for a member of the Communist Party to apply

1. *Gideon v. Wainwright,* 372 U.S. 335 (1963); *Malloy v. Hogan,* 378 U.S. 1 (1964).

2. *Draper v. Washington,* 372 U.S. 487 (1963).

3. *Murphy v. Waterfront Commission of New York Harbor,* 378 U.S. 52 (1964), overruling *U.S. v. Murdock,* 284 U.S. 141 (1931); *Feldman v. U.S.,* 322 U.S. 487 (1944); *Knapp v. Schweitzer,* 357 U.S. 371 (1958).

4. *Escobedo v. Illinois,* 378 U.S. 478 (1964).

5. *Rudolph v. Alabama,* 375 U.S. 889 (1963).

6. See, for example, *Watson v. City of Memphis,* 373 U.S. 526 (1963).

7. *Gibson v. Florida Legislative Investigation Committee,* 372 U.S. 539 (1963).

8. See, for example, *Edwards v. South Carolina,* 372 U.S. 229 (1963); *Peterson v. City of Greenville,* 373 U.S. 244 (1963).

9. *Bell v. Maryland.* 378 U.S. 226, 286 (1964).

10. *Cox v. Louisiana,* 379 U.S. 559 (1965).

11. *Wesberry v. Sanders,* 376 U.S. 1 (1964); *Reynolds v. Sims,* 377 U.S. 533 (1964).

12. *Griswold v. Connecticut,* 381 U.S. 479, 486 (1965).

13. *Kennedy v. Mendoza-Martinez,* 372 U.S. 144 (1963).

for and use a passport.[1] In March 1964, when the Court ruled that the First Amendment gave the press broad protection against libel suits brought by public officials, Goldberg urged the Court to go even further and hold that there was an "absolute, unconditional privilege" to criticize official conduct.[2]

Goldberg left the Court in July 1965, after only three terms, when President Lyndon Johnson asked him to take the post of ambassador to the United Nations. During his tenure on the bench, Goldberg demonstrated, according to one observer, "a sharp, analytical approach and a penchant for thoughtful, thorough analysis and precision of expression." All commentators agreed with legal scholar Henry J. Abraham that the Justice showed a "zest for innovation in the law that left an imprint far out of proportion to the brief period he served." Goldberg declared that it pained him to leave the high bench where he had spent the "richest and most satisfying period" of his career. But Johnson had told him he would have a direct hand in shaping American foreign policy and ending the Vietnam war, and Goldberg said he responded to the President's request out of a sense of duty.

On issues other than Vietnam Goldberg was able to play a significant role in developing and implementing American foreign policy at the United Nations. As part of an attempt to upgrade the world body into a forum for "negotiations" rather than "debate" Goldberg announced on Aug. 16, 1965 that the U.S. would drop its demand that General Assembly voting rights be denied to the Soviet Union, France and other states who had not paid their financial assessments for upkeep of the world organization. When the India-Pakistan war broke out in the late summer of 1965, Goldberg worked privately to secure a unanimous Security Council agreement on a cease-fire resolution demanding that both belligerents pull back to their original pre-war frontiers.

Goldberg demonstrated a degree of independence from the State Department during the October 1966 General Assembly debate over the status of Southwest Africa. He introduced a resolution, prepared by the U.S. delegation at the U.N., declaring that South Africa "forfeits all rights to continue to administer the territory." Goldberg's proposal, which was linked to formation of a new U.N. commission for Southwest Africa, was widely hailed by many of the new African and Asian states. However, the resolution put greater pressure on the South African regime than the U.S. State Department itself might have wished.

In the aftermath of the June 1967 Arab-Israeli war, Goldberg sought to avoid a U.N. condemnation of Israel apart from a general solution to the Middle East conflict. In July Goldberg helped defeat a Soviet-sponsored Security Council resolution condemning Israeli aggression. But during the fall he worked closely with Soviet U.N. Ambassador Anatoly Dobrynin on behalf of a British resolution that asserted Israel's right to exist, while at the same time calling for her withdrawal from land occupied during the Six Day War. The resolution, which served as the basic U.N. position on the Middle East conflict for the next six years, was adopted Nov. 22, 1967.

The Vietnam war dominated Goldberg's U.N. tenure, and much of his work at the world body was directed toward finding a formula that might start negotiations between the United States and North Vietnam. Goldberg was unsuccessful in this task. As the *Pentagon Papers* later showed, the progressive escalation of the air war was Johnson's chief strategy for resolving the conflict. In turn, the bombing of the North proved the main stumbling block to the start of negotiations, and Goldberg, who was not privy to the highest levels of Administration decision making, often found himself out of step with or unaware of American mili-

---

1. *Aptheker v. Secretary of State*, 378 U.S. 500 (1964). See also *Baggett v. Bullitt*, 377 U.S. 360 (1964); *U.S. v. Brown*, 381 U.S. 437 (1965).

2. *New York Times Co. v. Sullivan*, 376 U.S. 254, 297 (1964).

tary and political policy in Southeast Asia.

Goldberg began his term at the U.N. by announcing that the United States would "collaborate unconditionally" with the Security Council in the search for an "acceptable formula" to restore peace in Vietnam. Hanoi rejected Goldberg's request for U.N. intercession on Aug. 2, 1965 and reiterated its own conditions for an end to the conflict: an immediate halt in U.S. air attacks on the North and withdrawal of all U.S. troops from the South. (Later North Vietnam modified its second condition to one merely calling for an end to the U.S. troop buildup.) During the fall of 1965 Goldberg was involved in at least two other attempts to establish contact with the North Vietnamese, first through Communist U.N. delegations, and then in December through two Italian university professors who had recently returned from Hanoi. Both "peace feelers" collapsed.

Later in December 1965 Goldberg was part of a widely publicized Johnson Administration "peace offensive." The United States declared a halt to the bombing of North Vietnam on Dec. 24, and several high-ranking American officials, including Undersecretary of State Averell Harriman, Vice President Hubert Humphrey and Goldberg were dispatched to make contact with foreign heads of state in an effort to open negotiations with Hanoi. Goldberg conferred with Pope Paul VI in Rome on Dec. 29, with Italian Premier Aldo Moro on Dec. 30 and with French President Charles de Gaulle on Dec. 31. These diplomatic moves proved fruitless, in part because of the Johnson Administration's continuing commitment to the escalation of the air war.

In the fall of 1966 Goldberg made another effort, again only partially backed by the Administration, to start negotiations through the United Nations. For the previous several months U.N. Secretary General U Thant had proposed that peace talks might begin on the basis of three points: (1) cessation of U.S. bombing of North Vietnam (2) de-escalation of the ground war in South Vietnam and (3) inclusion of the National Liberation Front (NLF) in peace talks. On Sept. 22 Goldberg delivered a major speech at the U.N. responding to the U Thant proposals. He declared that the U.S. was prepared to halt the bombing and begin de-escalation of all military activity in Vietnam "the moment we are assured, privately or otherwise," that the U.S. moves would be matched by a reduction of North Vietnam's war effort. Goldberg also declared that inclusion of the NLF in any subsequent peace talks would not prove an "insurmountable problem."

Although the Goldberg speech was couched in terms somewhat more conciliatory than previous U.S. proposals, President Johnson declined to characterize the presentation as either new or important. North Vietnamese Premier Pham Van Dong rejected the Goldberg proposal on Sept. 25 and emphasized that a prerequisite to any negotiations was a "definite and unconditional" end to the bombing of the North. On Dec. 19 Goldberg called on U Thant to "take whatever steps you consider necessary to bring about negotiations leading to a cease-fire." But this appeal, which the *Pentagon Papers* described as "window dressing" to make up for the Administration's decision not to declare a lengthy Christmas cease-fire, was rejected by U Thant Dec. 30 when he declared that an unconditional cessation of the bombing was the "first and essential" part of any step toward negotiations.

Although Goldberg was excluded from White House decision-making on Vietnam, he played an important role in the March 1968 reassessment of American policy that reversed the escalation of the war and opened the way to negotiations with the North Vietnamese and the NLF. On March 15 Goldberg sent Johnson an eight-page memorandum arguing for a complete bombing halt in order to get talks started. Goldberg asserted that the efficacy of an unconditional pause "can best be determined by what actually happens during the talks rather than by any advance verbal commitments of the kind we have been seeking." According to Townsend Hoopes, then undersecretary of the Air Force, the Goldberg memo won a hostile, "volcanic response from the White House." Nevertheless, Goldberg's proposal, along with a similar suggestion from Ambassador to India Chester Bowles, became an important basis for discussion by the prestigious Senior Advisory Group on Vietnam, which undertook a complete reevaluation of U.S. policy during the latter part of March. Goldberg participated in many of these discussions, at one point seriously deflating the military assertion that the recent NLF-North Vietnamese Tet offensive had been an enemy defeat. Along with former Secretary of State Dean Acheson, former presidential special assistant McGeorge Bundy and Gen. Matthew Ridgway, Goldberg was among those who successfully argued for a bombing halt and deescalation of the war at the decisive meetings of the Senior Advisory Group on March 25 and 26.

Goldberg submitted his resignation as ambassador on April 25, 1968. Johnson accepted his departure in an unusually "chilly" letter that failed to praise the former Supreme Court Justice for his U.N. service. Goldberg joined the New York law firm of Paul, Weiss, Rifkind, Wharton and Garrison. Former Undersecretary of State George Ball succeeded Goldberg as chief U.S. representative at the U.N.

Goldberg became active in domestic politics after his resignation. In October 1968 he assumed command of Hubert Humphrey's presidential campaign in New York State. He joined other attorneys in appealing the conspiracy conviction of Benjamin Spock, William Sloan Coffin, Jr. and three other anti-war activists in January 1969. He spoke at the Oct. 15 Moratorium Day protests against the war and in December 1969 joined with Roy Wilkins and 25 other prominent citizens in a "searching inquiry" into recent clashes between the police and members of the Black Panther Party. In 1970 Goldberg challenged Nelson Rockefeller for the New York governorship but failed to unseat the three-term incumbent. He spoke out against the Nixon Administration's anti-crime and anti-busing proposals during the 1970s and opposed a plan put forward in December 1972 by a special study group for a new national court of appeals to screen petitions for review of cases filed in the Supreme Court.

HARLAN, JOHN MARSHALL

b. May 20, 1899; Chicago, Ill.
d. Dec. 29, 1971; Washington, D.C.
Associate Justice, U.S. Supreme
Court, 1955-71.

Grandson and namesake of a Supreme Court justice, John Marshall Harlan received a B.A. from Princeton in 1920 and was a Rhodes Scholar at Oxford for the next three years. He joined a major Wall Street law firm in 1923, obtained his law degree from New York Law School in 1924, and was admitted to the New York bar in 1925. Harlan undertook several public service jobs over the years, acting, for example, as an assistant to the U.S. attorney in New York from 1925 to 1927 and as chief counsel to the New York State Crime Commission from 1951 to 1953. However, the bulk of his career was spent in private practice. He became the principal litigation partner in his firm and was a specialist in corporate and antitrust cases. Harlan gradually emerged as a recognized leader of the New York bar.

A life-long Republican of proven legal ability, Harlan became a judge on the U.S. Second Circuit Court of Appeals in March 1954. Eight months later President Dwight D. Eisenhower named Harlan to the U.S. Supreme Court. The Senate Judiciary Committee held up action on the appointment, reportedly because some Southern senators hoped the delay would lead the Supreme Court to postpone implementation of its 1954 school desegregation decision.[1] Finally, in March 1955, the Senate confirmed Harlan's nomination by a vote of 71 to 11. He took his seat that month.

As his Southern opponents feared, Justice Harlan supported his colleagues view that school segregation was unconstitutional. He joined in the Court's May 1955 ruling that called for school desegregation with "all deliberate speed"[2] and voted in later cases against segregation in public facilities.[3] In June 1958 Harlan spoke for a unanimous Court to reverse a $100,000 fine imposed by the state of Alabama on the NAACP when the organization refused to turn over its membership lists. His opinion explicitly held that the right of free association was protected by the Constitution.[4]

In his earliest years on the Court, Harlan took a center position in loyalty-security cases. With the Court's liberal members he often opposed the government's position, but usually on narrow, technical grounds rather than on a broader, constitutional basis. He frequently spoke for the Court in important cases. In June 1956, for example, Harlan's majority opinion reversed the dismissal of a federal food and drug inspector on the ground that federal law authorized the summary dismissal of a government employe as a security risk only if he held a sensitive job.[5]

The Justice also spoke for a six-man majority in the June 1957 *Yates* case, which reversed the conviction of 14 California Communist Party leaders under the Smith Act. Harlan's opinion ruled that the Smith Act did not outlaw advocacy of forcible overthrow of the government as an abstract doctrine, but only such advocacy when directed at promoting concrete, unlawful action.[6] This interpretation made further convictions of Communists under the law's conspiracy clause virtually impossible. In the same month Harlan joined the majority in the *Watkins* case to reverse the contempt conviction of a witness who had refused to answer questions about former Communist associates before the House Un-American Activities Committee (HUAC).[7]

1. *Brown v. Board of Education,* 347 U.S. 483 (1954); *Bolling v. Sharpe,* 347 U.S. 497 (1954).

2. *Brown v. Board of Education,* 349 U.S. 294 (1955).

3. *Mayor and City Council of Baltimore v. Dawson,* 350 U.S. 877 (1955); *Holmes v. City of Atlanta,* 350 U.S. 879 (1955); *Gayle v. Browder,* 352 U.S. 903 (1956); *New Orleans City Park Improvement Assn. v. Detiege,* 358 U.S. 54 (1958).

4. *NAACP v. Alabama,* 357 U.S. 449 (1958).

5. *Cole v. Young,* 351 U.S. 536 (1956).

6. *Yates v. U.S.,* 354 U.S. 298 (1957).

7. *Watkins v. U.S.,* 354 U.S. 178 (1957).

After this, however, Harlan began taking a more conservative stance in most loyalty-security cases. In June 1959, for example, he wrote for a five-man majority to sustain the contempt conviction of a professor who had refused to answer the questions of a HUAC subcommittee about his Communist Party membership and activities. Balancing government interests against individual rights, Harlan ruled that the Committee had not violated the right to academic freedom and had met the necessary legal requirements in its questioning of the witness.[1]

The Justice's position in these later cases was more representative of his overall record on the bench and clarified the main principles in his judicial philosophy. Like Justice Felix Frankfurter, with whom he developed a close personal and intellectual relationship, Harlan thought the Court should exercise restraint and limit its role, leaving other branches of the government free to work out solutions to the nation's problems. He was deeply committed to the maintenance of federalism and believed Court interference should be minimal in areas where state power was preeminent. Harlan also respected the doctrine of separation of powers and was wary of invalidating federal legislative or executive action. He espoused an analytical, dispassionate approach to cases and contended that political and social ills should be remedied through political processes and not by the Court. Himself a "judge of cases and not of causes," as one commentator put it, Justice Harlan believed in following precedent unless there was a clear and strong demonstration that a past decision had been made in error.

In federal criminal cases Harlan was often willing to reverse lower court convictions if the defendant had not been afforded the proper procedural guarantees. He gave greater leeway to the states, however, and argued that the 14th Amendment's due process clause only required state criminal procedures to be "fundamentally fair." Harlan opposed the notion that the states had to give defendants all the guarantees designated in the Bill of Rights. He also rejected the idea that those guarantees were absolutes that could never be abridged by government. Harlan insisted instead that individual rights had to be balanced against government interests in each case.

Following Frankfurter's retirement in August 1962, Harlan became the Court's leading spokesman for a philosophy of judicial restraint. During the 1960s, however, a liberal, activist majority largely rejected this philosophy, and Harlan frequently dissented from the Warren Court's major trends. In criminal rights, for example, he fought the gradual extension of the Bill of Rights to the states. Harlan dissented in June 1961 when the majority overturned a 1949 decision and applied to the states the rule that illegally seized evidence was inadmissible in court.[2] He objected in June 1963 when the Court held that state and local law officers were subject to the same constitutional standards as federal agents in conducting searches and seizures.[3] The following year he dissented when the majority held the Fifth Amendment's privilege against self-incrimination applicable to the states.[4] Harlan also objected to the June 1966 *Miranda* decision, in which the Court set out rules governing police interrogation of arrested suspects. His dissenting opinion argued that the majority was departing from settled constitutional doctrine and creating unnecessary difficulties for law enforcement agencies.[5]

Justice Harlan was no inflexible conservative, however. His judicial views on matters like due process allowed for considerable discretion and made it hard to predict his stance in particular cases. He joined with the majority in June 1963, for example, to reverse a 21-year-old ruling and require the states to supply free coun-

---

1. *Barenblatt v. U.S.*, 360 U.S. 109 (1959).
2. *Mapp v. Ohio*, 367 U.S. 643 (1961), overruling *Wolf v. Colorado*, 338 U.S. 25 (1949).

3. *Ker v. California*, 374 U.S. 23 (1963).
4. *Malloy v. Hogan*, 378 U.S. 1 (1964).
5. *Miranda v. Arizona*, 384 U.S. 436 (1966).

sel to indigent criminal defendants.[1] In June 1965 Harlan concurred when the Court overturned a Connecticut law prohibiting the use of contraceptives by married couples.[2] The Justice again concurred when the Court in May 1967 extended certain constitutional safeguards such as the right to counsel to juvenile court proceedings.[3] He joined in a December 1967 ruling requiring federal agents to obtain a judicial warrant before using electronic eavesdropping devices.[4] He also joined with the majority in June 1962 and June 1963 decisions holding prayer and Bible-reading in public schools a violation of the First Amendment.[5]

In loyalty-security matters, Harlan continued to support congressional and state power to act against Communism. His majority opinion in two June 1961 cases upheld a provision in the 1940 Smith Act making it a crime to belong to an organization advocating violent overthrow of the government. Harlan rejected claims that the law violated the First and Fifth Amendments. However, he also ruled that the statute made illegal only active, not passive, membership in the Communist Party, a decision that made future prosecutions under the Act extremely difficult.[6] In March 1963 he voted to uphold the powers of a state legislative committee to investigate possible Communist infiltration into a nonsubversive organization.[7] Harlan dissented in June 1964 when the Court invalidated a federal law denying passports to members of the Communist Party.[8] In an exception to this pattern, the Justice did join in a November 1965 decision that held it a violation of the Fifth Amendment to require Communist Party

members to register with the government under the 1950 Subversive Activities Control Act.[9]

In dealing with obscenity legislation Harlan used a stricter standard when judging the constitutionality of federal rather than state laws. Since the states, he argued, had primary responsibility for protecting public morals and welfare, they should be given more leeway than the federal government in regulating expression that was allegedly obscene. As a result Harlan voted repeatedly to sustain convictions under state obscenity statutes but often favored reversal in federal obscenity cases such as the March 1966 *Ginzburg* decision.[10]

Harlan usually rejected constitutional claims based on the allegedly unequal treatment received by the poor. Thus in April 1956 he dissented when the majority held that states must supply an indigent convicted person with a free trial transcript when the right of appeal was conditioned on having such a transcript.[11] Harlan entered a sharp dissent to a March 1966 Court decision that held a Virginia poll tax unconstitutional because it discriminated against the poor.[12] He also disagreed with the majority when, in May 1968, it overturned state laws mandating different treatment for legitimate and illegitimate children as a denial of equal protection.[13] Justice Harlan generally supported state welfare regulations, but he did join the majority in March 1970 to hold that due process guaranteed welfare recipients the right to a hearing before their benefits could be terminated.[14] His majority opinion in a March 1971 decision also ruled that the states could not deny poor

---

. *Gideon v. Wainwright*, 372 U.S. 335 (1963).

2 . *Griswold v. Connecticut*, 381 U.S. 479 (1965).

3 . *In re Gault*, 387 U.S. 1 (1967).

4 . *Katz v. U.S.*, 389 U.S. 347 (1967).

5 . *Engel v. Vitale*, 370 U.S. 421 (1962); *Abington School District v. Schempp*, 374 U.S. 203 (1963).

6 . *Scales v. U.S.*, 367 U.S. 203 (1961); *Noto v. U.S.*, 367 U.S. 290 (1961).

7 . *Gibson v. Florida Legislative Investigation Committee*, 372 U.S. 539 (1963).

8 . *Aptheker v. Secretary of State*, 378 U.S. 500 (1964).

9 . *Albertson v. Subversive Activities Control Board*, 382 U.S. 70 (1965).

10. See, for example, Harlan's opinions in *Roth v. U.S.*, 354 U.S. 476 (1957); *Memoirs v. Massachusetts*, 383 U.S. 413 (1966); *Ginzburg v. U.S.*, 383 U.S. 463 (1966).

11. *Griffin v. Illinois*, 351 U.S. 12 (1956).

12. *Harper v. Virginia State Board of Elections*, 383 U.S. 663 (1966).

13. *Levy v. Louisiana*, 391 U.S. 68 (1968).

14. *Goldberg v. Kelly*, 397 U.S. 254 (1970). See also Harlan's dissent in *Shapiro v. Thompson*, 394 U.S. 618 (1969).

persons a divorce because they could not pay the court costs.[1]

Justice Harlan continued to join in major decisions outlawing racial segregation during the 1960s.[2] He also voted to sustain the public accommodations section of the 1964 Civil Rights Act in December 1964 and major portions of the 1965 Voting Rights Act in March 1966. In December 1961, when the Court overturned the breach of the peace convictions of 16 blacks involved in lunch counter sit-ins, Harlan entered a concurring opinion asserting that the sit-ins were comparable to verbal expression protected by the First Amendment.[4] He voted to overturn similar convictions from civil rights demonstrations in February 1963. However, by 1964 he had changed course, and he joined in opinions by Justice Hugo Black arguing for affirmance of such convictions.[5] Harlan also dissented in May 1967 when the Court voided a California constitutional amendment that had nullified earlier legislation prohibiting racial discrimination in housing.[6] He backed school desegregation orders in June and October 1969 decisions.[7] However, he dissented in December 1969 when the majority used an 1866 civil rights law to rule that a black family could not be excluded from membership in a community recreation club when a club share was included in their lease of a house in the neighborhood.[8]

In line with his views on the Court's limited role in a federal system, Harlan opposed extending the Court's jurisdiction into areas that he believed the Constitution left to other branches of govern-ment. He therefore dissented in March 1962 when the majority overturned a 1946 ruling and held that federal courts could try legislative apportionment cases. Harlan insisted that the federal courts had no jurisdiction in such suits and labeled the majority decision "an adventure in judicial experimentation."[9] The Justice also objected to February and June 1964 decisions in which the majority set forth a "one-man, one-vote" standard for congressional and state legislative apportionment.[10] In his dissenting opinion in the latter case, *Reynolds v. Sims,* Harlan summarized his objections to much of the Warren Court's activism. He labeled "mistaken" the view "that every major social ill in this country can find its cure in some constitutional 'principle,' and that this court should 'take the lead' in promoting reform when other branches of government fail to act." The Court, he added, as a judicial body, should not "be thought of as a general haven for reform movements."[11] Harlan maintained his opposition to the one-man, one-vote standard in all later reapportionment cases.[12]

Because of personnel changes, Justice Harlan found himself more often at the center of the Court during his final years on the bench. He remained, though, as thoughtful and dispassionate and as independent and difficult to predict as before. On criminal rights questions, for example, Harlan dissented in June 1969 when a majority applied the provision against double jeopardy to the states.[13] However, he concurred when the Court extended the right to counsel to preliminary hearings in June 1970 because recent Court

---

1. *Boddie v. Connecticut,* 401 U.S. 371 (1971).

2. See, for example, *Turner v. City of Memphis,* 369 U.S. 350 (1962); *Johnson v. Virginia,* 373 U.S. 61 (1963); *Loving v. Virginia,* 388 U.S. 1 (1967).

3. *Heart of Atlanta Motel v. U.S.,* 379 U.S. 241 (1964); *Katzenbach v. McClung,* 379 U.S. 294 (1964); *South Carolina v. Katzenbach,* 383 U.S. 301 (1966).

4. *Garner v. Louisiana,* 368 U.S. 157 (1961).

5. *Edwards v. South Carolina,* 372 U.S. 229 (1963); *Bell v. Maryland,* 378 U.S. 226 (1964.)

6. *Reitman v. Mulkey,* 387 U.S. 369 (1967).

7. *U.S. v. Montgomery County Board of Educa-tion,* 395 U.S. 225 (1969); *Alexander v. Holmes County Board of Education,* 396 U.S. 19 (1969).

8. *Sullivan v. Little Hunting Park, Inc.,* 396 U.S. 229 (1969).

9. *Baker v. Carr,* 369 U.S. 186 (1962), overruling *Colegrove v. Green,* 328 U.S. 549 (1946).

10. *Wesberry v. Sanders,* 376 U.S. 1 (1964); *Reynolds v. Sims,* 377 U.S. 533 (1964).

11. 377 U.S. at 624-625.

12. See, for example, *Avery v. Midland County,* 390 U.S. 474 (1968); *Kirkpatrick v. Preisler,* 394 U.S. 526 (1969); *Hadley v. Junior College District of Metropolitan Kansas City,* 397 U.S. 50 (1970).

13. *Benton v. Maryland,* 395 U.S. 784 (1969).

rulings supported such a decision, even though he personally disagreed with it.[1] The Justice joined in March 1970 and June 1971 rulings guaranteeing juvenile defendants the right to have their guilt proven "beyond a reasonable doubt" but not the right to trial by jury.[2] In two June 1971 cases Harlan's opinion for the Court held that the states did not deny due process by giving juries in capital cases complete discretion in deciding whether to impose the death penalty or by allowing such juries to determine both a defendant's guilt and his punishment in one proceeding.[3]

Since he demanded high procedural standards in federal criminal cases, Harlan voted in January 1969 and June 1971 to overturn federal convictions where he thought there had not been sufficient cause for a search warrent to be issued.[4] He also dissented from an April 1971 judgement upholding "third party bugging" in which a federal informer used an electronic device, without a warrant, to transmit a conversation between himself and another person.[5] In June 1970 the Justice concurred when the Court upheld the use of six-member juries in state trials. However, he objected when the majority at the same time overruled a long-standing precedent requiring 12 members for federal juries.[6]

Harlan maintained his opposition to the one-man, one-vote standard in reapportionment cases decided in 1969 and 1970. Because he believed that the states had the power to set reasonable voting requirements, he dissented in June 1969 and June l970 when the Court invalidated state laws limiting voting for school board members and on bond issues to those considered to have the most immediate stake in the results.[7] In December

1970 Harlan took the position that Congress could neither lower the voting age to 18 for state or federal elections nor limit state residency requirements for presidential elections to 30 days.[8]

In April 1969 Harlan spoke for a five man majority to reverse a conviction for making derogatory statements about the American flag as a violation of the First Amendment.[9] His majority opinion in a June 1971 case also overturned the conviction of a demonstrator who had entered a court house wearing a jacket inscribed with a vulgarism condemning the draft.[10] In June 1971, when a majority refused the government's request for an injunction to halt newspaper publication of a classified study of U.S. involvement in Indochina, Harlan strongly objected to the haste with which the case was handled. He maintained that the Court should have allowed more time for consideration of the serious issues involved. On the merits, the Justice dissented from the majority in the *Pentagon Papers* case because he thought that the Constitution gave control of foreign affairs to the executive branch and that the scope of judicial review of foreign policy matters was severely limited.[11]

Justice Harlan retired from the Court on Sept. 23, 1971 and died three months later of cancer. His retirement came when he was at the height of his intellectual powers, and his departure from the Court was mourned by commentators of every political persuasion. A diligent and disciplined worker, Harlan had been nearly blind during his last seven years on the Court, and yet, he continued to turn out meticulously crafted opinions which won universal praise. Often called a "judge's judge," Harlan wrote clear and learned opinions that analyzed the issues and op-

1. *Coleman v. Alabama*, 399 U.S. 1 (1970).

2. *In re Winship*, 397 U.S. 358 (1970); *McKeiver v. Pennsylvania*, 403 U.S. 528 (1971).

3. *McGautha v. California* and *Crampton v. Ohio*, 402 U.S. 183 (1971).

4. *Spinelli v. U.S.*, 393 U.S. 410 (1969); *U.S. v. Harris*, 403 U.S. 573 (1971).

5. *U.S. v. White*, 401 U.S. 745 (1971).

6. *Williams v. Florida*, 399 U.S. 78 (1970).

7. *Kramer v. Union Free School District No. 15*, 395 U.S. 621 (1969); *Phoenix v. Kolodziejski*, 399 U.S. 204 (1970).

8. *Oregon v. Mitchell*, 400 U.S. 112 (1970).

9. *Street v. New York*, 394 U.S. 576 (1969).

10. *Cohen v. California*, 403 U.S. 15 (1971).

11. *New York Times Co. v. U.S.*, 403 U.S. 713 (1971).

posing arguments in a case and fully explained the reasons for his decision. Even legal scholars who disagreed with Harlan's views had great respect for a jurist who, as Professor Alan Dershowitz said, "always brought sagacity and honesty to the deliberations of the Court." Admirers as well as critics of the Warren Court agreed with Norman Dorsen that Harlan had been the "conservative conscience to a highly active Court" and that he had rendered "conspicuous service" by acting as a "restraining force during a period of rapid change." Near the end of his career, when the Court seemed to be taking a conservative turn, many observers expected Harlan, with his unquestioned integrity and his commitment to consistency in the law, to apply the same critical standards to a new majority and to serve as a brake on any conservative activism as well. Harlan's 16-year career on the bench, wrote fellow jurist Henry J. Friendly, offered an outstanding example "of moral rectitude, of penetrating analysis, of unstinting labor" and "of utter devotion to the Constitution and respect for acts of Congress as he read them."

JACKSON, ROBERT H(OUGHWOUT)

b. Feb. 13, 1892; Spring Creek, Pa.
d. Oct. 9, 1954; Washington, D.C.
Associate Justice, U.S. Supreme
Court, 1941-54; U.S. Chief of
Counsel, Nuremberg War Crimes
Trials, 1945-46.

Raised in the small town of Frewsburg, N.Y., Jackson learned his law by the apprentice method, clerking in the legal offices of a cousin. Following his admission to the bar in 1913, he established a successful private practice in Jamestown, N.Y. A Democrat, he became general counsel to the Internal Revenue Bureau in 1934 and then rose rapidly in Washington, serving as an assistant attorney general from 1936 to 1938, Solicitor General from 1938 to 1939 and Attorney General from 1940 to 1941. He was named to the Supreme Court in June 1941 and took the oath of office the next month.

Beginning May 2, 1945, Jackson interrupted his judicial service for 18 months to serve as U.S. representative and chief prosecutor at the Nuremberg war crimes trials. He had a prominent role in developing the August 1945 London agreement on which the trials were based, and he helped draft the indictments and amass the evidence for the trials. Jackson headed the American prosecution team in the first trial of 22 top Nazis which began in November 1945. As an exceptionally skilled advocate, he made what was considered a masterful opening statement for the Allied prosecutors. After the tribunal found 19 of the Nazi leaders guilty on Oct. 1, 1946, Jackson resigned on Oct. 17. Despite all the controversy that then and later surrounded the Nuremberg trials, Jackson considered them "the most important, enduring and constructive work" of his life. He numbered among their achievements the recognition of aggressive war as a crime under international law and the historical documentation of totalitarian dictatorship in the Nazi era. Several commentators have labeled Jackson the primary architect of the trials. Telford Taylor, who succeeded the Justice as chief American counsel at the trials, stated that Jackson contributed more than anyone to the "integrity and dignity of the Nuremberg proceedings."

While at Nuremberg Jackson launched a public attack on Justice Hugo Black. The two had disagreed in the May 1945 *Jewell Ridge Coal* case where the Court, by a five-to-four vote, held that coal miners were entitled to portal-to-portal pay. They had also disputed the propriety of Black's participation in the case, which had been argued by a former law partner of the Alabaman.[1]

When Chief Justice Harlan Fiske Stone died in April 1946, Jackson was considered a possible successor. However reports circulated in the press that Black and one other justice had threatened to resign if Jackson were named Chief Justice; they cited as the reason Jackson's criticism of Black in the *Jewell Ridge* case. On June 10, 1946, after Fred Vinson had been appointed Chief Justice, Jackson released a statement from Nuremberg presenting his side of the *Jewell Ridge* story. Jackson's declaration came as a surprise in the U.S. Although commentators at the time differed on the merits of his charges against Black, many reproached him for turning their differences into a public feud.

The incident reflected deeper doctrinal differences between Jackson and the libertarian and activist Black. Jackson believed that the Court should exercise

---

1. *Jewell Ridge Coal Corp. v. Local No. 6167,* UMWA, 325 U.S. 161 (1945) and 325 U.S. 897 (1945).

restraint and leave economic and social policy-making to other branches of the government. The Justice also thought the Court should normally adhere to precedent. Based on his many years as a practicing attorney, he wanted the Court to strive for clear and consistent interpretations of the Constitution and federal statutes so that lawyers and their clients could know and apply the law with assurance.

On his return to the Court following the Nuremberg trials, Jackson, according to several analysts, showed more conservatism in civil liberties cases. Although he still regarded the First Amendment as a guarantor of the individual's right to believe what he wanted, Jackson did not think it gave anyone the right to express his beliefs in any manner or forum he chose.[1] The Justice thought that government had the authority to deal with threats to the public order, and in a series of cases between 1948 and 1951 he voted to uphold government restrictions on inflammatory speeches, the use of sound trucks and street meetings.[2] Jackson also believed the government should be accorded the powers reasonably necessary to safeguard national security. He viewed the Communist Party as a unique organization posing a special threat. In a separate opinion in a May 1950 case concerning the non-Communist oath provisions in the Taft-Hartley Act Jackson supported the law's compulsory pledge of nonmembership in the Communist Party although he rejected an accompanying oath that required union officials to swear they did not believe in forcible overthrow of the government.[3] Jackson voted in June 1951 to sustain the conviction of 11 American Communist Party leaders under the Smith Act.[4] His majority opinion in a

March 1953 case ruled that the Army could refuse a commission to an inducted psychiatrist who invoked the Fifth Amendment when asked whether he was a Communist.[5]

The Justice insisted that the government give individuals full and fair hearings in security cases, however, and he refused to uphold the government in several instances where he thought procedural standards had not been met. In March 1953, for example, when the majority held that the government could deny an alien reentry to the U.S. without any hearing and for unspecified reasons of security, Jackson dissented, arguing that the man was entitled to a fair hearing with notice of the charges against him.[6]

In cases involving state aid to religious education, Jackson took a strong stand against any form of government assistance. He voted against state payments for the transportation of children to parochial schools in February 1947 and against programs of released-time religious instruction for public school children in March 1948 and April 1952.[7]

In criminal cases Jackson gave more emphasis to the interests of society than to the rights of the defendant. He generally opposed requiring the states to conform to the procedural guarantees of the Bill of Rights, but he did join the majority in a June 1949 decision holding the Fourth Amendment applicable to the states.[8] Jackson believed unrestrained searches a prime tool of arbitrary and tyrannical governments, and he strongly favored giving full effect to the Fourth Amendment's prohibition on unreasonable searches and seizures. In federal cases he consistently voted to limit the scope of an allowable search conducted

1. Jackson's finest statement in favor of First Amendment freedoms came in *West Virginia State Board of Education v. Barnette*, 319 U.S. 624 (1943).

2. *Saia* v. *New York*, 334 U.S. 558 (1948); *Kovacs v. Cooper*, 336 U.S. 77 (1949); *Terminiello v. Chicago*, 337 U.S. 1 (1949); *Kunz v. New York*, 340 U.S. 290 (1951); *Feiner v. New York*, 340 U.S. 315 (1951).

3. *American Communications Assn. v. Douds*, 339 U.S. 382 (1950).

4. *Dennis v. U.S.*, 341 U.S. 494 (1951).

5. *Orloff v. Willoughby*, 345 U.S. 83 (1953).

6. *Shaughnessy v. U.S. ex rel Mezei*, 345 U.S. 206 (1953).

7. *Everson v. Board of Education*, 330 U.S. 1 (1947); *Illinois ex rel. McCollum v. Board of Education*, 333 U.S. 203 (1948), *Zorach v. Clauson*, 343 U.S. 306 (1952).

8. *Wolf v. Colorado*, 338 U.S. 25 (1949).

without a warrant.[1] However, Jackson also gave the opinion of the Court in a February 1954 case upholding a state conviction for gambling that was based on illegally obtained evidence. He strongly condemned the police's conduct in the case but said that the Fourth Amendment did not require the states to exclude illegally seized evidence at trial.[2]

Jackson was foremost among the justices of his day in insisting that the Constitution had established a national economic market that must be kept free of state and local restrictions. In an April 1949 case, for example, his majority opinion overturned New York State's effort to limit the amount of milk an out-of-state buyer could purchase. He asserted that a state could not burden interstate commerce to protect local economic interests.[3] In April 1952, however, in a case involving the question of inherent executive powers over the economy during an emergency, Jackson concurred in the Court's judgment that President Truman's seizure of the steel mills was invalid.[4]

Jackson suffered a heart attack on April 1, 1954, but he returned to the bench on May 17 when the Court handed down the decision in *Brown v. Board of Education*, holding racial segregation in public schools unconstitutional.[5] Jackson had largely supported the Court's expansion of the rights of blacks,[6] and his presence when Brown was announced vividly demonstrated the Court's unanimity in the case and Jackson's personal support for the decision. The Justice died of a heart attack in Washington on Oct. 9, 1954, just after the opening of a new Court term.

Overall Robert Jackson has been rated well by constitutional scholars. He was not an intellectual leader of the Court, but he had a strong, disciplined mind and was a superb writer with what Louis Jaffe has called "a 'big' virtuoso style, magnificent and athletic in exposition, powerful and ingenious in argument, racy, sardonic, alive with the passion and wit of his personality." A proponent of judicial self-restraint, Jackson stood somewhat right of center while on the Court. His views resulted from a thoughtful search for a practical, workable balance between the individual and society and from his belief that progress and liberty were achieved only with public order, not apart from it.

1. See, for example, *Harris v. U.S.* 331 U.S. 145 (1947), *U.S. v. DiRe*, 332 U.S. 581 (1948); *Johnson v. U.S.*, 333 U.S. 10 (1948), *McDonald v. U.S.*, 335 U.S. 451 (1948); *Brinegar v. U.S.*, 338 U.S. 160 (1949).

2. *Irvine v. California*, 347 U.S. 128 (1954).

3. *H.P. Hood & Sons v. DuMond*, 336 U.S. 525 (1949).

4. *Youngstown Sheet & Tube Co. v. Sawyer*, 343 U.S. 579 (1952)

5. *Brown v. Board of Education*, 347 U.S. 483 (1954); *Bolling v. Sharpe*, 347 U.S. 497 (1954).

6. See, for example, *Sipuel v. Board of Regents of Oklahoma*, 332 U.S. 631 (1948); *Sweatt v. Painter*, 339 U.S. 629 (1950); *McLaurin v. Oklahoma State Regents*, 339 U.S. 637 (1950); *Henderson v. U.S.*, 339 U.S. 816 (1950). An exception came in *Bob-Lo Excursion Co. v. Michigan*, 333 U.S. 28 (1948).

MARSHALL, THURGOOD
b. July 2, 1908; Baltimore, Md.
Director-Counsel, NAACP Legal
Defense and Educational Fund, 1940
– 61; Judge, U.S. Second Circuit
Court of Appeals, 1961–65; U.S.
Solicitor General, 1965–67; Associate
Justice, U.S. Supreme Court, 1967– .

Born and raised in Baltimore, Marshall graduated from Lincoln University in 1930 and from Howard University law school, where he was first in his class, in 1933. He then practiced in Baltimore until 1936, when he was named assistant special counsel to the NAACP. Two years later Marshall became special counsel; when the NAACP Legal Defense and Educational Fund was separately established in 1940, he was appointed its director-counsel. As head of the NAACP's legal program, Marshall became the nation's foremost civil rights attorney, coordinating attacks on racial discrimination in various fields. His Supreme Court victories included a 1944 decision prohibiting the exclusion of blacks from Democratic primaries because of their race[1] and a 1946 case outlawing segregation in interstate transportation.[2] A convivial and seemingly tireless individual, Marshall traveled thousands of miles throughout the South each year to represent black litigants in court and to encourage local NAACP chapters in their efforts to secure equal rights for blacks.

In perhaps the most significant court battle of his career, Marshall supervised the preparation of four cases challenging the validity of racial segregation in public schools. He personally represented the black plaintiffs from Clarendon Co., S.C., in one of the suits, and during oral arguments before the Supreme Court in December 1952 and December 1953, Marshall contended that state-enforced segregation violated the 14th Amendment. On May 17, 1954 the Supreme Court ruled unanimously in *Brown v. Board of Education* that segregation in public education was unconstitutional.[3] During argument in April 1955 on how the decision should be carried out, Marshall urged the Court to order complete desegregation of public schools no later than the fall term of 1956. The Court, however, announced a far more flexible standard in May 1955 and ordered school desegregation "with all deliberate speed."[4] Over the next several years Marshall and the NAACP led a massive program of litigation to enforce the *Brown* decision.

Along with several other NAACP lawyers, Marshall also represented Autherine Lucy in her suit to enter the University of Alabama and won a Supreme Court decision in October 1955 ordering her enrollment.[5] Marshall was with Lucy on Feb. 6, 1956, when she was attacked by a mob on the University's campus. After the University's trustees suspended Lucy the next day, Marshall secured a federal court order for her reinstatement. The trustees then expelled Lucy, and she withdrew from the case shortly afterwards.

Marshall was also counsel for the black students who desegregated Central High School in Little Rock, Ark., in the fall of 1957. When Gov. Orval Faubus tried to thwart integration of the high school in September 1957, Marshall got an injunction barring the Governor from further interference with the school's desegregation plan. Later in the school year the local school board sought to postpone its desegregation program for two-and-one-half years. In a special Supreme Court term in September 1958, Marshall argued against this delay and won a unanimous decision from the Court ordering continuance of school integration plans.[6]

1. *Smith v. Allwright*, 321 U.S. 649 (1944).

2. *Morgan v. Virginia*, 328 U.S. 373 (1946).

3. 347 U.S. 483 (1954).

4. *Brown v. Board of Education*, 349 U.S. 294 (1955).

5. *Lucy v. Adams*, 350 U.S. 1 (1955).

6. *Cooper v. Aaron*, 358 U.S. 1 (1958).

Marshall also handled cases extending the *Brown* principle to such areas as public recreation and public transit.[1] He participated in the suit growing out of the Montgomery, Ala., bus boycott, which resulted in a November 1956 Supreme Court ruling that segregation in local transportation was unconstitutional.[2] In his last oral argument before the Supreme Court in October 1960, Marshall successfully contended that segregation in restaurants at interstate bus terminals violated federal law.[3]

In his final years with the NAACP, Marshall aided the defense of hundreds of students arrested during the sit-ins, the Freedom Rides and similar nonviolent protests against segregation. He helped prepare the December 1961 case in which the Court reversed the convictions of blacks arrested for peaceful lunch counter sit-ins.[4] In all Marshall participated in 32 cases before the Supreme Court as NAACP counsel and won substantive victories in 27.

President John F. Kennedy nominated Marshall for a judgeship on the Second Circuit Court of Appeals on Sept. 23, 1961, and Marshall began serving in October under a recess appointment. Under the chairmanship of Sen. James O. Eastland (D, Miss), who opposed Marshall's appointment, the Senate Judiciary Committee delayed hearings in the nomination for nearly eight months and then held six days of hearings stretched out over four months. The Committee finally approved Marshall's appointment on Sept. 7, 1962 by a vote of 11 to 4. The full Senate confirmed the nomination on Sept. 11 by a vote of 54 to 16. All of the opposition came from Southern Democrats.

As a new judge, Marshall had little op-portunity to write majority opinions in significant civil or individual rights cases, and most of his written decisions concerned such areas as federal tort claims, admiralty law or patent and trademark cases. However, his votes on the Court and the opinions he did write identified him as a liberal jurist who usually granted the government broad powers in economic matters but barred it from infringing on the constitutional rights of the individual.[5]

President Johnson appointed Marshall U.S. Solicitor General in July 1965. The first black to serve in that post, Marshall argued a wide variety of cases for the government before the Supreme Court. In the field of civil rights, he won Court approval of the 1965 Voting Rights Act,[6] persuaded the Court to reinstate indictments in two cases against defendants charged with conspiracy to murder civil rights workers[7] and joined in a suit that successfully overturned a California constitutional amendment prohibiting open housing legislation.[8] Convinced that all electronic eavesdropping that involved an illegal trespass was unconstitutional, Marshall voluntarily informed the Supreme Court in two cases that the government had used electronic devices to collect information on suspects charged with violation of federal laws.[9] He had no similar qualms about the use of government informers, however, and he successfully argued in the Supreme Court that the government's use of an informer did not invalidate the convictions of James Hoffa and three other Teamster union officials for jury tampering.[10] Marshall argued 19 cases for the government before the Supreme court, winning all but five.

On June 13, 1967 President Johnson nominated Marshall as an associate jus-

---

1. *Mayor and City Council of Baltimore v. Dawson*, 350 U.S. 877(1955); *Holmes v. City of Atlanta*, 350 U.S. 879 (1955).

2. *Gayle v. Browder*, 352 U.S. 903 (1956).

3. *Boynton v. Virginia*, 364 U.S. 454 (1960).

4. *Garner v. Louisiana*, 368 U.S. 157 (1961).

5. See, for example, *U.S. ex rel. Angelet v. Fay*, 333 F.2d 12 (2 Cir. 1964); *New York v. Galamison*, 342 F.2d 255 (2 Cir. 1965); *U.S. ex rel. Hetenyi v. Wilkins*, 348 F.2d 844 (2 Cir. 1965).

6. *South Carolina v. Katzenbach*, 383 U.S. 301 (1966).

7. *U.S. v. Guest*, 383 U.S. 745 (1966); *U.S. v. Price*, 383 U.S. 787 (1966).

8. *Reitman v. Mulkey*, 387 U.S. 369 (1967).

9. *Black v. U.S.*, 385 U.S. 26 (1966); *Schipani v. U.S.*, 385 U.S. 372 (1966).

10. *Hoffa v. U.S.*, 385 U.S. 293 (1966).

tice of the U.S. Supreme Court to fill the vacancy created by the retirement of Justice Tom C. Clark. Once again Marshall was the first black appointed to this position. In announcing Marshall's nomination Johnson declared that this was "the right thing to do, the right time to do it, the right man and the right place." The Senate confirmed the nomination on Aug. 30 by a 69 to 11 vote, with all of the opposition coming from Southern senators. Marshall was sworn in on Oct. 2, 1967.

Marshall was not actively engaged in the civil rights movement after 1961 because of the government positions he held, but his career exemplified that segment of the movement that relied primarily on the judicial process to win political and social advancement for blacks. In a May 1969 speech at Dillard University in New Orleans, Marshall criticized those blacks who advocated violence saying, "Anarchy is anarchy, and it makes no difference who practices it, it is bad; it is punishable, and it should be punished." Younger black militants, in turn, criticized Marshall's and the NAACP's legal approach during the 1960s as ineffective "gradualism."

On the Supreme Court Marshall was a liberal and activist jurist who voted most often with Chief Justice Earl Warren and Justice William Brennan. He played a subordinate role in his first years on the bench, writing few majority opinions and rarely dissenting. As the Court became more conservative in the 1970s, however, Marshall became increasingly outspoken. The number of his dissents rose sharply, and he was identified as part of the left wing of the Burger Court.

In racial discrimination cases Marshall almost always voted to expand the civil rights of blacks. He supported school desegregation orders and dissented sharply in July 1974 when the Court upset an interdistrict busing plan to remedy school segregation in Detroit.[1] Marshall also objected to a June 1971 decision sanctioning the closing of public swimming pools in Jackson, Miss., to avoid desegregation and to a ruling a year later allowing private clubs with state liquor licenses to exclude blacks.[2] Although he generally voted in favor of blacks in employment discrimination cases, Marshall wrote the majority opinion in a February 1975 case holding that an employer could fire employes who bypassed their union's effort to resolve a dispute over racial discrimination and picketed on their own.[3]

In other equal protection cases, Marshall urged the Court to adopt a variable standard of review that would take into account the nature of the classification and of the interests involved in each case.[4] Even under the accepted approach to equal protection claims, however, the Justice took a strong stand against all forms of discrimination. He favored making sex a suspect classification that would be subject to strict judicial scrutiny and voted in almost every instance to overturn differences in treatment between men and women.[5] Marshall also opposed government distinctions between legitimate and illegitimate children and between citizens and aliens. However he did rule in a November 1973 majority opinion that the 1964 Civil Rights Act had not outlawed employment discrimination against aliens.[6] He opposed discrimination

---

1. *Milliken v. Bradley*, 418 U.S. 717 (1974). See also *Green v. County School Board*, 391 U.S. 430 (1968); *Alexander v. Holmes County Board of Education*, 396 U.S. 19 (1969); *Keyes v. School District No. 1, Denver*, 413 U.S. 189 (1973).

2. *Palmer v. Thompson*, 403 U.S. 217 (1971); *Moose Lodge No. 197 v. Irvis*, 407 U.S. 163 (1972).

3. *Emporium Capwell Co. v. Western Addition Community Organization*, 420 U.S. 50 (1975). See also *Franks v. Bowman Transportation Co.*, 424 U.S. 747 (1976); *Washington v. Davis*, 426 U.S. 229 (1976).

4. See his dissenting opinions in *Dandridge v. Williams*, 397 U.S. 471 (1970) and *San Antonio Independent School District v. Rodriguez*, 411 U.S. 1 (1973).

5. *Frontiero v. Richardson*, 411 U.S. 677 (1973). See also *Cleveland Board of Education v. LaFleur*, 414 U.S. 632 (1974); *Stanton v. Stanton*, 421 U.S. 7 (1975).

6. *Espinoza v. Farah Manufacturing Co.*, 414 U.S. 86 (1973). See also *Levy v. Louisiana*, 391 U.S. 68 (1968); *Labine v. Vincent*, 401 U.S. 532 (1971); *Sugarman v. Dougall*, 413 U.S. 634 (1973).

against the poor and voted in March 1973 to invalidate public school financing systems based on local property taxes.[1]

Justice Marshall supported expansions of the right to vote. His opinion in a June 1970 case held that residents of a federal enclave in Maryland could vote in state and local elections.[2] In a March 1972 majority opinion, Marshall overturned state residency requirements for voting of three months or more.[3] He opposed laws restricting voting on bond issues to property owners[4] and favored a federal law lowering the voting age to 18.[5] Marshall generally supported a strict one-man, one-vote standard of apportionment and dissented in cases which relaxed that standard at the state level.[6]

Marshall spoke for a six man majority in June 1969 to hold the Fifth Amendment's provision against double jeopardy applicable to the states.[7] In other criminal cases the Justice generally favored strong protection of the guarantees afforded by the Bill of Rights. He usually opposed searches without warrants[8] and believed a warrant necessary for electronic eavesdropping.[9] Marshall insisted that a waiver of rights was legitimate only if a defendant was fully informed and uncoerced.[10] As Solicitor General he had argued against the *Miranda* ruling, requiring the police

to inform suspects of their rights.[11] But as a justice, Marshall opposed most attempts to cut back that decision.[12] He dissented from rulings authorizing non-unanimous jury verdicts[13] and juries of less than 12 members in state and federal courts[14] and voted in several cases to expand the right to counsel.[15] Marshall took a broad view of the Fifth Amendment's privilege against self-incrimination[16] and he voted in June 1972 and July 1976 to hold the death penalty totally unconstitutional as a violation of the Eighth Amendment's ban on cruel and unusual punishment.[17]

Marshall took a liberal stance in most First Amendment cases. In a May 1968 opinion for the Court, he held peaceful labor picketing within a suburban shopping center protected by the Amendment.[18] He dissented vigorously when the Court narrowed this ruling in June 1972 and then overturned it in March 1976.[19] Marshall voted against prior restraints on the press.[20] However he did favor narrowing the protection against libel suits enjoyed by the press when the case involved a private citizen rather than a public figure.[21] In an April 1969 decision, his opinion for the Court held that the private possession of obscene materials within one's own home could not be made a crime.[22] He also joined in a dissenting opinion in several

1. *San Antonio Independent School District v. Rodriguez*, 411 U.S. 1 (1973).

2. *Evans v. Comman*, 398 U.S. 419 (1970).

3. *Dunn v. Blumstein*, 405 U.S. 330 (1972).

4. *Phoenix v. Kolodziejski*, 399 U.S. 204 (1970); *Hill v. Stone*, 421 U.S. 289 (1975).

5. *Oregon v. Mitchell*, 400 U.S. 112 (1970).

6. *Mahan v. Howell*, 410 U.S. 315 (1973); *Gaffney v. Cummings*, 412 U.S. 735 (1973); *White v. Regester*, 412 U.S. 755 (1973).

7. *Benton v. Maryland*, 395 U.S. 784 (1969).

8. See, for example, *Vale v. Louisiana*, 399 U.S. 30 (1970); *Wyman v. James*, 400 U.S. 309 (1971); *Almeida-Sanchez v. U.S.*, 413 U.S. 266 (1973); *U.S. v. Edwards*, 415 U.S. 800 (1974).

9. *U.S. v. White*, 401 U.S. 745 (1971).

10. See, for example, *Dukes v. Warden*, 406 U.S. 250 (1972); *Tollett v. Henderson*, 411 U.S. 258 (1973); *Schneckloth v. Bustamonte*, 412 U.S. 218 (1973); *U.S. v. Watson*, 423 U.S. 411 (1976).

11. *Miranda v. Arizona*, 384 U.S. 436 (1966).

12. See, for example, *Harris v. New York*, 401 U.S. 222 (1971); *Michigan v. Mosley*, 423 U.S. 96 (1975).

13. *Johnson v. Louisiana*, 406 U.S. 356 (1972); *Apodaca v. Oregon*, 406 U.S. 404 (1972).

14. *Williams v. Florida*, 399 U.S. 78 (1970); *Colgrove v. Battin*, 413 U.S. 149 (1973).

15. *Mempa v. Rhay*, 389 U.S. 128 (1967); *Coleman v. Alabama*, 399 U.S. 1 (1970); *Argersinger v. Hamlin*, 407 U.S. 25 (1972),

16. See, for example, *California v. Byers*, 402 U.S. 424 (1971); *Kastigar v. U.S.*, 406 U.S. 441 (1972); *U.S. v. Dionisio*, 410 U.S. 1 (1973); *U.S. v. Mara*, 410 U.S. 19 (1973).

17. *Furman v. Georgia*, 408 U.S. 238 (1972); *Gregg v. Georgia*, 428 U.S. 153 (1976).

18. *Amalgamated Food Employees Union v. Logan Valley Plaza*, 391 U.S. 308 (1968).

19. *Lloyd Corp. v. Tanner*, 407 U.S. 551 (1972); *Hudgens v. NLRB*, 424 U.S. 507 (1976).

20. *New York Times Co. v. U.S.* 403 U.S. 713 (1971); *Nebraska Press Assn. v. Stuart*, 427 U.S. 539 (1976).

21. *Rosenbloom v. Metromedia, Inc.*, 403 U.S. 29 (1971); *Gertz v. Robert Welch, Inc.*, 418 U.S. 323 (1974).

22. *Stanley v. Georgia*, 394 U.S. 557 (1969).

June 1973 cases urging the Court to ban all government suppression of allegedly obscene material for consenting adults.[1]

In March 1971, however, Marshall spoke for an eight-man majority to rule that Congress could deny conscientious objector status to draft registrants who opposed only the Vietnam war, not all wars, without violating the First Amendment's guarantee of freedom of religion.[2] In August 1973, while the Court was in recess, Marshall upheld a Second Circuit Court order allowing U.S. bombing of Cambodia to continue while the constitutionality of the action was being litigated. When Justice William O. Douglas intervened in the case several days later to order a halt in the bombing, Marshall immediately contacted the other members of the Court and issued an order with their support overriding Douglas's action.[3]

Even before joining the Court, Thurgood Marshall had won a place in history because of his pathbreaking legal work for the NAACP. He stood as a symbol of the fight for black equality through legal action, and in both his NAACP post and later federal appointments, as a symbol of black achievement. As a justice, he was not highly creative or outstanding, but over the years, he became an increasingly articulate advocate of a liberal judicial position. In steadfastly opposing all forms of discrimination and supporting the protection of individual rights, Marshall maintained the Warren Court's tradition of libertarian activism.

---

1. *Miller v. California*, 413 U.S. 15 (1973); *Paris Adult Theatre I v. Slaton*, 413 U.S. 49 (1973).

2. *Gillette v. U.S.*, 401 U.S. 437 (1971).

3. *Schlesinger v. Holtzman*, 424 U.S. 1321 (1973).

MINTON, SHERMAN

b. Oct. 20, 1890: Georgetown, Ind.
d. April 9, 1965: New Albany, Ind.
Associate Justice, U.S. Supreme
Court, 1949-56.

Minton was class valedictorian at Indiana University, where he earned an LL.B. in 1915. He received an LL.M. from Yale the following year and then practiced law in Indiana and Florida. In 1933 Minton was named counselor of the Indiana Public Service Commission. He was elected to the U.S. Senate from Indiana in 1934. A Democrat, Minton was a firm and outspoken supporter of the New Deal. A critic of the Supreme Court's anti-New Deal decisions in 1935–36, he backed Franklin D. Roosevelt's Court reorganization plan in 1937. Defeated for reelection in 1940, Minton was named a judge on the U.S. Court of Appeals for the Seventh Circuit in May 1941. As circuit judge Minton wrote several significant antitrust and pro-labor opinions.[1] In a 1948 case he upheld the anti-Communist oath requirement in the Taft-Hartley Act.[2]

Minton had become good friends with Harry Truman during their Senate years, and in March 1948, President Truman named the judge to a three-man board set up to investigate a 10-day strike by John L. Lewis's United Mine Workers. On Sept. 15, 1949 Truman nominated Minton to the Supreme Court. The following month the Senate confirmed the appointment. Minton was sworn in as associate justice on Oct. 12, 1949.

Minton's Senate record led many observers to believe he would be a liberal justice, but he soon emerged as one of the most conservative members of the Court. The Court fight of the 1930s had convinced him that judges must allow other branches of government to use the powers given them in the Constitution and refrain from ruling on the wisdom of executive or legislative action. As a result, the Justice supported a policy of judicial restraint. He applied it not only to economic and social welfare measures but also to the civil liberties questions that increasingly came before the Court during the Cold War era. Minton believed many government restrictions on individual freedoms were permissible under the Constitution. His appointment to the bench helped create a five-man conservative bloc which dominated the Court for the next four years.

On loyalty-security matters, Minton almost always supported the government against individual rights claims. In January 1950, in one of his first major opinions, Minton upheld the exclusion of an alien war bride from the U.S. without a hearing because the Attorney General considered her a security risk.[3] His majority opinion in a March 1952 case sustained New York's Feinberg Law barring members of subversive organizations from teaching in public schools.[4] Minton voted to uphold the conviction of 11 Communist Party leaders under the Smith Act in June 1951[5] and, in March 1952, to allow alien Communists facing deportation to be held without bail if the Attorney General thought them a danger to national security.[6] The Justice also dissented in June 1952, when the majority invalidated Truman's seizure of the steel industry and rejected the President's claim of an inherent executive power to seize private property in a national emergency.[7]

Under Chief Justice Earl Warren a

---

1. *U.S. v. New York Great Atlantic & Pacific Tea Co.*, 173 F. 2d 79 (7 Cir. 1949); *Western Cartridge Co. v. National Labor Relations Board*, 139 F. 2d 855 (7 Cir. 1943).

2. *Inland Steel v. National Labor Relations Board*, 170 F. 2d 247 (7 Cir. 1948).

3. *U.S. ex rel. Knauff v. Shaughnessy*, 338 U.S. 537 (1950).

4. *Adler v. Board of Education*, 342 U.S. 485 (1952).

5. *Dennis v. U.S.*, 341 U.S. 494 (1951).

6. *Carlson v. Landon*, 342 U.S. 524 (1952).

7. *Youngstown Sheet and Tube Co. v. Sawyer*, 343 U.S. 579 (1952).

more liberal trend gradually developed in loyalty-security decisions. Minton found himself dissenting far more than he had on the Vinson Court in such cases. He objected in April 1956 when the Court overturned a state sedition law on the ground that federal statutes had pre-empted this field.[1] In another case the same month, Minton objected to a majority ruling that a local government could not discharge without notice or hearing a teacher who invoked the Fifth Amendment during a federal investigation.[2] He again dissented in June 1956 when the Court held that federal employes could be summarily suspended as security risks only if they held sensitive jobs.[3] Minton joined the majority, however, in June 1955 to rule that the Civil Service Commission's Loyalty Review Board had exceeded its authority when it dismissed a consultant to the Public Health Service who had already been cleared twice by the Health Service's own loyalty board.[4]

In free speech cases that did not involve security questions, Justice Minton was somewhat more likely to support the individual against the government. In January 1951, for example, he voted to overturn a New York City ordinance requiring preachers to get a police permit for religious services held in city streets and parks.[5] On the same day Minton dissented when the Court upheld the arrest of a public speaker who was being threatened by hostile members of his audience.[6] However, the Justice also voted in April 1952 to approve an Illinois law prohibiting group libel against a challenge that this denied free speech.[7]

Minton generally favored the government in criminal cases. He hesitated to upset convictions when the defendant did not make any claim of innocence but only charged the government with procedural errors. In an important February 1950 case, Minton wrote for a five-man majority to approve the warrantless search of a defendant's office following his arrest there and to overturn a 1948 decision which required law enforcement officials to obtain search warrants wherever "reasonably practicable."[8] Minton also disliked interfering with the states' criminal justice systems. For that reason he dissented in April 1956, when the Court ruled that the states must furnish a trial transcript to an indigent defendant if the transcript was necessary to appeal a conviction.[9]

In civil rights cases Minton generally followed a liberal course, voting to outlaw racial and religious discrimination.[10] He believed that government had no constitutional power to discriminate, and so in this field he felt that the Court could legitimately intervene to protect minority rights against government infringement. Minton spoke for the Court in a June 1953 case holding that a homeowner could not be sued by his neighbors for violating a racial restrictive convenant by selling his property to blacks.[11] He also joined in the May 1954 decision in *Brown v. Board of Education*, which ruled that racial segregation in public schools was unconstitutional.[12]

Minton did not think the Constitution prohibited discrimination by private parties. On that ground he dissented in June 1952 when the Court ruled against the discriminatory practices of a railway labor union.[13] Minton was also the lone dissenter in a May 1953 case in which the majority decided that the pre-primary elections of the Jaybird Democratic As-

1. *Pennsylvania v. Nelson,* 350 U.S. 497 (1956).

2. *Slochower v. Board of Education,* 350 U.S. 551 (1956).

3. *Cole v. Young,* 351 U.S. 536 (1956).

4. *Peters v. Hobby,* 349 U.S. 331 (1955).

5. *Kunz v. New York,* 340 U.S. 290 (1951).

6. *Feiner v. New York,* 340 U.S. 315 (1951).

7. *Beauharnais v. Illinois,* 343 U.S. 250 (1952).

8. *U.S. v. Rabinowitz,* 339 U.S. 56 (1950), overruling *Trupiano v. U.S.,* 334 U.S. 699 (1948).

9. *Griffin v. Illinois,* 351 U.S. 12 (1956).

10. See, for example, *Sweatt v. Painter,* 339 U.S. 629 (1950); *McLaurin v. Oklahoma State Regents,* 339 U.S. 637 (1950); *Henderson v. U.S.,* 339 U.S. 816 (1950).

11. *Barrows v. Jackson,* 346 U.S. 249 (1953).

12. 347 U.S. 483 (1954); *Bolling v. Sharpe,* 347 U.S. 497 (1954).

13. *Brotherhood of Railroad Trainmen v. Howard,* 343 U.S. 768 (1952).

sociation in one Texas county were in effect state actions and therefore blacks could not be excluded from them. Minton asserted that the Association was purely private, and however undesirable its policy of barring blacks, the Constitution did not prohibit it.[1]

Justice Minton retired from the Court on Oct. 15, 1956 because of declining health. A warm, gregarious and unpretentious man who often used earthy language, "Shay" Minton was well liked by all his colleagues throughout his years on the bench. He was not, however, a leading figure on the Court, nor did he write many significant opinions. He did not have an outstanding intellect, and his strong regard for precedent and judicial restraint hampered the development of his legal creativity. Minton's career on the Court has generally been ranked as undistinguished. Following his retirement, Minton was active in the Indiana Bar Association. He died on April 9, 1965.

1. *Terry v. Adams,* 345 U.S. 461 (1953).

MURPHY, FRANK
b. April 13, 1890; Harbor Beach, Mich.
d. July 19, 1949; Detroit, Mich.
Associate Justice, U.S. Supreme Court, 1940-49.

Born into an Irish Catholic family, Frank Murphy received a law degree from the University of Michigan in 1914 and began his public career in 1919 as an assistant U.S. attorney in Detroit. He served as a judge on the Detroit Recorder's Court from 1923 to 1930 and became mayor of the city in 1930. A supporter of Franklin Roosevelt for the presidency in 1932, Murphy was named governor-general of the Philippine Islands in June 1933. Elected governor of Michigan in 1936, Murphy took office just as the sitdown strikes in Michigan auto plants began. He persistently refused to use force against the strikers and helped negotiate a settlement to the disputes. After losing a reelection bid in 1938, Murphy was appointed U.S. Attorney General in January 1939. A year later Roosevelt named him to the Supreme Court. He took the oath of office in February 1940.

Initially Murphy was often indecisive and diffident, looking to senior justices for guidance. By 1943, however, he had come into his own on the Court and had developed self-confidence as a justice. He started to carve out a role for himself as an ardent defender of civil liberties. Over the next six years he espoused the view that the Supreme Court had a duty to act as spokesman of the national conscience and protector of the weak. Murphy frankly asserted that reaching just, equitable and compassionate results in a case mattered more than adherence to legal rules and precedents. In perhaps the most famous instance of his use of these standards, he objected in December 1944 when the majority upheld the wartime relocation and internment of Japanese Americans. The Justice wrote a passionate dissent condemning the racial prejudice underlying the program.[1]

In the postwar years Murphy emerged as the foremost civil libertarian on the bench. Although often part of a four-man liberal "bloc" on the Court, the Michigan Justice surpassed all others in the consistency of his support for claims of individual liberty and civil rights. In February 1946, only he and Wiley Rutledge, the justice to whom Murphy was closest personally and judicially, voted to overturn the war crimes conviction of Japanese Gen. Yamashita on the ground that his trial lacked basic constitutional guarantees of due process.[2] A strong foe of racial discrimination, Murphy joined in several decisions advancing the rights of blacks and upsetting California anti-Japanese laws.[3] From 1942 to 1949 he repeatedly voted to sustain the rights of Jehovah's Witnesses to practice their religion freely.[4] Despite criticism from some fellow Catholics, Murphy joined the majority in two decisions in 1947 and 1948 involving state aid to parochial schools in which the Court held that the First Amendment placed a high wall of separation between church and state.[5]

Murphy went beyond the position advanced by Justice Hugo Black that the 14th Amendment made all of the Bill of Rights applicable to the states and insisted that the amendment also protected individuals against government intrusion on rights not specifically listed in the Bill of Rights.[6] Murphy favored strict observ-

---

1. *Korematsu v. U.S.*, 323 U.S. 214, 233 (1944).
2. *In re Yamashita*, 327 U.S. 1 (1946).
3. See, for example, *Steele v. Louisville & Nashville Railroad Co.*, 323 U.S. 192 (1944); *Shelley v. Kraemer*, 334 U.S. 1 (1948); *Oyama v. California*, 332 U.S. 633 (1948); *Takahashi v. Fish and Game Commission*, 334 U.S. 410 (1948).
4. See, for example, *Jones v. Opelika*, 316 U.S. 584 (1942); *Martin v. City of Struthers*, 319 U.S. 141 (1943); *West Virginia State Board of Education v. Barnette*, 319 U.S. 624 (1943).
5. *Everson v. Board of Education*, 330 U.S. 1 (1947); *Illinois ex rel. McCollum v. Board of Education*, 333 U.S. 203 (1948).
6. *Adamson v. California*, 332 U.S. 46, 123 (1947).

ance of the constitutional rights of the criminally accused and almost always voted in favor of a defendant's claim in criminal cases.[1] Favoring strong protection of the Fourth Amendment's guarantee against unreasonable searches and seizures, Murphy agreed when the Court in June 1949 applied the amendment to the states. However, he objected when it also held that illegally seized evidence did not have to be excluded from state courts as it was in federal courts.[2]

Murphy voted to sustain New Deal legislation[3] and argued that these statutes should be interpreted in accord with the humanitarian and reform goals of the New Deal.[4] In 1944 and 1945 he wrote the opinion of the Court in two cases that ruled that iron and coal miners were entitled to portal-to-portal pay under the Fair Labor Standards Act.[5]

Murphy, who had been in declining health for several years, died of a heart attack in Detroit on July 19, 1949. Both before and after his death, the Justice was deeply respected by libertarians for his devotion to civil liberties, but his reputation was low in professional legal circles. To his critics Murphy was a misfit on the Court, a doctrinaire libertarian without intellectual depth or a regard for legal traditions who decided cases on the basis of his own sympathies rather than the law. He became a symbol of the partisan and activist judge who voted his personal policy preferences into law. Later scholars have shown that Murphy was technically competent as a jurist and that his votes were independent of his personal political and religious affiliations. Moreover, many of the views he expressed in dissent concerning civil liberties and criminal rights were ultimately adopted by the Court. Yet Murphy still is rated as only an average justice, in part because he frequently was indifferent to legal technicalities when they stood in the way of achieving larger goals. This frankly instrumental view of the law remains rather unorthodox. He also often wrote, especially in dissent, in a crusading, evangelistic style that was consistent with his view of the Court as public conscience but seemed to some sanctimonious cant devoid of legal analysis. According to his biographer J. Woodford Howard, Jr., and others, Frank Murphy most resembled the ideal of the just judge who puts humane results and public policy ahead of book law and legal formalities. He was the "most underestimated member of the Supreme Court in our time," according to John P. Frank. Murphy, wrote another commentator, stands in the forefront of Supreme Court justices who have "applied their great talents, courage and devotion to the increase of individual liberty under law and to the amelioration of social and economic hardship."

---

1. See, for example, *Betts v. Brady*, 316 U.S. 455 (1942); *Canizio v. New York*, 327 U.S. 82 (1946); *Carter v. Illinois*, 329 U.S. 173 (1946).

2. *Wolf v. Colorado*, 338 U.S. 25, 41 (1949). See also *Harris v. U.S.*, 331 U.S. 145 (1947); *Trupiano v. U.S.*, 334 U.S. 699 (1948).

3. See, for example, *North American Co. v. SEC*, 327 U.S. 686 (1946); *American Power & Light Co. v. SEC*, 329 U.S. 90 (1946).

4. See, for example, his opinions in *A.H. Phillips Inc. v. Walling*, 324 U.S. 490 (1945), and *Morris v. McComb*, 332 U.S. 422, 438 (1947).

5. *Tennessee Coal, Iron & Railroad Co. v. Muscoda Local No. 123*, 321 U.S. 590 (1944); *Jewell Ridge Coal Corp. v. Local No. 6167, UMW*, 325 U.S. 161 (1945).

POWELL, LEWIS F(RANKLIN), JR.
b. Sept. 19, 1907; Suffolk, Va.
Associate Justice, U.S. Supreme
Court, 1972-.

Lewis Powell received a bachelor's degree in 1929 and a law degree in 1931 from Washington and Lee University. After another year's study at Harvard Law School, he joined an old Richmond, Va., firm in 1932, where he became a partner in 1937. A corporate attorney, Powell specialized in securities law, corporate mergers, acquisitions and reorganizations. He eventually became a director of a number of large companies such as Philip Morris and Ethyl Corp. Powell also engaged in a wide variety of public service work. He headed the Richmond Board of Education from 1952 to 1961 and helped bring peaceful school desegregation to the city at a time when other Virginia schools closed rather than integrate. Powell served on the state board of education, the Virginia constitutional revision commission and President Lyndon Johnson's National Crime Commission during the 1960s. Long active in the American Bar Association, Powell was president of the organization in 1964 and 1965. He headed the American College of Trial Lawyers from 1969 to 1970 and the American Bar Foundation from 1969 to 1971. Along with William H. Rehnquist, Powell was nominated to the Supreme Court on Oct. 21, 1971. A recognized leader of the legal profession, Powell faced no significant opposition, and the Senate confirmed his appointment on Dec. 6 by an 89 to 1 vote. He was sworn in on Jan. 7, 1972.

As a justice, Powell was frequently compared to John Marshall Harlan. Like Harlan, he showed great regard for the doctrines of federalism and separation of powers. Powell also was skeptical of the Court's ability to achieve social reform and favored a policy of judicial restraint. He was sensitive to jurisdictional limitations on the Court and adopted Harlan's practice of balancing conflicting interests in deciding cases. Uncomfortable with abstract theories and absolute rules, the Justice preferred a flexible approach that allowed him to accommodate the competing values in a suit.

In First Amendment cases, for example, Powell usually weighed free expression against other societal interests. His majority opinion in a June 1972 decision upheld the private property rights of a shopping center owner over the free speech rights of anti-war protesters and sustained the owner in barring the distribution of political pamphlets on his premises.[1] In April 1974 Powell voided the mail censorship system in California's prisons because it infringed on First Amendment rights more than was necessary to ensure prison security and discipline.[2] Two months later, for a five man majority, the Justice balanced freedom of the press against the right of privacy. He ruled that individuals who were not public figures or officials could recover actual damages for defamatory falsehoods if they proved negligence, not the more limited "actual malice," by the press.[3]

Justice Powell adhered to Harlan's view that state criminal procedures must be "fundamentally fair" but need not meet the standards set for the federal government in the Bill of Rights.[4] He also balanced the claims of defendants and the government in criminal cases but tended to give greater weight to society's interests. In June 1972 Powell voted to guarantee the right to counsel in certain misdemeanor cases and to afford defendants the right to a hearing before their parole could be revoked.[5] However, his majority opinion in a May 1972 case narrowed the scope of the immunity a person must receive before being forced to give up his

---

1. *Lloyd Corp. v. Tanner*, 407 U.S. 551 (1972).

2. *Procunier v. Martinez*, 416 U.S. 396 (1974).

3. *Gertz v. Robert Welch, Inc.*, 418 U.S. 323 (1974).

4. See, for example, Powell's concurring opinions in *Johnson v. Louisiana*, 406 U.S. 356 (1972), and *Argersinger v. Hamlin*, 407 U.S. 25 (1972).

5. *Argersinger v. Hamlin*, 407 U.S. 25 (1972); *Morrissey v. Brewer*, 408 U.S. 471 (1972).

privilege against self-incrimination.[1] The Justice took a restrictive view of the Fifth Amendment in other cases as well.[2] He also favored the government's position in most Fourth Amendment cases.[3] However, he did speak for the Court in June 1972 to hold that the President had no authority to use electronic surveillance in domestic security cases without a warrant.[4] He voted to uphold state death penalty laws in June 1972, arguing that capital punishment was constitutional and that the Court could only rule on the manner of execution used and the appropriateness of the death penalty for a particular crime.[5]

In race discrimination cases, Powell urged the Court to abandon the distinction between de facto and de jure school segregation and to establish instead a uniform national desegregation rule.[6] He voted in July 1974 against the use of interdistrict busing to remedy school segregation in Detroit[7] but two years later favored the inclusion of suburbs in a plan to correct intentional segregation in urban public housing.[8] For a five man majority in April 1977, Powell ruled that suburban zoning regulations, which effectively barred housing for low income minorities, were not unconstitutional unless a racially discriminatory motive for the regulations could be proven.[9] In other equal protection cases, Powell employed a balanced approach and frequently voted to overturn government distinctions based on illegitimacy, alienage and sex.[10] In March 1973, however, the Justice wrote for a five man majority to hold that school financ-

ing schemes based on property taxes did not violate the equal protection clause.[11]

Powell supported a trend narrowing the Court's jurisdiction and wrote several significant opinions in this area. His May 1974 opinion for the Court made class action suits more difficult by ruling that plaintiffs in such cases must bear the full cost of notifying all members of the class on whose behalf they were suing.[12] In a June 1975 opinion Powell tightened the requirement that plaintiffs have legal standing to bring a suit before the Court will hear their case.[13] In July 1976 he restricted federal court review of challenges to convictions based on the Fourth Amendment brought by state prisoners.[14]

The Justice approached due process claims on a case-by-case basis. He voted with the majority in January 1973 to overturn state laws restricting abortions during the first six months of pregnancy as a denial of due process.[15] However, he dissented in January 1975 when the Court held that due process required public school students to receive a notice and a hearing prior to suspension.[16] Powell was described as a friend of the businessman in Court. He often voted against the government in antitrust cases. In a June 1975 decision,[17] Powell ruled that a labor union was subject to antitrust laws if it tried to coerce a general contractor into dealing only with union subcontractors.[18]

A courtly man with a gentle demeanor, Powell was a conscientious and hardworking jurist. His opinions at their best were craftsmanlike products, precise,

1 *Kastigar v. U.S.*, 406 U.S. 441 (1972).

2. See, for example, *Couch v. U.S.*, 409 U.S. 322 (1973); *U.S. v. Dionisio*, 410 U.S. 1 (1973).

3. See, for example, *U.S. v. Calandra*, 414 U.S. 338 (1974); *U.S. v. Miller*, 425 U.S. 435 (1976).

4. *U.S. v. U.S. District Court*, 407 U.S. 297 (1972).

5. *Furman v. Georgia*, 408 U.S. 238 (1972).

6. *Keyes v. School District No. 1, Denver*, 413 U.S. 189 (1973).

7. *Milliken v. Bradley*, 418 U.S. 717 (1974).

8. *Hills v. Gautreaux*, 425 U.S. 284 (1976).

9. *Village of Arlington Heights v. Metropolitan Housing Development Corp.*, 429 U.S. 252 (1977).

10. See, for example, *Weber v. Aetna Casualty & Surety Co.*, 406 U.S. 164 (1972); *In re Griffiths*, 413 U.S. 717 (1973); *Frontiero v. Richardson*, 411 U.S. 677 (1973).

11. *San Antonio Independent School District v. Rodriguez*, 411 U.S. 1 (1973).

12. *Eisen v. Carlisle & Jacquelin*, 417 U.S. 156 (1974).

13. *Warth v. Seldin*, 422 U.S. 490 (1975).

14. *Stone v. Powell*, 428 U.S. 465 (1976).

15. *Roe v. Wade*, 410 U.S. 113 (1973); *Doe v. Bolton*, 410 U.S. 179 (1973).

16. *Goss v. Lopez*, 419 U.S. 565 (1975).

17. See, for example, *U.S. v. General Dynamics Corp.*, 415 U.S. 486 (1974); *U.S. v. Marine Bancorporation, Inc.*, 418 U.S. 602 (1974); *U.S. v. National Association of Securities Dealers, Inc.*, 422 U.S. 694 (1975).

18. *Connell Construction Co. v. Plumbers and Steamfitters Local Union No. 100*, 421 U.S. 616 (1975).

candid and cogent in argument. Many observers during his first years on the bench saw in Powell the potential for judicial leadership. Moderate and prudent by temperament, Powell was conservative but not inflexible, and he showed considerable independence of mind. Positioned near the center of the Court philosophically, he was considered capable of bringing other justices to his point of view and of acting as a spokesman for the Court on important issues.

REED, STANLEY F(ORMAN)
b. Dec. 31, 1884: Minerva, Ky.
Associate Justice, U.S. Supreme
Court, 1938-57.

After receiving B.A. degrees from Kentucky Wesleyan College in 1902 and Yale University in 1906, Reed studied law at the University of Virginia, Columbia University and the Sorbonne. From 1910 to 1929 he practiced law in Kentucky. He then served as counsel of the Federal Farm Board from 1929 to 1932 and as general counsel of the Reconstruction Finance Corp. from 1932 to 1935. A Democrat, Reed was named U.S. Solicitor General in March 1935, and over the next three years he defended before the Supreme Court such major New Deal legislation as the National Industrial Recovery Act, the Agricultural Adjustment Act and the Tennessee Valley Authority. President Franklin Roosevelt's second Supreme Court appointee, Reed had a reputation as a liberal Democrat with sound legal training and a judicious character when he was named a justice in January 1938.

As Solicitor General, Reed had seen a conservative Court majority overturn important New Deal measures. Probably as a result of that experience, the Kentuckian generally adhered to a policy of judicial restraint while on the bench. He regularly voted to uphold federal economic and social welfare laws and thus helped to legitimize the expansion of government regulatory powers that occurred during the 1930s. Although his belief in judicial deference to the executive and legislative branches produced a liberal record on economic matters, the same attitude led Reed to conservative positions on the civil liberties issues that became increasingly important during his years on the Court. The Justice voted to uphold most government security efforts against charges that they violated individual rights. He established one of the lowest records of support for civil liberties among the members of the Vinson Court.

Reed voted with the majority in May 1950, for example, to sustain the non-Communist oath provision in the Taft-Hartley Act and in June 1951 to uphold the conviction of American Communist Party leaders under the Smith Act.[1] He wrote the majority opinion in a March 1952 case in which a closely divided Court ruled that the Attorney General could hold without bail alien Communists who were facing deportation charges.[2] In June 1952 Reed dissented when the majority decided that President Harry S Truman's seizure of the steel industry was unconstitutional.[3]

Under Chief Justice Earl Warren, Reed objected when the Court in any way undermined loyalty-security programs. He dissented in June 1955 when the majority ruled that the Civil Service Commission's Loyalty Review Board had exceeded its authority in auditing a favorable loyalty judgment and had wrongfully commanded the dismissal of a Public Health Service employe.[4] In April 1956 Reed wrote the minority opinion in a case where the Court overturned Pennsylvania's antisubversive law.[5] Reed again dissented when the majority in June 1956 held that government employes could be summarily dismissed as security risks only if they held sensitive jobs.[6]

Outside the field of national security, Reed proved more responsive to individual rights claims involving the First Amendment. His majority opinion in a June 1946 case reversed the contempt of court conviction against a Miami newspaper for its criticism of local judicial proceedings.[7] In March 1948 Reed's opinion

---

1. *American Communications Assn. v. Douds,* 339 U.S. 382 (1950); *Dennis v. U.S.,* 341 U.S. 494 (1951).

2. *Carlson v. Landon,* 342 U.S. 524 (1952).

3. *Youngstown Sheet and Tube Co. v. Sawyer,* 343 U.S. 579 (1952).

4. *Peters v. Hobby,* 349 U.S. 331 (1955).

5. *Pennsylvania v. Nelson,* 350 U.S. 497 (1956).

6. *Cole v. Young,* 351 U.S. 536 (1956).

7. *Pennekamp v. Florida,* 328 U.S. 331 (1946).

for the Court overturned a New York State law barring publications that featured stories of violent crime.[1] In April 1952 the Justice voted to invalidate an Illinois law against group libel.[2]

In two 1951 cases Reed also voted to hold unconstitutional state licensing laws requiring persons to secure permits before speaking or meeting in public parks or streets because the laws gave too much discretion to the officials granting the licenses.[3] However, Reed believed some government regulation of expression was permissible. In April 1953 he wrote the majority opinion sustaining a similar New Hampshire licensing law because its standards were precise enough to make it constitutional.[4] Reed also wrote the majority opinion in a February 1947 case upholding the Hatch Act's ban on political activity by federal employes against a First Amendment challenge.[5] He upheld a city ordinance prohibiting door-to-door magazine sales in June 1951[6] and, in two cases in 1948 and 1949, voted to sustain local laws regulating the use of sound trucks.[7]

Reed favored a narrow interpretation of the First Amendment's clause barring the establishment of religion. He was the sole dissenter from a March 1948 decision in which the majority upset a program of released time religious education in public schools.[8] He took a conservative position on most criminal rights issues and in an important June 1947 case defended against challenges from four dissenters[9] the traditional view that the 14th Amendment did not extend all of the Bill of Rights guarantees to the states. Reed was also extremely reluctant to upset a convic-

tion on the grounds that a defendant's confession had been coerced. He would do so only when there was strong and clear evidence that a confession had been given involuntarily.[10]

Although a Southerner, Justice Reed joined in a series of decisions expanding the constitutional rights of blacks. He wrote for the Court in a June 1945 case sustaining the application of New York State's civil rights law to a labor union[11] and in a June 1946 suit holding state segregation laws inapplicable to interstate buses.[12]

However, Reed balked at holding racial segregation in and of itself unconstitutional. The issue was squarely presented to the Court during the 1952–53 session in five companion suits involving segregated schools. Reed evidently believed that segregation was allowable so long as blacks received equal treatment with whites. When the justices voted on the cases in conference early in 1954, Reed was alone in this view. After considering what would be best for the country and the Court, Reed yielded. He decided not to dissent and thus made unanimous the May 1954 decision in *Brown v. Board of Education*, which ruled that segregation in public schools violated the Constitution.[13]

A soft-spoken man of unfailing courtesy and kindliness, Reed retired from the Court in February 1957 at the age of 72. As a justice he was not easy to categorize because his liberalism in most economic, labor and civil rights cases was offset by his general conservatism on civil liberties and criminal rights issues. Assessing Reed's 19 years on the high bench, C.

---

1. *Winters v. New York*, 333 U.S. 507 (1948).

2. *Beauharnais v. Illinois*, 343 U.S. 250 (1952).

3. *Niemotko v. Maryland*, 340 U.S. 268 (1951); *Kunz v. New York*, 340 U.S. 290 (1951).

4. *Poulos v. New Hampshire*, 345 U.S. 395 (1953).

. *United Public Workers of America v. Mitchell*, 330 U.S. 75 (1947).

6. *Breard v. Alexandria*, 341 U.S. 622 (1951).

7. *Saia v. New York*, 334 U.S. 558 (1948); *Kovacs v. Cooper*, 336 U.S. 77 (1949).

8. *Illinois ex rel. McCollum v. Board of Education*, 333 U.S. 203 (1948).

9. *Adamson v. California*, 332 U.S. 46 (1947).

10. See, for example, *Ashcraft v. Tennessee*, 322 U.S. 143 (1944); *Gallegos v. Nebraska*, 342 U.S. 55 (1951); *Brown v. Allen*, 344 U.S. 443 (1953).

11. *Railway Mail Assn. v. Corsi*, 326 U.S. 88 (1945).

12. *Morgan v. Virginia*, 328 U.S. 373 (1946). See also *Smith v. Allwright*, 321 U.S. 649 (1944); *Sweatt v. Painter*, 339 U.S. 629 (1950); *McLaurin v. Oklahoma State Regents*, 339 U.S. 637 (1950); *Henderson v. U.S.*, 339 U.S. 816 (1950).

13. 347 U.S. 483 (1954); *Bolling v. Sharpe*, 347 U.S. 497 (1954).

Herman Pritchett called the Justice "a 'center judge,' occupying generally a middle position between the Court's conservative and liberal wings" but with a definite rightward bent in civil liberties cases. He was "a legal craftsman" who believed that the political branches of government, not the Court, had "the power and the responsibility for governing."

Following his retirement Reed spent time both in Washington and on his farm near Maysville, Ky. President Dwight D. Eisenhower named him chairman of the new six-member U.S. Civil Rights Commission in November 1957. However, Reed withdrew from the job in December because he feared his service in an investigatory and advisory post might lower public respect for the impartiality of the judiciary. In the years after this, he accepted many assignments to hear cases in the U.S. Court of Claims and the U.S. Court of Appeals for the District of Columbia.

REHNQUIST, WILLIAM H(UBBS)

b. Oct. 1, 1924; Milwaukee, Wisc.
Assistant Attorney General, 1969-72;
Associate Justice, U.S. Supreme
Court, 1972-.

Rehnquist received a B.A. from Stanford University in 1948 and graduated first in his class from Stanford Law School in 1952. He served as a law clerk to Supreme Court Justice Robert H. Jackson in 1952 and 1953 and then moved to Phoenix, Ariz., where he practiced privately from 1953 to 1969. Rehnquist also became active in the conservative wing of Arizona's Republican Party and supported Sen. Barry Goldwater (R, Ariz.) for the presidency in 1964. On the recommendation of Deputy Attorney General G. Richard Kleindienst, Rehnquist was appointed assistant attorney general in charge of the office of legal counsel in January 1969.

In that post Rehnquist gave legal advice to the Attorney General and the President and to other departments of government. Considered a brilliant attorney, Rehnquist also served as an articulate and well-informed spokesman for the Nixon Administration in Congress on a variety of controversial issues. He promoted the unsuccessful nominations of Clement F. Haynsworth, Jr. and G. Harrold Carswell to the Supreme Court. He defended the President's power to invade Cambodia, the mass arrests of anti-war demonstrators in Washington and the executive's privilege to withhold information from Congress. Rehnquist supported the Administration's criminal law proposals including authorization of wiretapping and electronic surveillance, preventive detention and "no-knock" entry. He aroused some controversy in March 1971, when he told a Senate subcommittee that the Justice Department opposed any legislation impairing the government's ability to collect information on citizens. He also said he saw no violation of the First Amendment in the Army's surveillance of civilian demonstrators.

On Oct. 21, 1971 President Nixon unexpectedly nominated Rehnquist and Lewis F. Powell, Jr., to the Supreme Court. Opposition to Rehnquist's appointment soon developed among civil rights, civil liberties and labor groups who criticized his conservative record on issues of individual and minority rights. Nonetheless, the Senate Judiciary Committee approved Rehnquist's nomination by a 12 to 4 vote on Nov. 23. After several days of debate, the Senate confirmed his appointment, 68 to 26. Rehnquist was sworn in as associate justice on Jan. 7, 1972.

The youngest justice at the time of his appointment, Rehnquist soon established himself as the most conservative member of the Court. He advanced a narrow conception of judicial review and insisted that policymaking was the function of the political branches of government. He argued that the Court should defer to the judgments of legislatures unless their actions were clearly unconstitutional, and he opposed expansive constitutional interpretations, which he thought allowed the justices to impose their own values on society.

Rehnquist objected, for example, to the Court's extension of the due process clause to a variety of new interests. In cases decided in 1974 and 1975, he voted against granting a right to a notice and a hearing to a federal civil service employe prior to his dismissal, to debtors prior to the seizure of their goods by creditors, and to public school students prior to a disciplinary suspension.[1] He dissented in January 1973 when the Court overturned state laws restricting abortions during the first six months of pregnancy as a violation of the due process right to privacy.[2] In

---

1. *Arnett v. Kennedy*, 416 U.S. 134 (1974); *Mitchell v. W.T. Grant Co.*, 416 U.S. 600 (1974); *North Georgia Finishing, Inc. v. Di-Chem, Inc.*, 419 U.S. 601 (1975); *Goss v. Lopez*, 419 U.S. 565 (1975).

2. *Roe v. Wade*, 410 U.S. 113 (1973); *Doe v. Bolton*, 410 U.S. 179 (1973).

a March 1976 majority opinion, Rehnquist stated that police did not deny due process when they identified an individual in a notice to shopkeepers as an "active shoplifter," even though he had never been convicted of theft.[1]

Similarly, Justice Rehnquist took a limited view of the equal protection clause. It was intended, he argued, to protect blacks from racial discrimination by the state and should not be used to overturn other forms of alleged discrimination unless there was no rational basis for the government's action. As a result of this view, Rehnquist voted, often alone, to uphold laws that established different treatment for illegitimate children, aliens and women.[2] He was the sole dissenter, for example, in May 1973, when the majority invalidated different eligibility requirements for dependency benefits for men and women in the military. He stood alone again in April 1975 when the Court overturned state laws setting a different age of majority for the sexes.[3] Rehnquist spoke for the Court, however, in December 1976 when he ruled that an employer did not violate the 1964 Civil Rights Act, which prohibited sex discrimination in employment, by excluding pregnancy and childbirth from coverage in a disability benefit plan.[4]

The Justice also used a rationality test to decide apportionment cases, and he wrote several significant opinions for the Court based on this standard. In February 1973 he upheld a state legislative districting plan that departed from a strict one-person, one-vote rule because the deviations helped the state achieve the goal of providing representation for local communities.[5] For a six-man majority Rehnquist ruled in March 1973 that the one-man, one-vote standard was not required for the election of officials to a special purpose governmental body, such as the board of directors of a state water storage district.[6]

In racial discrimination cases Rehnquist spoke for a unanimous Court in January 1973 to hold that a defendant must be allowed to question potential jurors about possible racial prejudice.[7] However, his majority opinion in a June 1972 case ruled that racial discrimination by a private club did not violate the Constitution, even though the club received a liquor license from the state.[8] In June 1976, for a six-man majority, the Justice declared that once school officials had complied with a desegregation order by establishing a racially neutral pupil assignment system, they could not be required to readjust attendance zones later on when population shifts caused resegregation.[9]

Justice Rehnquist generally voted to sustain governmental actions against individual rights claims, especially in criminal cases. On Fourth Amendment issues, where he was often the Court's spokesman, Rehnquist persistently upheld police searches and seizures against challenge. In a June 1972 decision he ruled that a policeman could stop and frisk a suspect for a weapon on the basis of an informant's tip and then, after arresting him for illegal possession of a handgun, could search the suspect's car without a warrant.[10] His opinion for the Court in a December 1973 case upheld the authority of the police to make a full personal search following a lawful custodial arrest, even for a minor offense such as a traffic violation.[11] In two decisions in April 1973 and April 1976, Rehnquist stated that a defendant could not claim entrapment into a

1. *Paul v. Davis*, 424 U.S. 693 (1976).

2. See, for example, *Weber v. Aetna Casualty & Surety Co.*, 406 U.S. 164 (1972); *Sugarman v. Dougall*, 413 U.S. 634 (1973); *Taylor v. Louisiana*, 419 U.S. 522 (1975).

3. *Frontiero v. Richardson*, 411 U.S. 677 (1973); *Stanton v. Stanton*, 421 U.S. 7 (1975).

4. *General Electric Co. v. Gilbert*, 429 U.S. 125 (1976).

5. *Mahan v. Howell*, 410 U.S. 315 (1973).

6. *Salyer Land Co. v. Tulare Lake Basin Water Storage District*, 410 U.S. 719 (1973).

7. *Ham v. South Carolina*, 409 U.S. 524 (1973).

8. *Moose Lodge No. 107 v. Irvis*, 407 U.S. 163 (1972).

9. *Pasadena City Board of Education v. Spangler*, 427 U.S. 424 (1976).

10. *Adams v. Williams*, 407 U.S. 143 (1972).

11. *U.S. v. Robinson*, 414 U.S. 218 (1973).

crime, no matter what the extent of government involvement, if he had shown a predisposition to violate the law.[1] The Justice also voted repeatedly to sustain state laws imposing capital punishment.[2]

In First Amendment cases Rehnquist also tended to give greater weight to society's interests than to individual free expression. He joined the majority in several June 1973 cases, for example, to set new guidelines for obscenity laws which allowed greater government control over pornography.[3] The Justice generally resolved federal-state conflicts in favor of the states. In a June 1976 majority opinion, he overturned a 1968 precedent and held federal minimum wage laws inapplicable to state and local governments.[4] Rehnquist also favored cutbacks in federal court jurisdiction. His opinion for a five-man majority in January 1976 ruled that a federal district judge exceeded his jurisdiction when he ordered Philadelphia officials to establish new procedures for handling complaints of police misconduct.[5]

Off the bench Justice Rehnquist was a frequent public speaker who agreed with Chief Justice Warren Burger that the Court's caseload was too heavy. On the Court he impressed all observers with his powerful intellectual ability and with opinions that were generally well-organized, able and articulate. Rehnquist's influence on the rest of the Court was a matter of debate. Some commentators believed him too dogmatically conservative in his views to sway other justices. One analyst, David Shapiro, labeled Rehnquist's judicial performance "markedly below" his "substantial capabilities," partly because of "the inflexibility of his ideological commitments." Other observers, however, suggested that the Justice's brilliance, self-confidence and persuasiveness, combined with the prospect of a lengthy tenure, made it likely that he would have a significant impact on the Court over the long run.

---

1. *U.S. v. Russell*, 411 U.S. 423 (1973); *Hampton v. U.S.*, 425 U.S. 484 (1976).

2. *Furman v. Georgia*, 408 U.S. 238 (1972) *Gregg v. Georgia*, 428 U.S. 153 (1976); *Proffitt v. Florida*, 428 U.S. 242 (1976); *Jurek v. Texas*, 428 U.S. 262 (1976); *Woodson v. North Carolina*, 428 U.S. 280 (1976); *Roberts v. Louisiana*, 428 U.S. 325 (1976); *Coker v. Georgia*, 433 U.S. 584 (1977).

3. *Miller v. California*, 413 U.S. 15 (1973); *Paris Adult Theatre I v. Slaton*, 413 U.S. 49 (1973); *U.S. v. 12 200-Foot Reels*, 413 U.S. 123 (1973); *U.S. v. Orito*, 413 U.S. 139 (1973).

4. *National League of Cities v. Usery*, 426 U.S. 833 (1976).

5. *Rizzo v. Goode*, 423 U.S. 362 (1976).

RUTLEDGE, WILEY B(LOUNT)
b. July 20, 1894; Cloverport, Ky.
d. Sept. 10, 1949; York, Me.
Associate Justice, U.S. Supreme
Court, 1943-49.

Wiley B. Rutledge graduated from the University of Wisconsin in 1914 and then taught high school. He received a law degree from the University of Colorado in 1922 and began his teaching career there in 1924. Rutledge went on to become professor of law and dean of the law school at Washington University in St. Louis between 1926 and 1935. He served as dean of Iowa College of Law from 1935 to 1939. He was active on the St. Louis Commission for Social Justice and was an ardent supporter of Franklin Roosevelt and the New Deal. A respected and influential figure in legal circles in the Midwest, Rutledge publicly criticized the anti-New Deal decisions of the Supreme Court and backed Roosevelt's Court-packing plan in 1937. His statements brought him to the attention of the President, and in March 1939, Rutledge was named to a judgeship on the U.S. Court of Appeals for the District of Columbia. In his four years there Rutledge wrote liberal opinions that reflected New Deal views on the economy and social welfare. He was nominated to the Supreme Court in January 1943 and easily won confirmation the next month.

On the bench Rutledge fulfilled expectations that he would be a liberal jurist. He supported the expansion of federal power over the economy and upheld broad interpretations of Congress's commerce and taxing powers. He generally voted in favor of workers in labor law cases and sustained the regulatory authority of federal administrative agencies.

At the same time Rutledge was careful to safeguard individual freedoms against government intrusion. He emerged as one of the foremost defenders of civil liberties in the Court's history. During his tenure Rutledge was part of a four-man liberal bloc, along with Hugo Black, William O. Douglas, and Frank Murphy, which sought to expand the scope of individual rights guarantees. He was most closely aligned with Murphy in voting, and like those of his colleague, Rutledge's decisions were influenced by his humanitarian philosophy and by his concern that the social and individual results of a decision serve justice as well as the law. He believed that the Constitution mandated rigorous protection of personal rights and that the Court was to be the primary guardian of individual liberties. Rutledge's only major lapse from a strong civil libertarian position came during World War II, when he voted to uphold the government program evacuating Japanese-Americans from the West Coast.[1]

Justice Rutledge took an expansive view of the guarantees in the Bill of Rights. He insisted that full constitutional protection be given those accused of crime in both federal and state courts.[2] He voted to uphold the right to counsel every time this issue came before the Court,[3] and he took strong stands against coerced confessions and denials of the privilege against self-incrimination.[4] Rutledge concurred when the Court held the Fourth Amendment applicable to the states in June 1949 but objected when a majority also ruled that state courts could admit illegally seized evidence.[5] The Justice thought basic rights of due process should be guaranteed even to an enemy belligerent. In what some consider his most important civil liberties opinion, he dissented in February 1946 when the majority upheld the conviction of Japanese

---

1. *Hirabayashi v. U.S.*, 320 U.S. 81 (1943); *Korematsu v. U.S.*, 323 U.S. 214 (1944).

2. *Adamson v. California*, 332 U.S. 46 (1947).

3. See, for example, Rutledge's opinions in *Foster v. Illinois*, 332 U.S. 134 (1947) and *Gryger v. Burke*, 334 U.S. 728 (1948).

4. See, for example, Rutledge's opinion in *Malinski v. New York*, 324 U.S. 401 (1945), and see *Adamson v. California*, 332 U.S. 46 (1947).

5. *Wolf v. Colorado*, 338 U.S. 25 (1949).

Gen. Tomoyuki Yamashita who had been tried by a U.S. military commission for violation of the laws of war. Rutledge attacked the legal basis of the commission, argued that its procedures had denied Yamashita a fair trial and insisted that the military tribunal had to meet the basic standards of fairness of the Anglo-American legal tradition.[1]

Rutledge adhered to the view that First Amendment freedoms have a preferred position and require special protection against government infringement.[2] He twice voted in 1948-49 to overturn local ordinances restricting the use of sound trucks[3] and, in a May 1949 case, to guarantee the free speech rights even of a man whose statements had stirred up a crowd and created a disturbance.[4] Rutledge almost always voted to sustain the right of Jehovah's Witnesses to distribute their religious literature free from government interference.[5] At the same time he took a strict view of the First Amendment's ban on the establishment of religion and contended that this provision barred the government from making any contributions from public funds to religious organizations. He thus dissented in February 1947 when the Court approved public payments for the transportation of children to parochial schools[6] and joined the majority in March 1948 to overturn a released-time program of religious education in public schools.[7]

Justice Rutledge joined in decisions which advanced the rights of blacks in public education and transit.[8] In February 1948 he wrote for a seven-man majority to uphold the application of Michigan's civil rights law to an excursion boat that had excluded blacks, even though the boat entered Canadian waters during its trips.[9] In one of the more famed cases of the Truman era, Rutledge dissented in March 1947 when the Court upheld the convictions of John L. Lewis and the United Mine Workers for civil and criminal contempt for having violated an anti-strike injunction issued by a lower federal court at a time when the U.S. government had taken over the coal mines. The Justice argued that the 1932 Norris-LaGuardia Act had withdrawn from federal courts the jurisdiction to issue injunctions in labor disputes, even when the federal government was involved, and he objected to the district court's mixing of civil and criminal proceedings in the same case.[10]

Justice Rutledge died on Sept. 10, 1949 while vacationing in Maine. By all accounts he was a man of great personal warmth and friendliness who showed a sincere interest and concern for all those around him. Although on the Court for only six-and-a-half years, Rutledge earned high ratings from legal analysts. He combined a strong humanitarian and democratic faith with scholarship, an able command of the law, and prodigious workmanship. All agree that his most enduring contribution came in the field of civil liberties. "Rigid, uniform protection of civil liberties," one commentator has observed, was for Rutledge "very nearly an absolute general principle." He had profound respect for the dignity of the individual and believed that this must be carefully safeguarded. Rutledge became, next to Frank Murphy, "the most consistent champion of substantive civil liberties on the Court." After both men died in the summer of 1949, the Supreme Court

1. *In re Yamashita*, 327 U.S. 1 (1946).

2. *Thomas v. Collins*, 323 U.S. 516 (1945).

3. *Saia v. New York*, 334 U.S. 558 (1948); *Kovacs v. Cooper*, 336 U.S. 77 (1949).

4. *Terminiello v. Chicago*, 337 U.S. 1 (1949).

5. *Jones v. Opelika*, 319 U.S. 103 (1943); *Murdock v. Pennsylvania*, 319 U.S. 105 (1943); *Martin v. Struthers*, 319 U.S. 141 (1943). See also *West Virginia State Board of Education v. Barnette*, 319 U.S. 624 (1943) and *Prince v. Massachusetts*, 321 U.S. 158 (1944).

6. *Everson v. Board of Education*, 330 U.S. 1 (1947).

7. *Illinois ex rel. McCollum v. Board of Education*, 333 U.S. 203 (1948).

8. *Sipuel v. Board of Regents*, 332 U.S. 631 (1948); *Morgan v. Virginia*, 328 U.S. 373 (1946).

9. *Bob-Lo Excursion Co. v. Michigan*, 333 U.S. 28 (1948).

10. *U.S. v. United Mine Workers*, 330 U.S. 258 (1947).

took a conservative turn. Not until the 1960s, when the activist Warren Court adopted many of his views, was the Court again as libertarian as it had been in Rutledge's day.

STEVENS, JOHN PAUL
b. April 20, 1920; Chicago, Ill.
Judge, U.S. Seventh Circuit Court of
Appeals, 1970-75; Associate Justice,
U.S. Supreme Court, 1975-.

Stevens received a B.A. from the University of Chicago in 1941 and graduated first in his class from Northwestern University Law School in 1947. He was law clerk to Supreme Court Justice Wiley Rutledge in 1947 and 1948. Stevens then entered private practice in Chicago, where he specialized in antitrust and corporate law. He also served in 1950 as counsel to the House Judiciary Subcommittee on Antitrust and Monopoly and as a member of the Attorney General's National Committee to Study Antitrust Laws in 1954 and 1955.

A Republican, Stevens was named a judge on the U.S. Seventh Circuit Court of Appeals in October 1970. During his five years on the appellate bench, he established an excellent reputation for judicial craftsmanship based on opinions that were consistently clear, scholarly and well-written. He was considered a generally moderate jurist with a nonideological approach to cases that made him difficult to categorize. Stevens usually emphasized the facts in each suit and applied the relevant law on a case-by-case basis. Within that framework, he tended to favor the prosecution in criminal cases but was responsive to claims of prisoners' rights.[1] He was moderate on discrimination and free expression issues and overall favored a policy of judicial restraint.[2]

On Nov. 28, 1975, President Gerald Ford nominated Stevens for the Supreme Court seat vacated by the retirement of Justice William O. Douglas. Stevens was strongly recommended for the post by Attorney General Edward H. Levi, who had known him in Chicago, and the nomination was generally well-received. Women's rights groups objected to Stevens because he had opposed women's claims in several sex discrimination cases.[3] However, he was confirmed by the Senate on Dec. 17 by a 98 to 0 vote and sworn in two days later.

Stevens proved to be an independent justice who demonstrated the same case-by-case approach to issues that he had shown on the circuit bench. Nondoctrinaire and individualistic, he was not clearly aligned with either the more liberal or conservative members of the Court. However, Stevens was more liberal in his votes than many observers had anticipated, and though hard to categorize, seemed to take a moderate to liberal approach on most issues.

During his first year on the bench, Justice Stevens concurred in an important June 1976 decision holding that a racially discriminatory purpose as well as a discriminatory effect was needed to make a government job test unconstitutional.[4] Later the same month, however, he joined the majority to declare racial discrimination in private nonsectarian schools illegal.[5] Stevens dissented several days later when the Court upheld a social security act provision discriminating against illegitimate children.[6] He also objected to a December 1976 decision ruling that pregnancy and childbirth could be excluded from coverage in a company disability insurance plan without violating a federal law prohibiting sex discrimination in employment.[7]

---

1. See, for example, *U.S. v. Walker*, 489 F.2d 1353 (7 Cir. 1973); *U.S. ex rel. Kirby v. Sturges*, 510 F.2d 397 (7 Cir. 1975); *U.S. ex rel. Miller v. Twomey*, 479 F.2d 701 (7 Cir. 1973).

2. See, for example, *Cousins v. City Council of Chicago*, 466 F.2d 830 (7 Cir. 1972); *Cohen v. Illinois Institute of Technology*, 524 F.2d 818 (7 Cir. 1975); *Gertz v. Robert Welch, Inc.*, 471 F.2d 801 (7 Cir. 1972), *reversed*, 418 U.S. 323 (1974); *Herzbrun v. Milwaukee County*, 504 F.2d 1189 (7 Cir. 1974).

3. See, for example, *Sprogis v. United Air Lines*, 444 F.2d 1194 (7 Cir. 1971).

4. *Washington v. Davis*, 426 U.S. 229, 252 (1976).

5. *Runyon v. McCrary*, 427 U.S. 160, 189 (1976).

6. *Mathews v. Lucas*, 427 U.S. 495 (1976); *Norton v. Mathews*, 427 U.S. 524 (1976).

7. *General Electric Co. v. Gilbert*, 429 U.S. 125 (1976).

Justice Stevens spoke for a five-man majority in June 1976 to hold that Civil Service Commission regulations barring resident aliens from federal jobs denied due process of law.[1] However, he also wrote the opinion in a case holding that the dismissal of a state policeman without a hearing did not deprive him of liberty or property without due process.[2] The Justice displayed a mixed pattern in First Amendment cases during his first term. His opinion for a five-man majority upheld a Detroit ordinance restricting the location of adult movie theaters.[3] However, Stevens took a strong stand a week later against judicial "gag" orders limiting publication of information about criminal cases.[4]

In July 1976 Stevens voted to overturn laws making death the mandatory penalty for murder.[5] However, he joined in rulings sustaining laws that established death as one possible penalty for murder and set guidelines for the judge or jury in determining the sentence.[6] The Justice took a conservative stance in several Fourth Amendment cases in his first months on the Court and was part of a six-man majority that limited state prisoners' right of appeal to federal courts on search and seizure issues.[7] He showed special sensitivity to claims of illegal treatment made by prison inmates. Stevens dissented in June 1976 when the Court ruled that inmates were not entitled to a hearing before being transferred from one prison to another, even when the move was a disciplinary action or conditions in the two prisons differed substantially.[8]

During the next few terms of the Court, Justice Stevens continued to pursue an independent and rather unpredictable course. Quiet and mild-mannered, he was considered a "swing" vote along with Justices Potter Stewart and Byron White. Of the three, he was the one most likely to join with the Court's liberals when the justices were divided. Commentators generally rated Stevens as an intelligent, thoughtful jurist who wrote well-regarded opinions.

---

1. *Hampton v. Mow Sun Wong*, 426 U.S. 88 (1976).

2. *Bishop v. Wood*, 426 U.S. 341 (1976).

3. *Young v. American Mini Theatres, Inc.*, 427 U.S. 50 (1976).

4. *Nebraska Press Assn. v. Stuart*, 427 U.S. 539, 617 (1976).

5. *Woodson v. North Carolina*, 428 U.S. 280 (1976); *Roberts v. Louisiana*, 428 U.S. 325 (1976).

6. *Gregg v. Georgia*, 428 U.S. 153 (1976); *Proffitt v. Florida*, 428 U.S. 242 (1976); *Jurek v. Texas*, 428 U.S. 262 (1976).

7. *South Dakota v. Opperman*, 428 U.S. 364 (1976); *U.S. v. Martinez-Fuerte*, 428 U.S. 543 (1976); *Stone v. Powell*, 428 U.S. 465 (1976).

8. *Meachum v. Fano*, 427 U.S. 215 (1976); *Montanye v. Haymes*, 427 U.S. 236 (1976).

STEWART, POTTER
b. Jan. 23, 1915; Jackson, Mich.
Associate Justice, U.S. Supreme
Court, 1958– .

Born into a Cincinnati family long prominent in Ohio Republican politics, Stewart graduated from Yale University in 1937 and received a degree from Yale Law School in 1941. He moved from a Wall Street law practice to a leading Cincinnati firm in 1947. There he also served two terms as a city councilman and one as vice-mayor before President Dwight D. Eisenhower appointed him to the Sixth Circuit Court of Appeals in April 1954. Stewart soon emerged as a leading federal circuit judge, admired for his closely reasoned and well-written opinions. He generally pursued a moderate course, especially in loyalty-security cases, and he showed a high regard for protecting the right to counsel.[1]

Mentioned as a possible Supreme Court nominee as early as 1957, Stewart was appointed to the high court when Harold Burton retired in October 1958. Stewart began serving on the Court under a recess appointment that month. The Senate confirmed his nomination in May 1959, by a vote of 70 to 17, with the opposition coming from Southern Democrats who disliked Stewart's stance on civil rights.[2]

In his early years on the Court, Stewart was often characterized as a "swing" justice who cast a pivotal ballot in cases dividing the Court's liberal and conservative wings. During his first term, for example, he joined the majority in two June 1959 cases in which the Court by a five-to-four vote upheld the contempt convictions of witnesses who had refused to answer questions or produce information for congressional and state anti-Communist investigations.[3] When a liberal majority emerged on the Warren Court in the early 1960s, Stewart's position was no longer decisive, but he remained a moderate and independent jurist. He tended toward a policy of judicial restraint, but he defended individual rights against government infringement when he believed there was a clear constitutional mandate for this or when the government violated principles of fair procedure. However, he usually preferred to overturn government action on narrow grounds, placing only limited restrictions on the power of the government.

Stewart was sensitive to First Amendment rights of free speech and association. In February 1960 he spoke for the majority to void the convictions of two Arkansas NAACP officials who had refused to give their membership lists to local authorities because the forced disclosure would cause unwarranted intrusion into the right of free association.[4] The Justice's opinion for the Court in a December 1960 case ruled unconstitutional an Arkansas law requiring public school teachers to list all organizations to which they had belonged in the past five years.[5] Stewart also displayed his concern for First Amendment rights in his opinion in a June 1959 case overturning New York State's ban on the showing of the film *Lady Chatterley's Lover.*[6]

In loyalty-security cases Stewart balanced individual rights against government needs. His majority opinions in two February 1961 cases upheld the power of the House Un-American Activities Committee (HUAC) to question individuals about their alleged prior membership in

---

1. See, for example, *NLRB v. Lannom Manufacturing Co.*, 226 F.2d 194 (6 Cir. 1955); *Wellman v. U.S.*, 227 F.2d 757 (6 Cir. 1955); *Henderson v. Bannan*, 256 F.2d 363 (6 Cir. 1958).

2. See his concurring opinion in *Clemons v. Board of Education of Hillsboro*, 228 F.2d 853, 858 (6 Cir. 1956).

3. *Uphaus v. Wyman*, 360 U.S. 72 (1959); *Barenblatt v. U.S.*, 360 U.S. 109 (1959).

4. *Bates v. City of Little Rock*, 361 U.S. 516 (1960).

5. *Shelton v. Tucker*, 364 U.S. 479 (1960).

6. *Kingsley International Pictures Corp. v. Board of Regents*, 360 U.S. 684 (1959).

the Communist Party! In June 1961 he was part of a five-man majority that sustained federal laws requiring Communist action organizations to register with the Justice Department and making illegal active membership in a party advocating violent overthrow of the government.[2] Writing the opinion of the Court in cases decided in June 1961 and May 1962, however, Stewart overturned contempt-of-Congress convictions of witnesses who had refused to answer HUAC's questions because statutory and procedural requirements necessary for a valid conviction had not been met.[3] Whether sustaining or invalidating government action, Stewart generally wrote narrowly based opinions limited to the facts of a case. His majority opinion in a December 1961 suit, for example, voided a Florida loyalty oath law but only on the ground that this particular statute was unconstitutionally vague.[4]

Stewart was the sole dissenter in three cases decided in June 1962 and June 1963 that held unconstitutional the use of a nondenominational prayer, the recitation of the Lord's Prayer and the reading of the Bible in public schools. Noncoercive, nondenominational religious exercises, Stewart argued, did not establish an official religion in violation of the First Amendment, and he suggested that prohibition of such practices denied the right to free exercise of religion without interference from government.[5] Stewart also dissented in two May 1961 cases in which the majority sustained state laws ordering Sunday closings of businesses against a challenge from Orthodox Jews, whose religion required them to close their stores on Saturdays. By forcing an individual to choose between his religion and economic gain, Stewart said, the state laws in this

case violated the free exercise clause of the First Amendment.[6]

Justice Stewart had a special concern for the right to counsel, and he joined in a March 1963 decision requiring the states to supply free counsel to indigent defendants.[7] In a May 1964 ruling Stewart's majority opinion held that incriminating statements deliberately elicited by the police after indictment and in the absence of counsel were inadmissible in federal courts since the defendant's right to counsel had been violated.[8] The Justice believed that many of the criminal safeguards in the Bill of Rights took effect only when formal judicial proceedings were instituted, however, and he dissented the next month when the Court extended the right to counsel to a suspect under police investigation but not yet formally indicted or arraigned.[9]

On other criminal rights issues, Stewart initially followed a relatively moderate course. In March 1959 he voted to hold that persons tried for the same offense in federal and state courts had not been subjected to double jeopardy.[10] However in a unanimous decision in March 1961, Stewart wrote that the Fourth Amendment prohibited the use of evidence obtained by an electronic eavesdropping device that physically intruded into a defendant's home.[11] His majority opinion in a June 1962 case held unconstitutional a California law that made drug addiction by itself, without any sale or possession of drugs, a crime.[12]

In the mid-1960s, however, as the Warren Court expanded criminal rights in a series of cases, Stewart repeatedly dissented, arguing that the rights of defendants should be balanced against society's interests. He objected, for example, to a

---

1. *Wilkinson v. U.S.*, 365 U.S. 399 (1961); *Braden v. U.S.*, 365 U.S. 431 (1961).

2. *Communist Party v. SACB*, 367 U.S. 1 (1961); *Scales v. U.S.*, 367 U.S. 203 (1961).

3. *Deutch v. U.S.*, 367 U.S. 456 (1961); *Russell v. U.S.*, 369 U.S. 749 (1962).

4. *Cramp v. Board of Public Instruction*, 368 U.S. 278 (1961).

5. *Engel v. Vitale*, 370 U.S. 421, 444 (1962); *School District of Abington Township v. Schempp* and *Murray v. Curlett*, 374 U.S. 203, 308 (1963).

6. *Braunfeld v. Brown*, 366 U.S. 599, 616 (1961); *Gallagher v. Crown Kosher Super Market*, 366 U.S. 617 (1961).

7. *Gideon v. Wainwright*, 372 U.S. 335 (1963).

8. *Massiah v. U.S.*, 377 U.S. 201 (1964).

9. *Escobedo v. Illinois*, 378 U.S. 478 (1964).

10. *Bartkus v. Illinois*, 359 U.S. 121 (1959); *Abbate v. U.S.*, 359 U.S. 187 (1959).

11. *Silverman v. U.S.*, 365 U.S. 505 (1961).

12. *Robinson v. California*, 370 U.S. 660 (1962).

June 1964 decision holding that the Fifth Amendment's privilege against self-incrimination applied to the states.[1] He protested the Court's June 1966 *Miranda* ruling, which placed limits on police interrogation of suspects.[2] Stewart also dissented from a May 1967 ruling applying the procedural rights of the Fifth and Sixth Amendments to juvenile court proceedings.[3] Writing the opinion of the Court in a December 1967 case, however, Stewart overturned a 39-year-old precedent to hold that electronic surveillance was subject to the Fourth Amendment's guarantee against unreasonable searches and seizures and to require police to obtain judicial warrants before using electronic eavesdropping devices.[4]

During this period Stewart continued to support most government security legislation, dissenting when the Court overturned a federal law prohibiting Communist Party members from serving as labor union officials in June 1965 and when it invalidated a set of New York State teacher loyalty laws in January 1967.[5] In obscenity cases, however, Stewart took positions that expanded the scope of free speech. In his concurring opinion in a June 1964 case, for example, Stewart defined obscene material as "hard core pornography," a definition narrower in effect than the one supported by some of the Court's more liberal members. But Stewart aroused much criticism by adding that while he could not define hard core pornography, "I know it when I see it."[6]

Justice Stewart concurred in a March 1962 ruling that federal courts could try legislative apportionment cases,[7] but he repeatedly dissented from Court decisions requiring that legislative districts be apportioned on an equal population basis. He objected in a February 1964 case to the application of this "one-man, one-vote" standard to congressional districting.[8] In a series of cases involving state legislative apportionment beginning in June 1964, Stewart insisted that such state plans must be rational and must not frustrate the will of the majority of the electorate. But aside from this, Stewart thought districts could be drawn to reflect economic, geographic and other interests in addition to population.[9]

Stewart opposed segregation laws and voted to uphold the major provisions of federal civil rights laws.[10] He wrote the majority opinion in a June 1968 case holding that an 1866 federal law prohibited racial discrimination in the private sale or rental of property and sustaining the law's constitutionality under the 13th Amendment.[11] The Justice dissented, however, in March 1966 when the Court voided a Virginia poll tax for state elections[12] and in June 1966 when it upheld a provision in the 1965 Voting Rights Act designed to guarantee the right to vote to Spanish-speaking citizens.[13] He initially voted to overturn the convictions of civil rights demonstrators and wrote the majority opinion in a February 1963 case reversing on First Amendment grounds the breach of the peace convictions of South Carolina protesters.[14] In later cases, though, Stewart voted to uphold state court convictions of

1. *Malloy v. Hogan*, 378 U.S. 1 (1964).

2. *Miranda v. Arizona*, 384 U.S. 436 (1966).

3. *In re Gault*, 387 U.S. 1 (1967).

4. *Katz v. U.S.*, 389 U.S. 347 (1967), overruling *Olmstead v. U.S.*, 277 U.S. 438 (1928).

5. *U.S. v. Brown*, 381 U.S. 437 (1965); *Keyishian v. Board of Regents*, 385 U.S. 589 (1967).

6. *Jacobellis v. Ohio*, 378 U.S. 184, 197 (1964). See also *Freedman v. Maryland*, 380 U.S. 51 (1965); *Ginzburg v. U.S.*, 383 U.S. 463 (1963).

7. *Baker v. Carr*, 369 U.S. 186 (1962).

8. *Wesberry v. Sanders*, 376 U.S. 1 (1964).

9. *Lucas v. Forty-Fourth General Assembly of Colorado*, 377 U.S. 713, 744 (1964).

10. See, for example, *State Athletic Commission v. Dorsey*, 359 U.S. 533 (1959); *Loving v. Virginia*, 388 U.S. 1 (1967); *Heart of Atlanta Motel v. U.S.*, 379 U.S. 241 (1964); *South Carolina v. Katzenbach*, 383 U.S. 301 (1966).

11. *Jones v. Mayer*, 392 U.S. 409 (1968).

12. *Harper v. Virginia State Board of Elections*, 383 U.S. 663 (1966).

13. *Katzenbach v. Morgan*, 384 U.S. 641 (1966).

14. *Edwards v. South Carolina*, 372 U.S. 229 (1963). See also *Garner v. Louisiana*, 368 U.S. 157 (1961); *Peterson v. City of Greenville*, 373 U.S. 244 (1963).

civil rights demonstrators.[1] His majority opinion in a June 1967 case sustained the contempt-of-court convictions of Martin Luther King and seven other black leaders resulting from the 1963 Birmingham demonstrations.[2]

On the Burger Court, Stewart, along with Byron White, once again became a "swing" justice whose vote was crucial in deciding close cases. He occupied a center position between the Court's liberal members and the four more conservative Nixon appointees. When those two groups disagreed in a case, Stewart was more likely to vote with the "Nixon bloc," but his progressive views on certain issues still established him as, overall, a moderate and somewhat unpredictable jurist.

Stewart continued, for example, to uphold the rights of free speech and assembly.[3] In June 1973 he went beyond his already liberal stance on obscenity to join in a dissent urging the Court to prohibit all attempts to regulate allegedly obscene material for willing adults.[4] Stewart took a broad view of freedom of the press and dissented in June 1972 when the Court held that journalists had no First Amendment right to refuse to identify confidential sources to a grand jury.[5] In an exception to his generally liberal First Amendment views, the Justice spoke for the Court in March 1976 to hold that a 1968 ruling which protected the right of union members to picket within a privately owned shopping center was no longer valid.[6]

Stewart usually opposed racial and sexual discrimination during this period.[7] However, he did vote in June 1972 to allow private clubs with state liquor licenses to exclude blacks.[8] He also wrote the opinion in a June 1974 case holding that a California job disability insurance program which excluded pregnancy from coverage did not deny women the equal protection of the laws.[9] In other discrimination cases, Stewart's judicial conservatism came to the fore. He believed the Court should normally defer to policy judgments made by legislatures, and so he voted to sustain laws that discriminated against illegitimate children and the poor.[10] In an April 1970 opinion, Stewart upheld a state ceiling on the amount of welfare benefits one family could receive and said that the economic, social and philosophical problems presented by welfare programs were not the business of the federal courts.[11] He also voted to uphold state laws limiting voting on bond issues to property owners or taxpayers.[12] The Justice maintained his opposition to a strict one-man, one-vote rule in reapportionment cases and supported February and June 1973 decisions relaxing that standard for state legislative districting.[13]

In accord with his insistence that the government meet strict procedural standards, Stewart voted in a series of cases beginning in 1969 to invalidate state laws that allowed creditors to seize a debtor's wages or goods without notice or hearing.[14]

---

1. See, for example, *Brown v. Louisiana*, 383 U.S. 131 (1966); *Adderley v. Florida*, 385 U.S. 39 (1966).

2. *Walker v. City of Birmingham*, 388 U.S. 307 (1967).

3. See, for example, *Tinker v. Des Moines School District*, 393 U.S. 503 (1969); *Coates v. Cincinnati*, 402 U.S. 611 (1971); *Cohen v. California*, 403 U.S. 15 (1971).

4. *Miller v. California*, 413 U.S. 15 (1973); *Paris Adult Theatre I v. Slaton*, 413 U.S. 49 (1973).

5. *Branzburg v. Hayes*, 408 U.S. 665 (1972).

6. *Hudgens v. NLRB*, 424 U.S. 507 (1976). The 1968 ruling was *Amalgamated Food Employees Union v. Logan Valley Plaza*, 391 U.S. 308 (1968).

7. See, for example, *Sullivan v. Little Hunting Park, Inc.*, 396 U.S. 229 (1969); *Wright v. Council of the City of Emporia*, 407 U.S. 451 (1972); *Hills v.*

Gautreaux, 425 U.S. 284 (1976); *Frontiero v. Richardson*, 411 U.S. 677 (1973); *Cleveland Board of Education v. LaFleur*, 414 U.S. 632 (1974).

8. *Moose Lodge No. 107 v. Irvis*, 407 U.S. 163 (1972).

9. *Geduldig v. Aiello*, 417 U.S. 484 (1974).

10. See, for example, *Labine v. Vincent*, 401 U.S. 532 (1971); *San Antonio Independent School District v. Rodriguez*, 411 U.S. 1 (1973).

11. *Dandridge v. Williams*, 397 U.S. 471 (1970).

12. See for example, *Kramer v. Union Free School District No. 15*, 395 U.S. 621 (1969); *Phoenix v. Kolodziejski*, 399 U.S. 204 (1970).

13. *Mahan v. Howell*, 410 U.S. 315 (1973); *Gaffney v. Cummings*, 412 U.S. 735 (1973).

14. See, for example, *Sniadach v. Family Finance Corp.*, 395 U.S. 337 (1969); *Fuentes v. Shevin*, 407 U.S. 67 (1972).

In a potentially far reaching June 1975 opinion, Stewart held that mental patients could not be confined in institutions against their will if they were not dangerous to others and could live outside the institution on their own.[1]

As he had on the Warren Court, Justice Stewart tended to favor law enforcement authorities in criminal cases. He supported several rulings cutting back on the *Miranda* decision.[2] He took a narrow view of the Fifth Amendment's privilege against self-incrimination[3] and, in Fourth Amendment cases, backed police "stop and frisk" practices, third-party bugging and grand jury use of illegally obtained evidence as the basis for questioning witnesses.[4] However, Stewart generally opposed warrantless searches, and in an important June 1969 opinion, he limited the scope of the search police could make incident to a lawful arrest.[5] In a June 1972 plurality opinion, he restricted the right to counsel at police line-ups to those conducted after a defendant's indictment or arraignment.[6]

Stewart voted in June 1972 to declare the death penalty as then imposed a violation of the Eighth Amendment's ban on cruel and unusual punishment.[7] He announced the judgement of the Court in several capital punishment cases decided in July 1976. In opinions joined by only two other Justices, Stewart argued that statutes making the death penalty mandatory for certain crimes were unconstitutional.[8] However, he voted to sustain laws setting death as one possible punishment for murder so long as standards were established to guide the judge or jury in imposing sentence.[9]

When Earl Warren retired from the Court in 1969, President Richard Nixon considered appointing Stewart to the chief justiceship. Stewart reportedly refused the post because he felt the new chief justice should be chosen from outside the Court. Throughout his years on the bench, Stewart was applauded for opinions that were concise, lucid and literate. He was known as a "cautious, judicious, fair-minded student of judicial power" who respected precedent and took a limited view of the judicial function. He followed a "progressive-conservative" course, and though not among the more influential justices on the Court, Stewart received a better-than-average rating from scholars.

---

1 . *O'Connor v. Donaldson*, 422 U.S. 563 (1975).

2. See, for example, *Harris v. New York*, 401 U.S. 222 (1971); *Michigan v. Mosley*, 423 U.S. 96 (1975).

3 . See, for example, *Kastigar v. U.S.*, 406 U.S. 441 (1972); *U.S. v. Dionisio*, 410 U.S. 1 (1973).

4 . *Adams v. Williams*, 407 U.S. 143 (1972); *U.S. v. White*, 401 U.S. 745 (1971); *U.S. v. Calandra*, 414 U.S. 338 (1974).

5 . *Chimel v. California*, 395 U.S. 752 (1969). See also *Vale v. Louisiana*, 399 U.S. 30 (1970); *U.S. v. Edwards*, 415 U.S. 800 (1974).

6 . *Kirby v. Illinois*, 406 U.S. 682 (1972).

7 . *Furman v. Georgia*, 408 U.S. 238 (1972).

8 . *Woodson v. North Carolina*, 428 U.S. 280 (1976); *Roberts v. Louisiana*, 428 U.S. 325 (1976).

9 . *Gregg v. Georgia*, 428 U.S. 153 (1976); *Profitt v. Florida*, 428 U.S. 242 (1976); *Jurek v. Texas*, 428 U.S. 262 (1976).

STONE, HARLAN FISKE

b. Oct. 11, 1872; Chesterfield, N.H.
d. April 22, 1946; Washington, D.C.
Chief Justice of the United States
1941-46.

Son of a New England farmer, Harlan Fiske Stone graduated from Amherst College in 1894 and from Columbia Law School in 1898. He then divided his time between teaching at Columbia, where he was dean of the law school from 1910 to 1923, and private practice as a corporate attorney in Wall Street firms. A Republican, Stone was named U.S. Attorney General in April 1924. In January 1925 he was appointed an associate justice on the U.S. Supreme Court. On June 12, 1941 President Franklin D. Roosevelt selected Stone as Chief Justice; the Senate confirmed the nomination later that month.

Throughout his years on the bench, Stone preached a philosophy of judicial restraint. Judges, he believed, must accord the legislature broad powers in social and economic affairs and must not allow their personal views on the desirability or wisdom of such legislation to determine its constitutionality. Stone also opposed the use of rigid legal formulae to settle cases and urged that each decision be based instead on a careful weighing of all relevant evidence including such elements as precedents, facts and legislative intent.

Through the mid-1930s these views led Stone to dissent repeatedly when a conservative majority overturned various economic and social welfare laws, including many important New Deal measures.[1] In a particularly sharp dissent written in 1936 when the Court invalidated the first Agricultural Adjustment Act, Stone chastised the majority for discarding any economic legislation it considered "undesirable" and thus usurping the function and powers of the legislature.[2] In 1937 the Court began to shift direction, and personnel changes helped create a new majority which sustained New Deal regulatory measures. With this, Justice Stone was more often in the majority, and he helped establish the legitimacy of wide-ranging federal power over the economy.[3] His opinions made important contributions to the law in areas such as intergovernmental tax immunities, commerce clause restrictions on the states, equity and patents.[4]

In the April 1938 *Carolene Products* case, Justice Stone suggested that outside the economic realm, the Court might have to practice less restraint and subject to close scrutiny laws which infringed on Bill of Rights guarantees or the rights of racial, religious or political minorities.[5] This statement was the foundation for the "preferred freedoms" doctrine, the notion that certain rights, particularly those listed in the First Amendment, are fundamental to all other liberties and must be given special protection by the judiciary. Stone's best-known application of the doctrine came in June 1940, when the Court upheld a state law requiring public school children to salute the flag against a challenge from Jehovah's Witnesses that this violated their religious scruples. Stone was the sole dissenter from this judgment. Three years later he was vindicated when several justices changed their minds and overturned a similar flag salute law in another case.[6]

1. See, for example, *Carter v. Carter Coal Co.*, 298 U.S. 238 (1936); *Morehead v. New York ex rel. Tipaldo*, 298 U.S. 587 (1936).

2. *U.S. v. Butler*, 297 U.S. 1, 78 (1936).

3. See, for example, *U.S. v. Darby*, 312 U.S. 100 (1941); *U.S. v. Wrightwood Dairy Co.*, 315 U.S. 110 (1942).

4. See, for example, *Helvering v. Gerhardt*, 304 U.S. 405 (1938); *Graves v. New York ex rel. O'Keefe*, 306 U.S. 466 (1939); *South Carolina State Highway Department v. Barnwell Brothers, Inc.*, 303 U.S. 177 (1938); *Southern Pacific Co. v. Arizona*, 325 U.S. 761 (1945); *Marconi v. U.S.*, 320 U.S. 1 (1943).

5. *U.S. v. Carolene Products Co.*, 304 U.S. 144, 152 n. 4 (1938).

6. *Minersville School District v. Gobitis*, 310 U.S. 586 (1940); *West Virginia State Board of Education v. Barnette*, 319 U.S. 624 (1943). See also *Jones v. Opelika*, 316 U.S. 584 (1942), *reversed*, 319 U.S. 103 (1943).

Stone's position in most economic and civil liberties cases won him a reputation as a liberal, but in his final years on the bench, he was often at odds with justices on the Court's left wing. Still a believer in judical restraint, Stone objected when he thought these jurists were trying to write their own liberal economic and social views into law, especially in cases involving statutory interpretation and the rulings of federal administrative agencies.[1] He also protested when he believed the "preferred freedoms" approach was used simplistically to invalidate any legislation affecting First Amendment rights.[2] Although he generally voted to support civil liberties, Stone did dissent in January 1946 when the majority upheld the right of Jehovah's Witnesses to distribute their literature in a company town.[3] The next month he also joined in a ruling sustaining the legality of the military tribunal that sentenced Japanese Gen. Tomoyuki Yamashita to death.[4]

"As an individual justice," John P. Frank wrote, "Stone was one of the great, dynamic contributors to American law," but as Chief Justice, "he was strikingly unsuccessful." Although his appointment to head the Court had been universally praised, Stone proved ineffective in the post. He disliked administrative work and lacked the skills needed to mass the Court and keep differences under control. Stone's Court was "the most frequently divided, the most openly quarrelsome in history," according to the Justice's biographer. The conflict included personal sniping and bickering as well as substantive differences on issues. By the end of Stone's tenure, critics asserted that the divisiveness had caused a decline in the Court's dignity and authority.

On April 22, 1946, Stone became ill while on the bench. He died later the same day at his Washington home. Despite his poor record as Chief Justice, Stone was ranked as one of the greatest Supreme Court jurists because of his "intellectual acumen" and "perception of constitutional fundamentals." He was a judge's judge, a superb legal craftsman who could sift through a mass of conflicting precedents to come up with a clear and solidly-based rule of law. He was calm, deliberate and balanced in his approach to issues and independent in his judgments. Stone combined, one scholar noted, "a basic faith in the dignity and worth of the individual with a firm belief in the right and capacity of the people to govern themselves."

---

1. See, for example, *U.S. v. South-Eastern Underwriters Assn.*, 322 U.S. 533 (1944); *Jewell Ridge Coal Corp. v. Local No. 6167, UMW*, 325 U.S. 161 (1945).

2. *Thomas v. Collins*, 323 U.S. 516 (1945).

3. *Marsh v. Alabama*, 326 U.S. 501 (1946).

4. *In re Yamashita*, 327 U.S. 1 (1946).

VINSON, FRED(ERICK) M(OORE)

b. Jan. 22, 1890; Louisa, Ky.
d. Sept. 8, 1953; Washington, D.C.
Chief Justice of the United States.
1946-53.

After receiving his law degree in 1911 from Centre College in Kentucky, Vinson practiced privately in Louisa and later in Ashland, Ky., and entered local Democratic politics. He was elected to the first of six terms in Congress in 1924. By the 1930s he had become a key figure on the House Ways and Means Committee. A loyal supporter of President Franklin Roosevelt, Vinson helped develop New Deal tax and coal programs. In May 1938 he was appointed a judge of the U.S. Court of Appeals for the District of Columbia. Beginning in May 1943 he served successively as Director of Economic Stabilization, Federal Loan Administrator and Director of War Mobilization and Reconversion.

When Harry S Truman assumed the presidency, Vinson quickly became a close friend and adviser. On July 16, 1945 Truman nominated the Kentuckian to be Secretary of the Treasury. Vinson soon emerged as the strongest figure in Truman's first Cabinet. He counseled the President not only on economic matters but on a broad range of domestic issues. As Treasury Secretary Vinson headed a team of American negotiators who worked out the terms of a major postwar loan to Britain in 1945. He was also a chief U.S. representative during the formation of the International Monetary Fund and the International Bank for Reconstruction and Development. At home, he successfully recommended a reduction in tax rates.

On June 6, 1946, Truman named Vinson Chief Justice of the United States. Aside from his compatible political philosophy and record in government service, the calm, patient and sociable Vinson was a skilled negotiator. Truman evident-

ly hoped he would be able to unify a faction-ridden Supreme Court. Although sworn in as Chief Justice on June 24, 1946, Vinson remained part of Truman's inner circle and often advised him throughout his Administration. Truman considered sending Vinson on a special diplomatic mission to Russia in 1948 and unsuccessfully urged him to enter the 1952 presidential race.

As Chief Justice, Vinson believed that the government needed broad powers to deal with the threat of Communism at home and abroad as well as other national and international problems. He favored a restrained, limited role for the Supreme Court and wanted the justices to give wide latitude to the executive and legislative branches, especially in loyalty-security cases. Thus, in civil liberties decisions, Vinson compiled a record that made him, according to C. Herman Pritchett, "very nearly the most negative member of the Court on libertarian claims." He voted to uphold state and federal loyalty programs, investigations of Communist activities and harsher treatment of aliens.[1] He wrote the opinion of the Court in two of the most important civil liberties cases of the period. In May 1950 Vinson upheld the non-Communist oath requirement in the Taft-Hartley Act against a First Amendment challenge.[2] He also sustained in June 1951 the convictions of 11 Communist Party leaders who were charged under the Smith Act with conspiracy to organize a party to teach and advocate overthrow of the government. Using a formula devised by Judge Learned Hand, Vinson held that the government could outlaw a conspiracy to advocate revolution when the individuals intended to overthrow the government as

---

1. See, for example, *U.S. ex rel. Knauff v. Shaughnessy*, 338 U.S. 537 (1950); *U.S. v. Bryan*, 339 U.S. 323 (1950); *Rogers v. U.S.*, 340 U.S. 367 (1951); *Joint Anti-Fascist Refugee Committee v. McGrath*, 341 U.S. 123 (1951); *Garner v. Board of Public Works*, 341 U.S. 716 (1951); *Shaughnessy v. U.S. ex rel. Mezei*, 345 U.S. 206 (1953).

2. *American Communications Assn. v. Douds*, 339 U.S. 382 (1950).

soon as circumstances would permit, even though the possibility of a successful revolution was not at all immediate.[1] The two decisions effectively curtailed the scope of the First Amendment's guarantees of free speech and association.

The Chief Justice's marked tendency to support government power was also displayed in the March 1947 Lewis case and the June 1952 steel seizure case. In the former Vinson's opinion for the Court sustained a contempt judgment and heavy fines against John L. Lewis and the United Mine Workers for their defiance of a district court order against striking. The order had been issued at a time when the government had assumed control of the coal mines.[2] In the steel seizure case, when a majority of the Court held Truman's takeover of the steel mills unconstitutional, Vinson dissented, arguing that in a time of genuine emergency the President had inherent power to move in defense of the nation's substantial interests.[3]

In criminal cases Vinson gave greater weight to government's interest than to the defendant's. He usually voted to reject claims that a confession was coerced or that counsel was improperly denied.[4] He was particularly conservative in Fourth Amendment cases. In a May 1947 case that surprised many observers, he wrote for a five-man majority to uphold a conviction based on evidence obtained in a long, detailed search of a defendant's apartment that was conducted without a warrant but had been incident to a valid arrest.[5] Vinson wrote his first dissenting opinion in June of the next year when another narrow Court majority reversed direction and held that search warrants must be obtained wherever reasonably

practicable.[6] In February 1950, when the latter decision was overturned, he was in the majority.[7]

On civil rights the Vinson Court established a liberal and relatively unified record. The Chief Justice wrote some of his most important opinions in this area. He spoke for a unanimous Court in May 1948 to hold restrictive covenants barring the sale of residential property to blacks and other minorities legally unenforceable.[8] In two June 1950 decisions Vinson ruled it a denial of equal protection to exclude a black student from the University of Texas law school and to segregate black graduate students in classes and other facilities at the University of Oklahoma.[9] The Chief Justice, though, was among the more cautious members of the Court on the race question. His opinions expanded the rights of minorities but went only as far as was needed to decide the issue at hand. Vinson occasionally dissented from majority rulings favorable to blacks.[10]

In his final term on the Court, Vinson again displayed his relative conservatism on racial issues. He was the lone dissenter in June 1953 when the majority extended the rule of his 1948 restrictive covenant decision and held that a white home owner could not be sued for damages by neighbors for having violated a covenant by selling to blacks.[11] The previous December the Court had heard arguments in five cases challenging the legality of segregated public schools and raising the fundamental question of whether segregation was constitutional even when facilities for the two races were equal. Rather than decide the issue the Court, on June 8, 1953, ordered reargument of the cases in the next term.[12] Vinson died before the

1. *Dennis v. U.S.*, 341 U.S. 494 (1951).
2. *U.S. v. United Mine Workers*, 330 U.S. 258 (1947).
3. *Youngstown Sheet & Tube Co. v. Sawyer*, 343 U.S. 579 (1952).
4. See, for example, *Haley v. Ohio*, 332 U.S. 596 (1948); *Bute v. Illinois*, 333 U.S. 640 (1948); *Gallegos v. Nebraska*, 342 U.S. 55 (1951).
5. *Harris v. U.S.*, 331 U.S. 145 (1947).
6. *Trupiano v. U.S.*, 334 U.S. 699 (1948).
7. *U.S. v. Rabinowitz*, 339 U.S. 56 (1950).
8. *Shelley v. Kraemer*, 334 U.S. 1 (1948); *Hurd v. Hodge*, 334 U.S. 24 (1948).
9. *Sweatt v. Painter*, 339 U.S. 629 (1950); *McLaurin v. Oklahoma State Regents*, 339 U.S. 637 (1950).
10. For example, *Bob-Lo Excursion Co. v. Michigan*, 333 U.S. 28 (1948).
11. *Barrows v. Jackson*, 346 U.S. 249 (1953).
12. *Brown v. Board of Education*, 345 U.S. 972 (1953).

suits were finally disposed of, but the available evidence suggests that had he lived he would most likely have voted to hold segregation *per se* constitutional. Ultimately, in May 1954 under Chief Justice Earl Warren the Court voted unanimously that public school segregation violated the Constitution.[1]

In June 1953 Vinson and the Court were briefly caught up in the case of Julius and Ethel Rosenberg, who had been sentenced to death for giving atomic secrets to the Soviet Union. The Supreme Court three times refused to review the Rosenbergs' conviction and on June 15, 1953 denied what seemed to be all final motions in their case. Two days later, however, Justice William O. Douglas granted a stay of execution because a new legal argument had been raised on behalf of the convicted couple. Vinson immediately called a special session of the Court which, on June 18, heard oral argument on whether to uphold Douglas's stay. On June 19 Vinson read the decision of a six-man majority that the legal question raised was "not substantial," that further proceedings to litigate it were "unwarranted" and that the stay of execution was

therefore vacated.[2] Later that day the Rosenbergs were executed.

On Sept. 8, 1953, Vinson died of a heart attack at his home in Washington, D.C. A man of action rather than reflection, he had a pragmatic mind and a common sense approach to problems. Vinson was not a judicial philosopher or legal theorist while on the Court nor was he its intellectual leader. After 1949 he was part of a five-man bloc which largely controlled the Court, especially in civil liberties cases, but Vinson never succeeded in unifying or personally dominating a Court on which justices of strong intellect and convictions were often divided on basic issues. The Chief Justice was widely recognized as a man of integrity and great devotion to the nation who as a justice helped advance the rights of racial minorities. However, he was also one of the most conservative members of the Court on other civil liberties issues. Critics have charged Vinson with overemphasizing the needs of the state to the detriment of individual rights. The Court under Vinson followed the policy of restraint he favored. Later analysts questioned whether such a passive Court role was necessary or wise at the time, particularly in civil liberties matters.

---

1. *Brown v. Board of Education*, 347 U.S. 483 (1954); *Bolling v. Sharpe*, 347 U.S. 497 (1954).

2. *Rosenberg v. U.S.*, 346 U.S. 273 (1953).

WARREN, EARL

b. March 19, 1891; Los Angeles, Calif.
d. July 9, 1974; Washington, D.C.
Governor, Calif., 1943-53; Chief
Justice of the United States, 1953-69.

Of Scandanavian heritage, Earl Warren grew up in Bakersfield, Calif. As a youth he spent summers working for the Southern Pacific Railroad, which employed his father as a car repairer. He attended college and law school at the University of California at Berkeley, receiving his law degree in 1914. After working a few years for private firms, Warren enlisted in the Army in 1917 and spent most of the war training recruits. In 1919 he joined the staff of the Oakland city attorney but left a year later to be a prosecutor for Alameda Co.

Advancing to chief deputy in 1923, Warren became district attorney two years later, a position he held until 1938. He earned a reputation as a strict and aggressive prosecutor, cracking down particularly hard on vices such as gambling, bootlegging and prostitution. None of the convictions obtained by Warren's office were ever reversed by a higher court. Raymond Moley of Columbia University in 1931 called him "the most intelligent and politically independent district attorney in the United States."

From 1934 to 1936 Warren served as chairman of the Republican state central committee. In 1938, pledging a non-partisan regime, he was elected California attorney general as the nominee of the Republican, Democratic and Progressive parties. For four years Warren carried out his law enforcement duties with the same vigor and sternness he had shown as district attorney. He waged an energetic campaign against racketeering and offshore gambling enterprises. At the outset of World War II, he zealously advocated the internment of Japanese-Americans. Warren argued at the time that Americans of German and Italian descent need not receive the same treatment. He later regretted his actions.

In 1942 Warren was elected governor over the Democratic incumbent, Culbert Olson. With his hearty public persona, plain manner of expression and pragmatic style, Warren created a personal following in the state that transcended party labels. His liberal Republicanism angered conservatives but won over enough Democrats to achieve handsome majorities in his reelection contests. Warren characterized his middle of the road politics as "progressive conservatism."

During Warren's tenure California raised old age pensions, widened unemployment coverage and reorganized its penal system. His sponsorship of a plan to enact "prepaid medical care through a system of compulsory health insurance" aroused the vociferous opposition of the state's medical association, which denounced it as "socialized medicine" and waged a successful campaign to defeat the measure in the legislature.

Presiding over the state government during a period of economic prosperity and tremendous growth, Warren was constantly engaged in expanding public services to accommodate the swelling population. He supported public development of hydroelectric power and proposed an increase in the gasoline tax to finance highway construction. He testified before congressional committees in favor of state ownership of offshore oil. In the battle over loyalty oaths at the University of California, Warren opposed the dismissal of professors who refused to sign a special pledge required of faculty members. He did not oppose a loyalty oath per se but argued that the professors had already subscribed to the loyalty oath taken by all state employes. Warren also criticized the clause of the Taft-Hartley Act requiring loyalty oaths from union officials on the grounds that such oaths "ought to apply mutually to both sides."

A declared candidate for the presidency at the Republic National Convention in 1948, Warren swung California's delegates to New York Gov. Thomas E. Dewey on the final ballot. Dewey chose Warren as his running mate, and the Convention unanimously endorsed

154

the selection. At one point in the campaign, President Truman answered Warren's criticism by saying of the California Governor: "He is really a Democrat and doesn't know it." The Dewey-Warren ticket went down to a surprising defeat in November.

Warren again made a bid for his party's presidential nomination in 1952. At the Republican National Convention that July, the California delegation, which Warren led, voted at an important moment to seat delegates supporting Dwight D. Eisenhower. Warren campaigned for the General in California that fall.

Following the election, according to Warren, Eisenhower promised him the first Supreme Court vacancy. However, when Chief Justice Fred Vinson died early in September 1953, the President considered other possible appointees before settling on Warren. Eisenhower announced Warren's nomination as Chief Justice on Sept. 30, saying he had chosen the Californian for his unquestioned integrity, middle-of-the-road philosophy and experience in government and law. Warren was given a recess appointment and sworn in less than a week later on Oct. 5, the day the Court's new term started. The Senate confirmed his nomination by a unanimous voice vote on March 1, 1954.

In December 1953, soon after Warren took his seat, the Court heard arguments in five cases held over from its previous sessions which challenged the legality of racial segregation in public schools. Contrary to their usual practice, the justices did not vote on the cases at their weekly conference following the argument but instead continued to discuss the suits over the next few months. After a vote was finally taken in late February or March 1954, Warren undertook the

writing of the opinion himself. On May 17, 1954 he delivered his first major opinion as Chief Justice in *Brown v. Board of Education.* In a deliberately brief and low-key manner, he announced that the justices had unanimously decided that racially segregated public schools deprived children of equal educational opportunities. Citing both law and sociology, Warren stated that separate educational facilities were inherently unequal. Therefore, he ruled, they violated the Constitution. He left open the question of how this desegregation decision should be implemented and called for further argument on this issue.[1] A year later, on May 31, 1955, Warren again spoke for a unanimous Court to rule that school desegregation must proceed "with all deliberate speed."[2]

The *Brown* decision was called the "supreme achievement" of the Warren Court and it was unquestionably a momentous decree. It overturned the nearly 60-year-old "separate-but-equal" doctrine, which had held that segregated facilities were constitutional so long as blacks and whites received equivalent treatment. In the next few years the Court extended its judgment that racial barriers imposed by law were invalid to an array of public facilities including parks, playgrounds, golf courses, transportation and courtrooms.[3] *Brown* ended the legality of the South's system of segregation, help set in motion major changes in American race relations and also led to the first major controversy over a Warren Court decision with many white Southerners denouncing the justices for their ruling.

Warren's special contribution in *Brown* may well have been his success in winning unanimity among the justices. Although several prior rulings strongly suggested that the Court would outlaw segregation in *Brown,*[4] a unanimous decision

1. 347 U.S. 483 (1954); *Bolling v. Sharpe,* 347 U.S. 497 (1954).

2. *Brown v. Board of Education,* 349 U.S. 294 (1955).

3. *Mayor and City Council of Baltimore v. Dawson,* 350 U.S. 877 (1955); *Holmes v. City of Atlanta,*

350 U.S. 879 (1955); *Gayle v. Browder,* 352 U.S. 903 (1956); *New Orleans City Park Improvement Assn. v. Detiege,* 358 U.S. 54 (1958); *Johnson v. Virginia,* 373 U.S. 61 (1963).

4. See, for example, *Sweatt v. Painter,* 339 U.S. 629 (1950); *McLaurin v. Oklahoma State Regents,* 339 U.S. 637 (1950).

was by no means assured. According to several fellow justices as well as some outside analysts of the cases, Warren contributed significantly to the Court's unity by his handling of the issue in conference, his discussion of the cases with individual justices and the moderate phrasing of the final opinion. Some supporters as well as opponents of the *Brown* decision, however, criticized Warren's opinion as being deficient in solid legal analysis and argument, and many civil rights advocates expressed dissatisfaction with the gradualist "all deliberate speed" formula adopted by the Court.

Aside from *Brown*, Warren in his first years on the bench was the moderate and rather cautious jurist most observers expected him to be when he was appointed. In his first term, for example, he voted to uphold a state gambling conviction based on illegally seized evidence[1] and to sustain New York State medical authorities when they suspended a doctor's license to practice because he had refused to cooperate with a congressional investigation into Communism.[2]

By mid-1956, however, Warren had moved away from the center and had aligned himself with the Court's more libertarian members. His shift was most evident in a series of controversial cases involving loyalty-security issues in which he consistently voted in favor of individual claimants and against the government, though on a variety of grounds. In April 1956 Warren's opinion for a six-man majority overturned a state conviction for sedition against the U.S. on the grounds that Congress had preempted this field from the states with the 1940 Smith Act.[3] In the *Watkins* decision of June 1957, the Chief Justice again spoke for the Court to reverse the contempt conviction of an individual who had refused to answer questions about former Communist Party associates before a subcommittee of the House Un-American Activities Committee. The subcommittee had failed, Warren said, to show the witness that the questions asked were pertinent to the subject under investigation, but he added to this narrow holding a lengthy essay which insisted that congressional committees were subject to constitutional limitations and that Congress had no power to expose the private beliefs and affairs of individuals solely for the sake of exposure.[4]

In a companion case reversing a similar state contempt conviction, Warren's plurality opinion also discussed in broad terms the limits on state investigatory powers, but its actual holding was again fairly narrow.[5] The language of both opinions led many people to believe that the Court had cut significantly into congressional and state authority to inquire into possible subversion, and they aroused considerable controversy. Two years later, however, in June 1959, the Court by a five-to-four vote upheld contempt convictions in two cases very similar to the 1957 suits, and the majority opinions emphasized the limits of the earlier rulings. The Chief Justice dissented from both of the later decisions.[6] Warren's liberalism in these and other cases ultimately led President Eisenhower to call the appointment one of the biggest mistakes he made while in office.

Under Warren the Supreme Court also rewrote the law on the administration of criminal justice and extended its rulings to the states as well as the federal government. It also changed the operation of the political system by ordering legislative reapportionment on a "one-man, one-vote" basis, prohibited religious exercises in public schools, significantly broadened the rights of free speech and artistic expression and restricted the government's power to penalize individual beliefs and associations. With the exception of obscenity rulings, Warren supported every

---

1. *Irvine v. California*, 347 U.S. 128 (1954).

2. *Barsky v. Board of Regents*, 347 U.S. 442 (1954).

3. *Pennsylvania v. Nelson*, 350 U.S. 497 (1956).

4. *Watkins v. U.S.*, 354 U.S. 178 (1957).

5. *Sweezy v. New Hampshire*, 354 U.S. 234 (1957).

6. *Uphaus v. Wyman*, 360 U.S. 72 (1959); *Barenblatt v. U.S.*, 360 U.S. 109 (1959).

major change in constitutional law ultimately made by the Court.

During the Kennedy years, when the
civil rights movement entered a new
phase with widespread use of nonviolent
protest, Warren delivered the Court's first
ruling on sit-in demonstrations. In a December 1961 opinion he overturned the
breach-of-the-peace convictions of 16
black protesters on the ground that there
was no evidence to support the state's
charge.[1] He again spoke for the Court in a
May 1963 ruling that voided the convictions of civil rights demonstrators in six
cases[2] and concurred in similar rulings in
June 1962 and February 1963.[3] Warren
also joined the majority in decisions that
prohibited the exclusion of blacks from
private restaurants situated on state-
owned property and held invalid pupil
transfer plans designed to thwart school
desegregation.[4]

In December 1964 the Court unanimously sustained the public accommodations section of the 1964 Civil Rights Act.[5]
The Chief Justice then wrote the majority
opinion in a March 1966 case upholding
seven major parts of the 1965 Voting
Rights Act.[6] Warren spoke for the Court in
an April 1965 decision that invalidated a
Virginia law substituting a special registration procedure for the poll tax outlawed by the 24th Amendment.[7] In June
1967 Warren, speaking for a unanimous
Court, found unconstitutional state anti-
miscegenation laws, one of the last bas-
tions of legalized segregation.[8] The following year he joined in a Court decision

ruling that an 1866 federal statute prohibited racial discrimination in the private
sale or rental of housing and other property.[9] In November 1966, a five-man majority reversed the Court's trend in cases involving civil rights demonstrators and
upheld the trespass convictions of protesters who had gathered outside a Florida jail. Warren dissented from this judgment and from a similar Court ruling in
June 1967.[10]

In a series of cases involving Communism, the Chief Justice continued to vote
against the government. He dissented in
June 1961, when a five-man majority sustained provisions in two federal anti-
subversive laws.[11] Warren also opposed
February 1961 rulings upholding the contempt-of-Congress convictions of individuals who refused to answer questions before the House Un-American Activities Committee.[12] He joined with the
majority to overturn similar convictions
in June 1961, May 1962 and June 1963.[13]

In the mid-1960s the Court consistently
restricted government action against
members of the Communist Party. Warren himself wrote the opinion in an important June 1965 case that overturned a
federal law barring Party members from
serving as labor union officials.[14] He again
spoke for the majority in a December
1967 decision that nullified a federal statute making it a crime for Communists to
work at defense facilities. The law was
voided on the grounds that it was over-
broad and thus an unconstitutional violation of the right of free association.[15] In ad-

1. *Garner v. Louisiana*, 368 U.S. 157 (1961).

2. *Peterson v. City of Greenville*, 373 U.S. 244
(1963); *Shuttlesworth v. City of Birmingham*, 373
U.S. 262 (1963); *Lombard v. Louisiana*, 373 U.S.
267 (1963); *Wright v. Georgia*, 373 U.S. 284 (1963);
Gober v. City of Birmingham, 373 U.S. 374 (1963);
Avent v. North Carolina, 373 U.S. 375 (1963).

3. *Taylor v. Louisiana*, 370 U.S. 154 (1962); *Edwards v. South Carolina*, 372 U.S. 229 (1963).

4. *Burton v. Wilmington Parking Authority*, 365
U.S. 715 (1961); *Goss v. Board of Education*, 373
U.S. 683 (1963).

5. *Heart of Atlanta Motel v. U.S.*, 379 U.S. 241
(1964); *Katzenbach v. McClung*, 379 U.S. 294
(1964).

6. *South Carolina v. Katzenbach*, 383 U.S. 301
(1966).

7. *Harman v. Forssenius*, 380 U.S. 528 (1965).

8. *Loving v. Virginia*, 388 U.S. 1 (1967).

9. *Jones v. Mayer*, 392 U.S. 409 (1968).

10. *Adderley v. Florida*, 385 U.S. 39 (1966);
Walker v. City of Birmingham, 388 U.S. 307 (1967).

11. *Communist Party v. Subversive Activities
Control Board*, 367 U.S. 1 (1961); *Scales v. U.S.*, 367
U.S. 203 (1961).

12. *Wilkinson v. U.S.*, 365 U.S. 399 (1961); *Brad-
en v. U.S.*, 365 U.S. 431 (1961).

13. *Deutch v. U.S.*, 367 U.S. 456 (1961); *Russell v.
U.S.*, 369 U.S. 749 (1962); *Yellin v. U.S.*, 374 U.S.
109 (1963).

14. *U.S. v. Brown*, 381 U.S. 437 (1965).

15. *U.S. v. Robel*, 389 U.S. 258 (1967).

dition to limiting federal anti-subversive legislation, the Court knocked down numerous state loyalty oath laws between 1964 and 1968.[1] Although he generally favored individual liberty over a claim of government security interests, Warren in May 1965 did sustain the Secretary of State's authority to refuse a citizen a passport valid for travel to Cuba.[2]

Warren's majority opinion in four May 1961 cases held that state "blue laws," prohibiting certain types of business on Sundays, did not violate the First Amendment. Although their origin was religious, Warren ruled that the laws had become secular in character and were designed to prevent overwork and unfair competition rather than to promote religious observance.[3] In three cases decided in June 1962 and June 1963, Warren joined the majority to hold prayer and Bible-reading in public schools a violation of the First Amendment's guarantee of freedom of religion.[4] The decisions resulted in a storm of criticism from certain congressmen and religious leaders and generated unsuccessful attempts to adopt a constitutional amendment restoring prayer to public schools.

In March 1962 Warren was part of a six-man majority that overturned a 1946 precedent and held that federal courts could try legislative apportionment cases.[5] Two years later the Court laid down a "one-man, one-vote" standard for congressional apportionment.[6] Warren's majority opinion in six June 1964 cases held that the equal protection clause required the same standard for state legislative districting.[7] These decisions resulted in reap-

portionment in nearly every state of the Union. In later years Warren labeled them the most significant action taken by the Court during his tenure.

In December 1966 Warren spoke for a unanimous Court in ruling that the Georgia House of Representatives had violated activist Julian Bond's right of free speech when it excluded him from his seat in the legislature because of his opposition to the draft and the Vietnam war.[8] Although he normally favored expanding the right to free expression, the Chief Justice proved to be less tolerant in the realm of obscenity. He dissented from several Court decisions that restricted government suppression of allegedly obscene materials and that resulted in much greater freedom of expression in this area.[9] In May 1968 Warren, speaking for a seven-man majority, upheld a provision in the Selective Service Act that made it a criminal offense to burn one's draft card and rejected the argument that this type of conduct was a form of symbolic speech protected by the First Amendment.[10]

Of all the Warren Court's rulings, those advancing the rights of criminal defendants aroused perhaps the most sustained debate. The Court gradually nationalized the most important criminal guarantees in the Bill of Rights, extending them to the states. In June 1961, with Warren in the majority, it held that illegally seized evidence could not be used in state courts.[11] A unanimous Supreme Court in June 1963 also ruled that the Sixth Amendment's right to counsel applied to the states.[12] Between 1964 and 1968, a majority which included Warren held that the Fifth

---

1. See, for example, *Baggett v. Bullitt,* 377 U.S. 360 (1964); *Keyishian v. Board of Regents,* 385 U.S. 589 (1967).

2. *Zemel v. Rusk,* 381 U.S. 1 (1965).

3. *McGowan v. Maryland,* 366 U.S. 420 (1961); *Two Guys from Harrison Allentown, Inc. v. McGinley,* 366 U.S. 582 (1961); *Braunfeld v. Brown,* 366 U.S. 599 (1961); *Gallagher v. Crown Kosher Super Market,* 366 U.S. 617 (1961).

4. *Engel v. Vitale,* 370 U.S. 421 (1962); *School District of Abington Township v. Schempp and Murray v. Curlett,* 374 U.S. 203 (1963).

5. *Baker v. Carr,* 369 U.S. 186 (1962).

6. *Wesberry v. Sanders,* 376 U.S. 1 (1964).

7. *Reynolds v. Sims,* 377 U.S. 533 (1964). *WMCA, Inc. v. Lomenzo,* 377 U.S. 633 (1964); *Maryland Committee for Fair Representation v. Tawes,* 377 U.S. 656 (1964); *Davis v. Mann,* 377 U.S. 678 (1964); *Roman v. Sincock,* 377 U.S. 695 (1964); *Lucas v. Forty-Fourth General Assembly of Colorado,* 377 U.S. 713 (1964).

8. *Bond v. Floyd,* 385 U.S. 116 (1966).

9. See, for example, *Jacobellis v. Ohio,* 378 U.S. 184 (1964).

10. *U.S. v. O'Brien,* 391 U.S. 367 (1968).

11. *Mapp v. Ohio,* 367 U.S. 643 (1961).

12. *Gideon v. Wainwright,* 372 U.S. 335 (1963).

158

Amendment's privilege against self-incrimination and the Sixth Amendment's right to confront witnesses, to a speedy trial and to trial by jury applied to state as well as federal courts.[1]

The Court also liberalized the interpretation of these criminal rights. A series of decisions on the admissibility of confessions, for example, culminated in the June 1966 *Miranda* ruling, one of the Court's most controversial criminal justice decisions. Speaking for a five-man majority Chief Justice Warren laid down a set of protections for a criminal suspect immediately following his arrest. These included requirements that he be informed of his right to remain silent and his right to counsel and that he be supplied with an attorney if unable to afford one.[2]

The landmark ruling was denounced by many who felt it would hinder law enforcement agencies. Republican presidential candidate Richard M. Nixon made *Miranda* and other Court rulings on criminal rights a major issue in his 1968 campaign. However, other observers noted that although the Court enhanced the rights of the accused, it also upheld the right of police to use informants and made it clear that both wiretapping and eavesdropping would be approved if properly authorized by judicial warrants.[3] An opinion written by Warren in June 1968 also upheld the authority of police to stop and frisk persons for weapons when necessary to protect their own or others' safety.[4]

In addition to his work on the Court, Warren, at the urging of President Lyndon Johnson, reluctantly accepted in November 1963 the chairmanship of a commission to investigate the assassination of John F. Kennedy. After 10 months of work, which Warren later called "the un-happiest time of my life," the Commission produced a unanimous report, concluding that Lee Harvey Oswald, acting alone, had killed Kennedy. The Warren Commission report was later disputed by other researchers who insisted that Kennedy's assassination was the result of a conspiracy. However, their arguments never led Warren to doubt the Commission's findings.

On June 13, 1968 Warren submitted his resignation to President Johnson, who accepted it pending confirmation of a new chief justice. Johnson nominated Associate Justice Abe Fortas to the post, but withdrew the nomination in October 1968 after a coalition of Republicans and conservative Democrats effectively blocked Senate confirmation of the appointment. Warren then announced that he would retire at the end of the Court's term in June 1969.

During his final months on the bench, the Chief Justice dissented from a decision overturning state residency requirements for welfare,[5] but joined in a ruling barring garnishment of a debtor's wages prior to notice and hearing.[6] He was also part of a six-man majority that in June 1969 extended the Fifth Amendment's provision against double jeopardy to the states.[7] In his last opinion for the Court on June 16, 1969, Warren reversed an appeals court decision written by Warren Burger and held that the House of Representatives had acted unconstitutionally in excluding Adam Clayton Powell from membership.[8] A week later, Warren stepped down from the bench.

A thoughtful man with a friendly, affable manner, Warren devoted a part of his retirement years to the fishing, hunting and spectator sports he so enjoyed. He also did some writing and lecturing and spoke out in 1973 in opposition to a pro-

1. *Malloy v. Hogan,* 378 U.S. 1 (1964); *Pointer v. Texas,* 380 U.S. 400 (1965); *Klopfer v. North Carolina,* 386 U.S. 213 (1967); *Duncan v. Louisiana,* 391 U.S. 145 (1968).

2. *Miranda v. Arizona,* 384 U.S. 436 (1966).

3. *Hoffa v. U.S.* 385 U.S. 293 (1966); *Katz v. U.S.,* 389 U.S. 347 (1967).

4. *Terry v. Ohio,* 392 U.S. 1 (1968).

5. *Shapiro v. Thompson,* 394 U.S. 618 (1969).

6. *Sniadach v. Family Finance Corp.,* 395 U.S. 337 (1969).

7. *Benton v. Maryland,* 395 U.S. 784 (1969).

8. *Powell v. McCormack,* 395 U.S. 486 (1969), *affirming in part and reversing in part* 395 F.2d 577 (D.C. Cir. 1968).

posal for a new appeals court below the Supreme Court. He died in Washington on July 9, 1974.

During his years on the bench, Earl Warren served as a symbol for the entire Court to both its admirers and its critics. Denunciations of the Court's rulings often turned into attacks on Warren personally, and he was often picketed and heckled when he delivered public speeches. His actual role in making the Warren Court the activist, liberal body it became was debated. One skeptic, noting Warren's greater liberalism as a justice than as a politician, concluded it would be most accurate to say "that Warren has not formed the Court but rather that the Court has formed him." A larger number of observers, however, gave Warren great credit for supplying the leadership needed to carry forward the Court's constitutional changes. Warren was not the author of many of the opinions adopted by the Court or of the judicial philosophy underlying them, but his political and administrative skills were judged essential for achieving a new consensus and direction on the Court.

Legal scholars directed their strongest criticism of both Warren and his Court at the style rather than the substance of their decisions. The Court's liberal jurists, many argued, were so oriented toward achieving desirable results that they too easily discarded precedents, failed to explain or justify their rulings with any solid legal reasoning and left themselves open to the charge that they interpreted the Constitution solely on the basis of their political preferences. Warren's own concern for fairness over precedent or theory became legendary among Court watchers. He was reported to have frequently interrupted counsel during oral argument to ask if particular actions had been fair. His opinions were criticized for being unanalytical and more ethical than legal. His opinion in *Miranda,* setting forth a detailed code of conduct for the police, was considered a prime example of the Court's tendency to act more like a legislative than a judicial body.

To those who charged that the Court reached out to decide controversial issues and was too result-oriented, Warren answered that the Court had an obligation to decide all cases properly placed before it, however controversial the issues. In the judicial process, Warren also wrote, the "basic ingredient of decision is principle and it should not be compromised and parceled out a little in one case, a little more in another, until eventually someone receives the full benefit. If the principle is sound and constitutional, it is the birthright of every American" and should be accorded "to everyone in its entirety whenever it is brought into play." For Warren the Court's special function lay in guaranteeing the constitutional protections afforded the individual, especially for those least likely to receive them. Unless "the Court has the fiber to accord justice to the weakest member of society," he stated, "we never can achieve our goal of 'life, liberty and the pursuit of happiness' for everyone."

Warren was not a great legal scholar or judicial philosopher, but most analysts consider him to have been a preeminent Chief Justice. His personal dedication to the ideal of equal justice for all Americans and to the protection of individual liberties was widely praised. All observers agreed that the Court he presided over had an enormous impact on American law and life, giving support and impetus to significant social change. Under Warren's leadership, according to Archibald Cox, the Court gave "creative and enduring impetus" to the "responsibility of government for equality among men, the openness of American society to change and reform and the decency of the administration of criminal justice."

WHITE, BYRON R(AYMOND)
b. June 8, 1917; Fort Collins, Colo.
Associate Justice, U.S. Supreme
Court, 1962- .

White grew up in Wellington, a small town in Colorado near the Wyoming border. He graduated in 1938 from the University of Colorado, where he was valedictorian of his class and an All-America in football. "Whizzer" White played professional football for the Pittsburgh Steelers in 1938 and the Detroit Lions in 1940 and 1941; he was named to the National Football Hall of Fame in 1954. A Rhodes Scholar at Oxford University in 1939, White graduated from Yale Law School in November 1946 and served as law clerk to Supreme Court Chief Justice Fred Vinson during the 1946-47 term. At this time he became friendly with Rep. John F. Kennedy (D, Mass.), whom he had earlier known in England and as a naval officer in the Pacific during World War II. In 1947 White joined a prestigious Denver law firm, eventually becoming a partner and working primarily on corporate cases.

An early supporter of John Kennedy's bid for the 1960 Democratic presidential nomination, White marshaled the Kennedy forces in Colorado prior to the Democratic National Convention and headed a nation-wide Citizens for Kennedy-Johnson organization during the 1960 campaign. Named deputy attorney general in January 1961, White assisted Attorney General Robert F. Kennedy in recruiting highly qualified attorneys for the Justice Department. Considered an able administrator, White oversaw much of the day-to-day administration of the department, supervised antitrust and civil rights suits and evaluated candidates for federal judicial appointments.

On May 20, 1961 the Freedom Riders, civil rights demonstrators challenging segregated transportation, were assaulted by a mob in Montgomery, Ala. White personally commanded the more than 400 federal marshals ordered to Montgomery later that day by the Attorney General. He also conferred with Alabama Gov. John Patterson and the head of the Alabama National Guard during the crisis. With the retirement of Associate Justice Charles Whittaker, President Kennedy selected White as his first Supreme Court nominee on March 30, 1962. Confirmed by the Senate on April 11, White was sworn in five days later.

As a jurist White was not easy to categorize. He refrained from broad statements of philosophy in his opinions and had a pragmatic, nondoctrinaire approach that made it difficult to predict his stance in many cases. Over time, though, his votes showed that he tended to favor government authority over individual rights in First Amendment and criminal cases. White generally supported judicial deference to legislative judgments because he believed it better for the nation to resolve many controversial questions through the political process rather than the courts. The Justice also preferred to resolve cases without making dramatic changes in existing law.

As a result of such views, White proved to be far more conservative on the bench than had been expected, especially on criminal rights and civil liberties issues, and he surprised many observers who had expected this New Frontier Democrat to align himself with the Court's liberals. He registered his first dissent, for example, in June 1962 in a case in which the majority overturned a California law that made drug addiction a crime.[1] White then went on to object to some of the Warren Court's most significant criminal rights rulings. He dissented from two 1964 decisions in which the majority extended the right to counsel to include preliminary police investigation of a suspect[2] and held the Fifth Amendment's privilege against self-incrimination applicable to the

---

1. *Robinson v. California*, 370 U.S. 660 (1962).

2. *Escobedo v. Illinois*, 378 U.S. 478 (1964).

161

states.[1] White also dissented from the 1966 *Miranda* ruling, in which the majority placed restrictions on police interrogation of arrested suspects. White accused the Court of making "new law and new public policy" and warned that the decision would result in the return of "a killer, a rapist, or other criminal to the streets . . . to repeat his crime."[2] However, Justice White spoke for the majority in a 1967 decision holding that a routine municipal housing inspection of a private dwelling, conducted without a warrant, was an unreasonable search in violation of the Fourth Amendment.[3]

White also voted consistently to sustain federal laws regarding citizenship and Communists. He dissented in May 1964 when the Court nullified a law canceling the citizenship of naturalized Americans who returned to their native lands for three years[4] and in June when it overturned a provision in the 1950 Internal Security Act denying passports to members of the Communist Party.[5] He was again with the minority in June 1965 when the Court overturned a provision in the Landrum-Griffin Act that barred Communist Party members[6] from serving as labor union officials. Justice White also dissented in January 1967 when the majority held unconstitutional three New York State laws requiring public school and state college teachers to sign oaths disavowing membership in the Communist Party and ordering the removal of teachers for treasonous or seditious acts or statements.[7]

Justice White took a more liberal position in many racial discrimination cases, however. He voted to uphold the public

accommodations section of the 1964 Civil Rights Act in December 1964[8] but did dissent when the Court ruled that the law barred state prosecution of peaceful demonstrators who had tried to desegregate the places covered by the act prior to the law's passage.[9] He backed major provisions of the 1965 Voting Rights Act in March 1966[10] and joined the majority later that month in voiding a poll tax for state elections.[11] In May 1967 White wrote the majority opinion in *Reitman v. Mulkey* overturning a California state constitutional amendment that had nullified earlier legislation prohibiting racial discrimination in the sale or rental of housing.[12]

Because he believed in solving national problems through political means where possible, White also considered it important that the political process accurately reflect popular interests and views. To that end he voted consistently from 1964 through 1968 in favor of the Court's one-man, one-vote rule for reapportionment of legislative districts.[13] In an April 1968 decision White's majority opinion extended the reapportionment decisions to elections for local political units having general governmental powers over their area.[14]

On the Burger Court White occupied a center position and was identified, along with Potter Stewart, as a "swing" justice whose vote decided cases in which the Court's liberal members were at odds with the more conservative Nixon appointees. When the two groups were sharply divided, White was more likely to vote with the conservatives, especially in criminal cases. He backed police "stop and frisk"[15] practices, upheld warrantless

1. *Malloy v. Hogan*, 378 U.S. 1 (1964).

2. *Miranda v. Arizona*, 384 U.S. 436, 526 (1966).

3. *Camara v. Municipal Court of San Francisco*, 387 U.S. 523 (1967).

4. *Schneider v. Rusk*, 377 U.S. 163 (1964).

5. *Aptheker v. Secretary of State*, 378 U.S. 500 (1964)

6. *U.S. v. Brown*, 381 U.S. 437 (1965).

7. *Keyishian v. Board of Regents*, 385 U.S. 589 (1967).

8. *Heart of Atlanta Motel v. U.S.*, 379 U.S. 241 (1964); *Katzenbach v. McClung*, 379 U.S. 294 (1964).

9. *Hamm v. City of Rock Hill*, 379 U.S. 306 (1964).

10. *South Carolina v. Katzenbach*, 383 U.S. 301 (1966).

11. *Harper v. Virginia State Board of Elections*, 383 U.S. 663 (1966).

12. 387 U.S. 369 (1967).

13. *Wesberry v. Sanders*, 376 U.S. 1 (1964); *Reynolds v. Sims*, 377 U.S. 533 (1964).

14. *Avery v. Midland County*, 390 U.S. 474 (1968).

15. *Terry v. Ohio*, 392 U.S. 1 (1968); *Adams v. Williams*, 407 U.S. 143 (1972).

searches he considered reasonable[1] and urged the Court to limit the application of the exclusionary rule which barred the use of illegally seized evidence at trial.[2] In a March 1969 opinion, White ordered the government to let defendants examine the transcripts of illegal electronic eavesdropping against them, even in national security cases.[3] In April 1971, however, he upheld "third-party bugging" in which an informer, without a warrant, used an electronic device to transmit his conversation with another person to government agents.[4]

White also joined in decisions cutting back on the 1966 *Miranda* ruling.[5] In three May 1970 cases, he upheld plea bargains against charges from defendants that their guilty pleas had been involuntary or improperly induced.[6] In a June 1970 opinion, White sustained the use of six member juries in state courts, and in May 1972, he spoke for the Court to sanction non-unanimous jury verdicts. Justice White joined the Court's liberals in June 1972 to hold the death penalty as then imposed a violation of the Eighth Amendment's ban on cruel and unusual punishment.[9] However, he voted four years later to sustain capital punishment as the penalty for murder under newer state laws which either made the penalty mandatory or else established guidelines restricting the judge's or jury's discretion in imposing the death sentence.[10]

Justice White opposed the Court's use of an 1866 civil rights law to overturn racial discrimination in housing and in private nonsectarian schools.[11] His majority opinion in a significant June 1976 case held that government action must have a discriminatory purpose as well as a racially disproportionate effect in order to violate the 14th Amendment.[12] However, White dissented in June 1971, when a majority allowed a city to close its public swimming pools rather than desegregate them[13] and in July 1974 when the Court rejected an interdistrict remedy for school segregation in Detroit.[14] He favored a strict standard of review in sex discrimination cases and voted to overturn most laws discriminating against women and against illegitimate children.[15] White also dissented in March 1973 when the Court held that public school financing systems based on local property taxes did not deny children in poorer districts the equal protection of the laws.[16]

Because he preferred political solutions of controversial issues, White opposed the Court's January 1973 decision invalidating anti-abortion laws for the first six months of pregnancy.[17] He also supported virtually all state and federal laws providing aid to parochial schools.[18] In June 1973 he was part of a five-man majority which granted the states greater leeway in regulating allegedly obscene mate-

---

1. See, for example, *Chimel v. California*, 395 U.S. 752 (1969); *U.S. v. Edwards*, 415 U.S. 800 (1974).

2. See his dissenting opinion in *Stone v. Powell*, 428 U.S. 465, 536 (1976)

3. *Alderman v. U.S.*, 394 U.S. 165 (1969).

4. *U.S. v. White*, 401 U.S. 745 (1971).

5. See, for example, *Harris v. New York*, 401 U.S. 222 (1971); *Michigan v. Mosley*, 423 U.S. 96 (1975).

6. *Brady v. U.S.*, 397 U.S. 742 (1970); *McMann v. Richardson*, 397 U.S. 759 (1970); *Parker v. North Carolina*, 397 U.S. 790 (1970).

7. *Williams v. Florida*, 399 U.S. 78 (1970).

8. *Johnson v. Louisiana*, 406 U.S. 356 (1972); *Apodaca v. Oregon*, 406 U.S. 404 (1972).

9. *Furman v. Georgia*, 408 U.S. 238 (1972).

10. *Gregg v. Georgia*, 428 U.S. 153 (1976); *Proffitt v. Florida*, 428 U.S. 242 (1976); *Jurek v. Texas*, 428 U.S. 262 (1976); *Woodson v. North Carolina*, 428

U.S. 280 (1976); *Roberts v. Louisiana*, 428 U.S. 325 (1976).

11. *Jones v. Mayer*, 392 U.S. 409 (1968); *Sullivan v. Little Hunting Park, Inc.*, 396 U.S. 229 (1969); *Runyon v. McCrary*, 427 U.S. 160 (1976).

12. *Washington v. Davis*, 426 U.S. 229 (1976).

13. *Palmer v. Thompson*, 403 U.S. 217 (1971).

14. *Milliken v. Bradley*, 418 U.S. 717 (1974).

15. See, for example, *Frontiero v. Richardson*, 411 U.S. 677 (1973); *Taylor v. Louisiana*, 419 U.S. 522 (1975); *Labine v. Vincent*, 401 U.S. 532 (1971); *Weber v. Aetna Casualty & Surety Co.*, 406 U.S. 164 (1972).

16. *San Antonio Independent School District v. Rodriquez*, 411 U.S. 1 (1973).

17. *Roe v. Wade*, 410 U.S. 113 (1973); *Doe v. Bolton*, 410 U.S. 179 (1973).

18. See for example, *Board of Education v. Allen*, 392 U.S. 236 (1968); *Lemon v. Kurtzman*, 403 U.S. 602 (1971).

rial.[1] To ensure that the political system would be responsive to the popular will, White favored expansion of the electoral process. His opinion in a June 1970 case, for example, opened voting on local bond issues to tenants as well as property owners,[2] and the Justice supported a federal law lowering the voting age to 18 in December 1970.[3] Although he had endorsed the one-man, one-vote rule in reapportionment cases, White objected in these years to a very strict application of that standard. For a six-man majority in June 1973, he declared that the states did not have to justify minor deviations from the one-man, one-vote rule in the apportionment of their own legislatures.[4]

In First Amendment cases Justice White most often voted to sustain government power against individual rights claims.[5] He did vote to deny the government's request for an injunction in June 1971 to halt newspaper publication of the *Pentagon Papers*.[6] However, he wrote the opinion in a five-to-four decision a year later holding that journalists had no First Amendment right to refuse to testify before a grand jury about information obtained from confidential sources.[7] In June 1969 White spoke for the Court to sustain the Federal Communications Commission's "fairness doctrine" requiring radio and television stations to air both sides of important issues.[8]

A straightforward man with a quick intellect, White wrote very direct, blunt opinions. He was not a leader on the Court and was considered an average justice by most Court observers. Although conservative on criminal rights issues, White was evaluated as an independent and a "thoughtful moderate" on other constitutional questions.

---

1. *Miller v. California*, 413 U.S. 15 (1973); *Paris Adult Theatre I v. Slaton*, 413 U.S. 49 (1973).

2. *Phoenix v. Kolodziejski*, 399 U.S. 204 (1970).

3. *Oregon v. Mitchell*, 400 U.S. 112 (1970).

4. *Gaffney v. Cummings*, 412 U.S. 735 (1973); *White v. Regester*, 412 U.S. 755 (1973). See also *Wells v. Rockefeller*, 394 U.S. 542 (1969); *Mahan v. Howell*, 410 U.S. 315 (1973).

5. See, for example, *Baird v. State Bar of Arizona*, 401 U.S. 1 (1971); *Cole v. Richardson*, 405 U.S. 676 (1972); *U.S. Civil Service Commission v. National Association of Letter Carriers*, 413 U.S. 548 (1973).

6. *New York Times Co. v. U.S.*, 403 U.S. 713 (1971).

7. *Branzburg v. Hayes*, 408 U.S. 665 (1972).

8. *Red Lion Broadcasting Co. v. Federal Communications Commission*, 395 U.S. 367 (1969).

WHITTAKER, CHARLES E(VANS)
b. Feb. 22, 1901: Troy, Kan.
d. Nov. 26, 1973: Kansas City, Mo.
Associate Justice, U.S. Supreme
Court, 1957-62.

Charles E. Whittaker worked his way through law school at the University of Kansas City, Mo., and passed the state bar exam in 1923, a year before his graduation. He joined a prestigious Kansas City law firm, eventually becoming a senior partner, where he specialized in litigation and business planning for a largely corporate clientele. Although not active politically, Whittaker was a Republican and a close friend of President Dwight D. Eisenhower's brother Arthur, and he was well regarded by state political leaders. He was named to a federal district court judgeship in Kansas City in July 1954 and promoted to a seat on the Eighth Circuit Court of Appeals in June 1956. In both posts Whittaker demonstrated great industry and efficiency. Eisenhower nominated him to the Supreme Court in March 1957, and he was quickly confirmed by the Senate.

On the bench Whittaker soon aligned himself with the Court's more conservative members. In June 1957 he wrote the majority opinion in a case upholding a section of the 1952 McCarran Act which resulted in the deportation of an alien for committing an offense that had not been grounds for deportation when he committed it.[1] A year later Whittaker was part of a five-man majority that sustained the dismissal of a public school teacher who had refused to answer questions about possible Communist affiliations in the past.[2] He also dissented in June 1958 when the Court ruled that Congress had not authorized the Secretary of State to refuse a citizen a passport because of his political beliefs.[3] In two June 1959 cases the Justice voted to uphold the contempt convictions of witnesses who had refused to answer questions or produce records for congressional and state investigations of Communism.[4]

Whittaker joined the majority in a series of five to four decisions in 1961 involving loyalty-security matters. In two decisions handed down in February, he voted to uphold the investigative power of the House Un-American Activities Committee and to sustain the contempt-of-Congress convictions of witnesses who had refused to answer committee questions.[5] Whittaker also voted in June to uphold the requirement in the 1950 Internal Security Act for Communist-action organizations to register with the government and the clause in the 1940 Smith Act that made it a crime to be an active member of a party advocating violent overthrow of the government.[6] He was part of a five-man majority in another 1961 case which upheld a Chicago ordinance that barred public showing of movies without prior approval of city censors.[7]

Whittaker did occasionally vote with the Court's liberals in First Amendment and loyalty-security cases. His opinion for the Court in a January 1958 decision declared unconstitutional a local ordinance that required union organizers to obtain permits before they could solicit membership in a union.[8] Whittaker also voted in two March 1958 cases to overturn federal statutes taking away the citizenship of wartime deserters or individuals who voted in a foreign election.[9] Gen-

1. *Lehmann v. U.S. ex rel. Carson*, 353 U.S. 685 (1957).

2. *Beilan v. Board of Education*, 357 U.S. 399 (1958).

3. *Kent v. Dulles*, 357 U.S. 116 (1958).

4. *Uphaus v. Wyman*, 360 U.S. 72 (1959); *Barenblatt v. U.S.*, 360 U.S. 109 (1959).

5. *Wilkinson v. U.S.*, 365 U.S. 399 (1961); *Braden v. U.S.*, 365 U.S. 431 (1961).

6. *Communist Party v. Subversive Activities Control Board*, 367 U.S. 1 (1961); *Scales v. U.S.*, 367 U.S. 203 (1961).

7. *Times Film Corp. v. Chicago*, 365 U.S. 43 (1961).

8. *Staub v. City of Baxley*, 355 U.S. 313 (1958).

9. *Trop v. Dulles*, 356 U.S. 86 (1958); *Perez v. Brownell*, 356 U.S. 44 (1958).

erally, however, he voted in a conservative vein, and in the 1959 and 1960 Court terms, the Justice had the lowest civil liberties record of any member of the Court.

In criminal rights cases Whittaker again leaned toward conservatism. He joined the majority in a March 1959 case which held that an individual acquitted in a federal court could then be tried for the same offense in a state court without violating the safeguard against double jeopardy.[1] He dissented when the Court decided in June 1961 in *Mapp v. Ohio* that illegally seized evidence was inadmissible in state courts.[2] However, Whittaker wrote the opinion for a unanimous Court in a 1961 case holding that an uneducated and mentally ill defendant needed the assistance of counsel in a state prosecution for assault.[3] He also delivered the majority opinion in an eight to one decision the same year that overturned a federal conviction based on an illegal search by state police.[4] In many criminal cases, such as those involving an allegedly coerced confession, Whittaker was accused of inconsistency because he would vote opposite ways in largely similar cases without clearly explaining his reasons for doing so.[5]

On March 16, 1962 Whittaker entered the hospital suffering from exhaustion.

He resigned from the Court on March 29, explaining that the "great volume and continuous stresses of the Court's work" had brought him to the "point of physical exhaustion" and that his doctors had warned him that staying on the Court would jeopardize his health. According to legal scholar Henry J. Abraham, Whittaker had not found genuine satisfaction on the Supreme Court and had been overwhelmed by both the volume and gravity of the Court's business.

A modest, sincere man who worked extremely hard while on the Court, Whittaker has been considered by most commentators a failure as a justice. He had a very limited view of his role, was not outstanding either as a judicial thinker or legal craftsman and wrote almost no significant opinions. He articulated no judicial philosophy and "was not," according to Leon Friedman, "fitted intellectually or physically for the job" of a Supreme Court justice. Whittaker retained his Supreme Court commission after he left the Court, but then resigned the commission in October 1965 to take a position on the legal staff of General Motors. In April 1966 he was appointed a consultant to the Senate Committee on Standards and Conduct to help work on a code of senatorial ethics. Whittaker died in November 1973.

---

1. *Bartkus v. Illinois,* 359 U.S. 121 (1959).

2. 367 U.S. 643 (1961).

3. *McNeal v. Culver,* 365 U.S. 109 (1961).

4. *Chapman v. U.S.,* 365 U.S. 610 (1961).

5. Compare, for example, *Thomas v. Arizona,* 356 U.S. 390 (1958) with *Payne v. Arkansas,* 356 U.S. 560 (1958).

Appendix

Chronology of Supreme Court Appointments

1920				
1930	**Harlan Fiske Stone** March 2, 1925 (Stone took another oath when named Chief Justice on July 3, 1941) died April 22, 1946			
1940		**Hugo L. Black** August 19, 1937 retired September 17, 1971	**Stanley F. Reed** January 31, 1938 retired February 25, 1957	**Felix Frankfurter** January 30, 1939 retired August 28, 1962
1950	**Fred M. Vinson** June 24, 1946 died September 8, 1953			
1960	**Earl Warren** October 5, 1953 retired June 23, 1969		**Charles Whittaker** March 25, 1957 retired April 1, 1962	
1970	**Warren E. Burger** June 23, 1969		**Byron R. White** April 16, 1962	**Arthur J. Goldberg** October 1, 1962 resigned July 26, 1965 **Abe Fortas** October 4, 1965 resigned May 14, 1969
1980		**Lewis F. Powell, Jr.** January 7, 1972		**Harry A. Blackmun** June 9, 1970

The first date after each justice's name is the date on which he took the oath of office. The second date is the date on which his service on the Court ended.

William O. Douglas April 17, 1939 retired November 22, 1975				
	Frank Murphy February 5, 1940 died July 19, 1949 **Tom C. Clark** August 24, 1949 retired June 12, 1967	**Robert H. Jackson** July 11, 1941 died October 9, 1954	**Wiley B. Rutledge** February 15, 1943 died September 10, 1949	**Harold H. Burton** October 1, 1945 retired October 13, 1958
		John Marshall Harlan March 28, 1955 retired September 23, 1971	**Sherman Minton** October 12, 1949 retired October 15, 1956 **William J. Brennan, Jr.** October 16, 1956	**Potter Stewart** October 14, 1958
	Thurgood Marshall October 2, 1967			
John Paul Stevens December 19, 1975		**William H. Rehnquist** January 7, 1972		

Significant Decisions: 1945-1976

Marsh v. Alabama, 326 U.S. 501, January 7, 1946

The Court upheld the right of Jehovah's Witnesses to distribute their religious literature on the streets of a privately owned company town.

Thomas v. Collins, 323 U.S. 516, January 8, 1945

The Court overturned a Texas law requiring labor union organizers to get an organizer's card from the state before soliciting union members as an infringement on freedom of speech. Justice Wiley Rutledge's opinion for the Court was notable for its strong advocacy of the view that First Amendment rights constituted "preferred freedoms."

In re Yamashita, 327 U.S. 1, February 4, 1946

By a six-to-two vote, the Court sustained the legality of the military tribunal that tried and sentenced to death Japanese Gen. Tomoyuki Yamashita on charges of violating the laws of war.

Colegrove v. Green, 328 U.S. 549, June 10, 1946

In a case from Illinois, Justice Felix Frankfurter spoke for the Court to hold that legislative apportionment was a political question and therefore not a proper subject for judicial consideration. The decision was overturned in *Baker v. Carr* (1962).

Everson v. Board of Education, 330 U.S. 1, February 10, 1947

This was the first major case concerning the First Amendment's clause banning government establishment of religion. The Court upheld state payments for the transportation of children to parochial schools on the ground that this constituted a social welfare measure rather than an aid to religious education.

United Public Workers of America v. Mitchell, 330 U.S. 75, February 10, 1947

The Court ruled that the Hatch Act provision prohibiting political activity by federal employes did not violate the employes' First Amendment rights.

U.S. v. United Mine Workers, 330 U.S. 258, March 6, 1947

The Court sustained the contempt-of-court judgment and heavy fines imposed on John L. Lewis and the United Mine Workers for their defiance of a district court order prohibiting a strike. The order was issued at a time when the federal government had seized control of the coal mines.

Adamson v. California, 332 U.S. 46, June 23, 1947

A five-man majority held that the Fifth Amendment's privilege against self-incrimination did not apply to the states. The majority and dissenting opinions presented the major theories regarding "incorporation," i.e., the degree to which the 14th Amendment's due process clause made the guarantees in the Bill of Rights applicable to the states.

Illinois ex rel. McCollum v. Board of Education, 333 U.S. 203, March 8, 1948

The First Amendment was held to prohibit released time religious instruction of public school students in public school buildings.

Shelley v. Kraemer, 334 U.S. 1; **Hurd v. Hodge,** 334 U.S. 24, May 3, 1948

The Court ruled that restrictive covenants, which barred the sale of residential property to blacks and other minorities, were legally unenforceable in federal and state courts. The Justices did not outlaw restrictive covenants per se but held that court enforcement of them would violate the 14th Amendment, in the case of state courts, and the 1866 Civil Rights Act, in the case of federal courts.

Takahashi v. Fish and Game Commission, 334 U.S. 410, June 7, 1948

This decision invalidated a California law barring Japanese aliens from commercial fishing as a denial of equal protection.

Wolf v. Colorado, 338 U.S. 25, June 27, 1949

The Court unanimously held that the Fourth Amendment's prohibition on unreasonable searches and seizures applied to the states. But by a six-to-three vote, the Court also decided that the exclusionary rule, which barred the use of evidence obtained in violation of the amendment in federal courts, did not apply to state courts. The judgment concerning the exclusionary rule was overturned in *Mapp v. Ohio* (1961).

U.S. v. Rabinowitz, 339 U.S. 56, February 20, 1950

A five-man majority upheld the right of police to make a "reasonable" search without a warrant incident to a valid arrest.

American Communications Assn. v. Douds, 339 U.S. 382, May 8, 1950

The Court ruled that the provision in the Taft-Hartley Act requiring labor union officials to file non-Communist affidavits did not violate the First Amendment.

Sweatt v. Painter, 339 U.S. 629, June 5, 1950

A unanimous Court held that a recently-established state law school for blacks was inferior to the law school at the University of Texas for whites. Therefore, the state violated the guarantee of equal protection by excluding black students from the University of Texas law school.

McLaurin v. Oklahoma State Regents, 339 U.S. 637, June 5, 1950

A unanimous Court ruled that a state denied equal protection when it admitted a black to the graduate school at a state university and then segregated the student in classrooms and other facilities.

Joint Anti-Fascist Refugee Committee v. McGrath, 341 U.S. 123, April 30, 1951

By a five-to-three vote, the Court ruled in favor of three organizations challenging their placement on the Attorney General's list of subversive organizations. It determined that the presidential order establishing the federal loyalty program had not given the Attorney General the authority to arbitrarily designate an organization as subversive.

Dennis v. U.S., 341 U.S. 494, June 4, 1951

The Court sustained the conviction of 11 American Communist Party leaders for violation of the Smith Act. Chief Justice Fred Vinson broadened the "clear and present danger" rule to hold that the government could outlaw a conspiracy to teach and advocate overthrow of the government when the individuals intended to overthrow the government as soon as circumstances would permit, even though the possibility of a successful revolution was remote.

Adler v. Board of Education, 342 U.S. 485, March 3, 1952

The Court held constitutional New York State's Feinberg Law which barred members of subversive organizations from teaching in public schools. The decision was eventually overruled in *Keyishian v. Board of Regents* (1967).

Zorach v. Clauson, 343 U.S. 306, April 28, 1952

The Court upheld a released-time program of religious instruction for New York City public school students. Justice William O. Douglas distinguished this ruling from *Illinois ex rel. McCollum v. Board of Education* (1948) by noting that in the New York case the instruction did not take place in the public schools or at public expense.

Burstyn, Inc. v. Wilson, 343 U.S. 495, May 26, 1952

The Court extended First Amendment protection to movies. It overturned a New York State ban on the showing of a film judged "sacrilegious" by censors as an unconstitutional prior restraint on freedom of speech and of the press.

Youngstown Sheet & Tube Co. v. Sawyer, 343 U.S. 579, June 2, 1952

By a six-to-three vote the Court ruled that President Harry S Truman had no authority to seize the nation's steel mills in order to avert a strike by steelworkers during the Korean war.

Brown v. Board of Education. 347 U.S. 483; **Boling v. Sharpe.** 347 U.S. 497, May 17, 1954

In a historic decision, the Court unanimously ruled that separate educational facilities for black children were inherently unequal. Therefore, racially segregated public schools required by law were unconstitutional. Based on this ruling, the Court went on to outlaw segregation in all public facilities.

Brown v. Board of Education, 349 U.S. 294, May 31, 1955

In a follow-up to the *Brown* decision of the previous term, the Court ordered school desegregation to proceed "with all deliberate speed."

Pennsylvania v. Nelson, 350 U.S. 497, April 2, 1956

This controversial decision overturned a state conviction for sedition against the United States on the ground that Congress had pre-empted this field from the states with the 1940 Smith Act.

Griffin v. Illinois, 351 U.S. 12, April 23, 1956

The Court held that states must supply an indigent convict with a free trial transcript if the transcript was essential to the appeal of a criminal conviction.

Jencks v. U.S. 353 U.S. 657, June 3, 1957

The Court ruled that in federal criminal trials the government must let the defense examine FBI reports made by individuals who testify as government witnesses.

Watkins v. U.S., 354 U.S. 178, June 17, 1957

In the first of three controversial decisions delivered on the same day, Chief Justice Earl Warren overturned the contempt-of-Congress conviction of an individual who had refused to answer certain questions before a House Un-American Activities subcommittee. Warren held that the subcommittee had failed to show the witness that the questions asked were pertinent to the subject under investigation.

Sweezy v. New Hampshire, 354 U.S. 234, June 17, 1957

In a ruling similar to *Watkins,* the Court reversed the contempt conviction of an individual who had refused to answer several questions posed by New Hampshire's Attorney General. Chief Justice Warren's opinion for the Court held that the state legislature, in authorizing the Attorney General's investigation into possible subversion, had not set clear and proper limits on the investigation and had not explicitly authorized the particular inquiries at issue in this case.

Yates v. U.S., 354 U.S. 298, June 17, 1957

This decision reversed the conviction of 14 California Communist Party leaders for violation of the Smith Act. Justice John Marshall Harlan ruled that the term 'organize' in the Act applied only to the initial formation of the party, not to continuing organizing efforts after that date. He then found that the statute of limitations had run on this charge against the defendants. Harlan also held that the Smith Act did not outlaw advocacy of forcible overthrow of the government as an abstract doctrine, but only such advocacy when directed at promoting concrete unlawful actions. This interpretation made further convictions of Communists under the conspiracy clause of the Smith Act almost impossible.

Mallory v. U.S., 354 U.S. 449, June 24, 1957

Extending a ruling made in *McNabb v. U.S.,* 318 U.S. 332 (1943), the Court held that when there was any unnecessary delay between the arrest and arraignment of a federal defendant, a confession obtained during that period was inadmissible in federal courts.

Roth v. U.S., 354 U.S. 476, June 24, 1957

The Court ruled that obscene materials were not protected by the First Amendment's guarantees of free speech and free press. It defined the test of obscenity as whether, to the average person applying contemporary community standards, the dominant theme of the material taken as a whole appealed to the prurient interest.

Perez v. Brownell, 356 U.S. 44; **Trop v. Dulles,** 356 U.S. 86, March 31, 1958

By a five-to-four vote in *Perez,* the Court upheld a provision in the 1940 Nationality Act removing citizenship from any American who voted in a foreign election as a valid exercise of Congress's power to regulate foreign affairs. In *Trop,* however, a five-man majority overturned another section in the same law providing for the expatriation of an individual convicted of desertion in wartime. The Court held that this provision violated the Eighth Amendment's ban on cruel and unusual punishment.

Kent v. Dulles, 357 U.S. 116, June 16, 1958

The Court overturned the State Department's policy of denying passports to members of the Communist Party. William O. Douglas's opinion held that the Department lacked congressional authorization for this policy and also declared that the Fifth Amendment's due process clause protected the right to travel.

NAACP v. Alabama, 357 U.S. 449, June 30, 1958

A unanimous Court reversed a $100,000 fine imposed by the state of Alabama on the NAACP for refusal to turn over its membership lists. The Court explicitly held that the right of free association was protected by the Constitution and ruled that Alabama had shown no compelling reason to justify its infringement on NAACP members' right of association.

Cooper v. Aaron, 358 U.S. 1, September 12, 1959

The Court denied a request from the Little Rock, Ark., school board for a delay in its school desegregation plan. The Court reaffirmed its decision in *Brown v. Board of Education* (1954) and said integration must proceed despite opposition from state and local officials and public hostility.

Uphaus v. Wyman, 360 U.S. 72, June 8, 1959

Retreating from the position taken in *Sweezy v. New Hampshire* (1957), a five-man majority sustained the contempt conviction of a minister who had refused to turn over to New Hampshire's Attorney General the guest list of a summer camp suspected of being a Communist meeting place. Justice Tom Clark's opinion for the Court held that the state's interest in discovering the presence of possible subversive individuals outweighed any rights of privacy and association involved.

Barenblatt v. U.S., 360 U.S. 109, June 8, 1959

In a companion case to *Uphaus,* the Court by a five-to-four vote sustained the contempt-of-Congress conviction of a professor who refused to answer questions before a House Un-American Activities subcommittee about his Communist Party membership and activities. Justice John Marshall Harlan's opinion limited the Court's holding in *Watkins v. U.S.* (1957). The Court ruled that the requirement of pertinency had been met in this instance, and denied that the subcommittee's inquiry violated the witness's First Amendment rights.

Greene v. McElroy, 360 U.S. 474, June 29, 1959

An eight-man majority invalidated a Defense Department industrial security program that denied individuals the right to confront and cross-examine witnesses against them on the ground that neither Congress nor the President had authorized the use of this procedure.

Thompson v. City of Louisville, 362 U.S. 199, March 21, 1960

The Court held it a denial of due process of law to convict an individual of loitering and disorderly conduct when there was no evidence to support the charge.

Communist Party v. Subversive Activities Control Board, 367 U.S. 1, June 5, 1961

By a five-to-four vote, the Court sustained the requirement in the Subversive Activities Control Act of 1950 that Communist-action organizations register with the government.

Scales v. U.S., 367 U.S. 203, June 5, 1961

The Court upheld the provision in the 1940 Smith Act making it a crime to belong to an organization advocating violent overthrow of the government. However, Justice John Marshall Harlan's opinion for the Court ruled that the act made only active, not passive, membership in such an organization illegal. This interpretation made future prosecutions under this provision extremely difficult.

Mapp v. Ohio, 367 U.S. 643, June 19, 1961

The Court overruled *Wolf v. Colorado* (1949) to hold that illegally seized evidence could not be admitted in state courts.

Baker v. Carr, 369 U.S. 186, March 26, 1962

By a six-to-two vote, the Court overturned *Colegrove v. Green* (1946) and held that federal courts could hear cases challenging state legislative apportionment.

Engel v. Vitale, 370 U.S. 421, June 25, 1962

This controversial decision held that the use of an official, nondenominational prayer in New York State's public schools violated the First Amendment's ban on establishment of religion.

Robinson v. California, 370 U.S. 660, June 25, 1962

The Court invalidated a California law that made drug addiction in and of itself, without any sale or possession of drugs, a crime. It ruled that the law violated the Eighth Amendment's ban on cruel and unusual punishment which, it held, applied to the states.

Gideon v. Wainwright, 372 U.S. 335, March 18, 1963

The Court unanimously reversed *Betts v. Brady,* 316 U.S. 455 (1942) and held that the states must supply free counsel to any indigent charged with a felony.

Abington School District v. Schempp, 374 U.S. 203, June 17, 1963

By an eight-to-one vote, the Court held that state and local rules requiring recitation of the Lord's Prayer and Bible-reading in public schools violated the First Amendment.

Wesberry v. Sanders 376 U.S. 1, February 17, 1964

The Court extended the doctrine of *Baker v. Carr* (1962) and held that federal courts could hear cases involving congressional districting. It then established a "one-man, one-vote" standard for congressional apportionment by ruling that Article I of the Constitution required congressional districts to be as equal in population as possible.

New York Times Co. v. Sullivan, 376 U.S. 254, March 9, 1964

In a major First Amendment ruling, the Court held that a public official could not recover damages for a defamatory falsehood relating to his official conduct unless he proved that the statement was made with "actual malice." The decision, based on the guarantees of free speech and free press, was the first to put constitutional limits on the law of libel.

Reynolds v. Sims, 377 U.S. 533, June 15, 1964

In this and five companion cases, Chief Justice Earl Warren's opinions for the Court held that the equal protection clause required both houses of state legislatures to be apportioned on an equal population basis. This establishment of a "one-man, one-vote" standard led to legislative redistricting in nearly every state in the country.

Malloy v. Hogan, 378 U.S. 1, June 15, 1964

Reversing *Adamson v. California* (1947), the Court held the Fifth Amendment's privilege against self-incrimination applicable to the states. It also ruled that the same standards used in federal tribunals for determining whether a likelihood of incrimination had been shown should be used in state tribunals.

Murphy v. Waterfront Commission of New York Harbor, 378 U.S. 52, June 15, 1964

Decided on the same day as *Malloy,* this case held that when an individual was compelled to testify in either a state or federal proceeding under a grant of immunity, the Fifth Amendment barred the other jurisdiction from using his testimony to prosecute him for a crime.

Bell v. Maryland, 378 U.S. 226, June 22, 1964

In this and several companion cases, the Court reversed or vacated and remanded the convictions of sit-in demonstrators for trespass. It avoided deciding the key constitutional issue of whether the state's use of its trespass laws to enforce a private business's discriminatory practices violated the equal protection clause. However, several Justices expressed their views on this question in multiple concurring and dissenting opinions.

Escobedo v. Illinois, 378 U.S. 478, June 22, 1964

A five-man majority ruled that incriminating statements obtained from a state criminal defendant who was not told of his right to silence and was not allowed to consult his attorney during police questioning were inadmissible at trial because the defendant's right to counsel had been violated. The decision extended the right to counsel to the investigation stage of state criminal cases.

Aptheker v. Secretary of State, 378 U.S. 500, June 22, 1964

The Court overturned a provision in the 1950 Subversive Activities Control Act making it a crime for members of the Communist Party to apply for or use a passport as an unconstitutional curtailment of the right to travel.

Heart of Atlanta Motel v. U.S., 379 U.S. 241; **Katzenbach v. McClung,** 379 U.S. 294, December 14, 1964

The Court unanimously upheld the constitutionality of the public accommodations section of the 1964 Civil Rights Act.

Hamm v. City of Rock Hill, 379 U.S. 306, December 14, 1964

By a five-to-four vote, the Court held that the passage of the 1964 Civil Rights Act in effect abated the convictions of sit-in demonstrators who had been trying to desegregate the business places covered by the new law prior to its enactment.

Freedman v. Maryland, 380 U.S. 51, March 1, 1965

The Court invalidated Maryland's film censorship system because it provided inadequate safeguards against the suppression of films protected by the First Amendment. The Justices set out strict procedural guidelines for a constitutionally acceptable film censorship system.

U.S. v. Brown 381 U.S. 437, June 7, 1965

In a five-to-four decision, the Court overturned a provision in the 1959 Labor-Management Reporting and Disclosure Act barring members of the Communist Party from serving as labor union officials as a violation of the constitutional ban on bills of attainder.

Griswold v. Connecticut, 381 U.S. 479, June 7, 1965

The Court upset a state law forbidding the use of contraceptives as an unconstitutional invasion of a right to marital privacy. The case was notable for the multiple opinions discussing the scope of the due process clause and the Bill of Rights.

Estes v. Texas, 381 U.S. 532, June 7, 1965

The Court ruled that the televising of a criminal trial had denied the defendant, financier Billie Sol Estes, due process of law.

Albertson v. Subversive Activities Control Board, 382 U.S. 70, November 15, 1965

In a unanimous ruling, the Court held the provision in the 1950 Subversive Activities Control Act requiring individual members of Communist-action organizations to register with the government a violation of the Fifth Amendment. Admission of membership in such organizations, the Court pointed out, could subject the individuals to prosecution under other federal laws such as the Smith Act.

South Carolina v. Katzenbach, 383 U.S. 301, March 7, 1966

Taking a broad view of congressional power under the 15th Amendment, the Court upheld the major provisions of the 1965 Voting Rights Act.

Memoirs v. Massachusetts, 383 U.S. 413; **Ginzburg v. U.S.,** 383 U.S. 463; **Mishkin v. New York,** 383 U.S. 502, March 21, 1966

Justice William Brennan's opinions of the Court in two of these cases narrowed the basic test of obscenity established in *Roth v. U.S.* (1957). In *Ginzburg,* however, he ruled that pandering in the sale and publicity of a work could be used to determine obscenity.

Harper v. Virginia State Board of Elections, 383 U.S. 663, March 24, 1966

The Court invalidated a poll tax for state elections on the ground that it denied equal protection to make affluence a qualification for voting.

Sheppard v. Maxwell, 384 U.S. 333, June 6, 1966

The Court ruled that massive publicity and the disruptive behavior of reporters in the courtroom had denied the defendant a fair trial. The Court's opinion suggested several ways in which a trial judge could limit the prejudicial effect of extensive publicity.

Miranda v. Arizona, 384 U.S. 436, June 13, 1966

In an opinion by Chief Justice Earl Warren, a five-man majority held that the Fifth Amendment's privilege against self-incrimination applied to custodial police interrogations of a suspect. To secure the privilege, the Court said, police must follow certain procedural safeguards in dealing with an arrested suspect. These included warning him of his right to silence, his right to counsel and his right to a court-appointed attorney, if indigent.

Katzenbach v. Morgan, 384 U.S. 641, June 13, 1966

The Court upheld a section of the 1965

Voting Rights Act designed to guarantee the right to vote to non-English speaking Puerto Ricans as a proper exercise of congressional power under the 14th Amendment.

Adderley v. Florida, 385 U.S. 39, November 14, 1966

For the first time, the Court upheld the convictions of participants in a peaceful civil rights demonstration. By a five-to-four vote, it sustained the trespass convictions of demonstrators who had gathered outside a Florida jail to protest the arrest of fellow demonstrators and who had refused to disperse when so ordered.

Hoffa v. U.S., 385 U.S. 293, December 12, 1966

The Court upheld the constitutionality of the government's use of an informer in a criminal investigation.

Time, Inc. v. Hill, 385 U.S. 374, January 9, 1967

The Court extended the "actual malice" rule of *New York Times Co. v. Sullivan* (1964) to invasion of privacy suits against the press.

Keyishian v. Board of Regents, 385 U.S. 589, January 23, 1967

Reversing *Adler v. Board of Education* (1952), a five-man majority ruled that New York State's loyalty laws for public school teachers were unconstitutionally vague.

In re Gault, 387 U.S. 1, May 15, 1967

The Court extended to juvenile court proceedings many of the constitutional safeguards required in adult trials including the right to counsel, the right of confrontation and the privilege against self-incrimination.

Afroyim v. Rusk, 387 U.S. 253, May 29, 1967

A five-man majority overruled *Perez v. Brownell* (1958) and held unconstitutional a federal law providing for loss of citizenship for voting in a foreign election. Justice Hugo Black's opinion of the Court asserted that Congress had no power to remove an individual's citizenship involuntarily.

Reitman v. Mulkey, 387 U.S. 369, May 29, 1967

The Court invalidated a California constitutional amendment that nullified existing "fair housing" legislation and barred the state and municipalities from adopting future laws against racial discrimination in the sale or rental of housing.

Berger v. New York, 388 U.S. 41, June 12, 1967

This decision held that the use of an electronic device to record conversations constituted a search within the meaning of the Fourth Amendment. The Court overturned a permissive state eavesdropping law because it did not include sufficient safeguards to prevent violations of the amendmant.

U.S. v. Wade, 388 U.S. 218; **Gilbert v. California,** 388 U.S. 263, June 12, 1967

In two controversial rulings, the Court held that the right to counsel extended to a police lineup and ruled inadmissible at trial any identifications or testimony based on a lineup conducted in the absence of a defendant's counsel.

Katz v. U.S., 389 U.S. 347, December 18, 1967

The Court ruled that the Fourth Amendment protected people, not places. Therefore, all electronic surveillance was subject to the Fourth Amendment, regardless of whether it involved a physical trespass. The Court also held that police must secure judicial warrants before using electronic eavesdropping devices.

Avery v. Midland County, 390 U.S. 474, April 1, 1968

The Court extended the one-man, one-vote rule of apportionment to elections for local political units having general governmental powers over a geographic area.

Levy v. Louisiana, 391 U.S. 68, May 20, 1968

By a six-to-three vote, the Court extended the guarantee of equal protection to illegitimate children. It overturned a state law that denied illegitimates certain rights granted to legitimate offspring.

Duncan v. Louisiana, 391 U.S. 145, May 20, 1968

This case held the Sixth Amendment's right to trial by jury applicable to the states.

Green v. County School Board, 391 U.S. 430, May 27, 1968

In a unanimous ruling, the Court invalidated "freedom of choice" plans for school desegregation when they did not actually eliminate the vestiges of racial discrimination and result in a unitary school system.

Terry v. Ohio, 392 U.S. 1, June 10, 1968

An eight-man majority upheld the right of police to stop and frisk individuals for weapons, without a warrant, when the action seemed necessary for the safety of the police and others present.

Jones v. Mayer, 392 U.S. 409, June 17, 1968

The Court held that the 1866 Civil Rights Act prohibited private racial discrimination in the sale or rental of housing and other property. It then sustained the constitutionality of the law as construed under the 13th Amendment.

Tinker v. Des Moines School District, 393 U.S. 503, February 24, 1969

By a seven-to-two vote, the Court held that the First Amendment guaranteed public school students a right to peaceful, nondisruptive political expression, such as wearing black armbands to protest the Vietnam war.

Shapiro v. Thompson, 394 U.S. 618, April 21, 1969

A six-man majority overturned state residency requirements for welfare as a denial of equal protection and an unconstitutional restriction on the right to travel.

Sniadach v. Family Finance Corp., 395 U.S. 337, June 9, 1969

The Court invalidated state laws allowing garnishment of a debtor's wages prior to any hearing as a denial of property without due process of law.

Powell v. McCormack, 395 U.S. 486, June 16, 1969

An eight member majority ruled that the House of Representatives had unconstitutionally excluded Adam Clayton Powell (D, N.Y.) from membership in 1967. The Court held that the House could exclude members only for failure to meet the age, citizenship and residency requirements set forth in the Constitution.

Chimel v. California, 395 U.S. 752, June 23, 1969

By a six-to-two vote, the Court overturned *U.S. v. Rabinowitz* (1950) and limited the scope of the warrantless search that police could make incident to a valid arrest to the suspect's person and the area within his immediate control.

Benton v. Maryland, 395 U.S. 784, June 23, 1969

A six-man majority held that the Fifth Amendment's guarantee against double jeopardy applied to the states.

Alexander v. Holmes County Board of Education, 396 U.S. 19, October 29, 1969

In a unanimous *per curiam* ruling, the Court held that the "all deliberate speed" standard for school desegregation established in *Brown v. Board of Education* (1955) was no longer constitutionally permissible. It declared that every school district must end dual school systems "at once" and operate only unitary school systems "now and hereafter."

Goldberg v. Kelly, 397 U.S. 254, March 23, 1970

This decision held that the guarantee of due process required states to give welfare recipients notice and a hearing before termination of welfare benefits.

Dandridge v. Williams, 397 U.S. 471, April 6, 1970

By a five-to-three vote, the Court held that a state ceiling on the amount of welfare benefits one family could receive did not violate the Social Security law or the constitutional guarantee of equal protection.

Brady v. U.S., 397 U.S. 742; **Parker v. North Carolina,** 397 U.S. 790, May 4, 1970

The Court sustained guilty pleas entered by defendants against claims that the pleas had been improperly induced. These cases removed doubts about the constitutionality of plea bargaining.

Williams v. Florida, 399 U.S. 70, June 22, 1970

The Court upheld the constitutionality of a jury of six rather than 12 members in a state court.

Oregon v. Mitchell, 400 U.S. 112, December 21, 1970

Ruling on 1970 amendments to the Voting Rights Act, the Court upheld a congressional ban on the use of literacy tests as a qualification for voting and a limitation on state residency requirements for voting in presidential elections to a maximum of 30 days. With Justice Hugo Black casting the deciding vote, the Court also upheld, five to four, a provision lowering the voting age to 18 in federal elections, but overturned, five to four, a similar provision for state and local elections.

Harris v. New York, 401 U.S. 222, February 24, 1971

In a modification of *Miranda v. Arizona* (1966), a five-man majority held that a confession obtained by police in violation of *Miranda,* which would ordinarily be inadmissible in court, could be introduced at trial to impeach the defendant's credibility as a witness.

Griggs v. Duke Power Co., 401 U.S. 424, March 8, 1971

This decision held that Title VII of the 1964 Civil Rights Act, which prohibited racial discrimination in employment, barred the use of job tests that disproportionately disqualified blacks and were not significantly related to successful job performance.

Swann v. Charlotte-Mecklenburg Board of Education, 402 U.S. 1, April 20, 1971

A unanimous Court held that a federal district judge could make limited use of racial quotas, rezone school attendance districts and order busing of students in order to eliminate state-imposed segregation in Southern schools.

Palmer v. Thompson, 403 U.S. 217, June 14, 1971

In a five-to-four decision, the Court ruled that officials in Jackson, Miss., had not denied equal protection when they closed all public swimming pools rather than desegregate them.

Bivens v. Six Unknown Named Agents, 403 U.S. 388, June 21, 1971

The Court held that a violation of the Fourth Amendment by a federal agent acting under covor of his authority gave rise to a cause of action for damages by the person whose rights were violated. The case was notable for the attack on the exclusionary rule found in the dissenting opinion.

Lemon v. Kurtzman, 403 U.S. 602; **Tilton v. Richardson,** 403 U.S. 672, June 28, 1971

The Court established a three-pronged test to determine whether government aid to parochial education was constitutional. In *Lemon* it invalidated several state aid programs because they would result in "excessive government entanglement with religion" in violation of the First Amendment. However, in *Tilton,* the Court found permissible a federal program of construction grants to religious colleges and universities, so long as the buildings were used solely for secular educational purposes.

New York Times Co. v. U.S., 403 U.S. 713, June 30, 1971

By a six-to-three vote, the Court denied the government's request for an injunction to halt newspaper publication of the *Pentagon Papers,* a classified government study of U.S. involvement in Vietnam.

Reed v. Reed, 404 U.S. 71, November 22, 1971

For the first time, the Court applied the 14th Amendment's guarantee of equal protection to women. It overturned a state law favoring men over women in the administration of estates as unconstitutional sex discrimination.

Dunn v. Blumstein, 405 U.S. 330, March 21, 1972

The Court invalidated as a denial of equal protection a voting requirement that an individual be a resident of the state for one year and of a county for three months prior to an election.

Johnson v. Louisiana, 406 U.S. 356; Apodaca v. Oregon, 406 U.S. 404, May 22, 1972

A five-man majority sanctioned non-unanimous jury verdicts in state criminal trials.

Kastigar v. U.S., 406 U.S. 441, May 22, 1972

This decision held that the government only had to give a witness a limited grant of immunity from prosecution in order to compel him to give up his Fifth Amendment privilege against self-incrimination and testify. The Court held that "use immunity," under which a witness's testimony and any leads developed from it may not be used against him, satisfied the Fifth Amendment. The government did not have to grant the broader "transactional immunity," which guaranteed a witness complete immunity from prosecution for crimes related to his testimony, even from independently developed evidence.

Argersinger v. Hamlin, 407 U.S. 25, June 12, 1972

The Court unanimously extended the right to counsel to misdemeanor cases and held that an indigent defendant could not be imprisoned for any offense, however petty, unless afforded free counsel.

Moose Lodge No. 107 v. Irvis, 407 U.S. 163, June 12, 1972

The Court refused to expand the concept of "state action." It held that the grant of a state liquor license to a private club did not make the club's refusal to serve black guests state action in violation of the 14th Amendment.

U.S. v. U.S. District Court, 407 U.S. 297, June 19, 1972

The Court ruled that the President had no authority to use electronic surveillance in domestic security cases without a warrant.

Furman v. Georgia, 408 U.S. 238, June 29, 1972

In a five-to-four decision, the Court held that the death penalty as then imposed violated the Eighth Amendment's ban on cruel and unusual punishment.

Morrissey v. Brewer, 408 U.S. 471, June 29, 1972

The Court held that due process guaranteed parolees the right to a hearing before revocation of their parole.

Branzburg v. Hayes, 408 U.S. 665, June 29, 1972

The Court ruled, five to four, that journalists did not have a First Amendment right to refuse to testify before a grand jury about information obtained from confidential sources.

Roe v. Wade, 410 U.S. 113; Doe v. Bolton, 410 U.S. 179, January 22, 1973

By a seven-to-two vote, the Court held that state laws prohibiting abortions during the first six months of pregnancy unconstitutionally violated women's rights to privacy.

Mahan v. Howell, 410 U.S. 315, February 21, 1973

The Court for the first time made a distinction between the standards for state legislative and congressional districting. A majority ruled that the Constitution permitted greater flexibility in state legislative apportionment and that the state could deviate from a strict one-man, one-vote standard in order to achieve a rational policy goal.

San Antonio Independent School District v. Rodriguez, 411 U.S. 1, March 21, 1973

A five-man majority decided that school financing schemes based on property taxes did not violate the equal protection guarantee.

Frontiero v. Richardson, 411 U.S. 677, May 14, 1973

The Court held unconstitutional a distinction made between male and female members of the armed forces in the award of dependency benefits, but it stopped short of declaring classifications based on sex inherently "suspect" and therefore subject to strict judicial scrutiny.

Miller v. California, 413 U.S. 15, June 21, 1973

In a five-to-four decision, the Court reaffirmed the principle of *Roth v. U.S.* (1957) that obscenity was not protected by the First Amendment. It defined as obscene works those that, "taken as a whole, appeal to the prurient interest in sex, which portray sexual conduct in a patently offensive way and which, taken as a whole, do not have serious literary, artistic, political, or scientific value." The majority also held that local, rather than national, community standards were to be applied in deciding prurience.

U.S. v. Robinson, 414 U.S. 218, December 11, 1973

By a six-to-three vote, the Court upheld the authority of police to make a full personal search following a lawful custodial arrest, even for a minor offense such as a traffic violation.

U.S. v. Calandra, 414 U.S. 338, January 8, 1974

The Court ruled that grand juries can use illegally seized evidence as the basis for questioning witnesses, even though the exclusionary rule barred the use of such evidence in federal and state trials.

Geduldig v. Aiello, 417 U.S. 484, June 17, 1974

In a six-to-three decision, the Court held that a California job disability insurance program that excluded pregnancy from coverage did not deny women equal protection of the law.

Gertz v. Robert Welch, Inc., 418 U.S. 323, June 25, 1974

The Court held that private individuals could recover actual, though not punitive, damages in defamation suits against the news media if they proved negligence by the media. Unlike public officials and public figures, private individuals did not have to prove "actual malice" by the press.

U.S. v. Nixon, 418 U.S. 683, July 24, 1974

In a celebrated ruling, the Court ordered President Richard Nixon to surrender the tapes and documents subpoenaed by the government's special prosecutor for the pending Watergate coverup trial of six former presidential aides. By an eight-to-zero vote, the Court held that a claim of executive privilege had to yield to the demonstrated need for evidence in a pending criminal trial.

Milliken v. Bradley, 418 U.S. 717, July 25, 1974

In a ruling on the validity of metropolitan-wide school desegregation plans, a five-man majority held that such plans, which combined city and suburban school districts, were impermissible when unconstitutional segregation had been proven in only one school district and there was no evidence that school district lines had been drawn in a discriminatory fashion.

Goss v. Lopez, 419 U.S. 565, January 22, 1975

In a five-to-four ruling, the Court held that due process guaranteed public school students a right to notice and an informal hearing prior to a disciplinary suspension.

O'Connor v. Donaldson, 422 U.S. 563, June 26, 1975

This decision held that mental patients could not be confined in institutions against their will if they were not dangerous to others and could live outside the institution on their own.

Buckley v. Valeo, 424 U.S. 1, January 30, 1976

In ruling on the 1974 amendments to the Federal Election Campaign Act, the Court overturned limits placed on a candidate's personal expenditures and on overall campaign expenditures. It upheld, however, ceilings on campaign contributions, disclosure and recordkeeping requirements, and public financing of presidential election campaigns. It also ruled that the Federal Election Commission as then established was unconstitutional.

Paul v. Davis, 424 U.S. 693, March 23, 1976

The Court dismissed a suit brought by an individual who was included in a list of "active shoplifters" that police distributed to area merchants, even though he had not been convicted of any theft. The person might well have a claim for defamation under state law, a majority ruled, but the police's action had not denied him of "liberty" or "property" within the meaning of the due process clause. He therefore had no constitutional claim for the federal courts to hear.

Virginia State Board of Pharmacy v. Virginia Citizens Consumer Council, Inc., 425 U.S. 748, May 24, 1976

The Court invalidated a state law prohibiting the advertisement of prescription drug prices as a violation of the First Amendment. It set aside the older doctrine that commercial speech, such as ads, had no First Amendment protection.

Washington v. Davis, 426 U.S. 229, June 7, 1976

The Court ruled that government action with a racially disproportionate effect did not violate the guarantee of equal protection unless it was discriminatorily motivated.

Runyon v. McCrary, 427 U.S. 160, June 25, 1976

The Court decided that the 1866 Civil Rights Act prohibited racial discrimination by private nonsectarian schools.

Nebraska Press Assn. v. Stuart, 427 U.S. 539, June 30, 1976

The Court unanimously overturned a judicial "gag" order restricting pretrial news coverage of a mass murder case as an unjustified prior restraint on the press.

Gregg v. Georgia, 428 U.S. 153, July 2, 1976

In this and four companion cases, the Court held unconstitutional state laws that made the death penalty mandatory punishment for murder. However, it upheld state laws that established death as one possible penalty for murder and set forth standards to guide the judge or jury in determining the sentence.

General Electric Co. v. Gilbert, 429 U.S. 125, December 7, 1976

A six-man majority ruled that an employer had not violated the ban on sex discrimination in employment in the 1964 Civil Rights Act by excluding pregnancy and childbirth from coverage in a company disability benefits plan.

Bibliography

THE JUSTICES

General works include Leon Friedman and Fred L. Israel, eds., *The Justices of the United States Supreme Court, 1789-1969* (New York, 1969) which contains a biographical article and representative opinions for each justice through 1969. Henry J. Abraham, *Justices and Presidents* (New York, 1974) focuses on the appointment process, and John P. Frank, *The Warren Court* (New York, 1964) has portraits of each of the justices on the Court as of 1964. Alan Westin, ed., *The Supreme Court: Views from Inside* (New York, 1961) is a collection of speeches by several justices discussing the operation and role of the Supreme Court. A similar collection but one that covers a longer period of Court history and also includes speeches on some basic constitutional issues is Alan Westin, ed. *An Autobiography of the Supreme Court: Off-the-Bench Commentary by the Justices* (New York, 1963).

Virginia Van Der Veer Hamilton, *Hugo Black: The Alabama Years* (Baton Rouge, 1972) is a well-researched biography of Black up through his appointment to the Court. Black's own reminiscences of his days in law school may be found in the *Alabama Law Review,* 18 (Fall, 1965), pp. 3-11. William E. Leuchtenburg, "A Klansman Joins the Court: The Appointment of Hugo L. Black," *University of Chicago Law Review,* 41 (Fall, 1973), pp. 1-31, gives a detailed account of Black's appointment to the bench and of the controversy over his past membership in the Ku Klux Klan. Charlotte Williams, *Hugo L. Black* (Baltimore, 1950) and John P. Frank, *Mr. Justice Black* (New York, 1949) are early biographies covering Black's Court career through the 1940s. The most recent biography of Black is Gerald T. Dunne, *Hugo Black and the Judicial Revolution (New York, 1977)* which surveys major trends and cases during Black's years on the Court. An excellent overview of Black's judicial philosophy and his views on different questions of constitutional law may be found in Sylvia Snowiss, "The Legacy of Justice Black," *The Supreme Court Review 1973* , ed. Philip B. Kurland (Chicago, 1974), pp. 187-252. Stephen P. Strickland, ed. *Hugo Black and the Supreme Court* (Indianapolis, 1967) offers a series of essays examining Black's contribution in various fields of law. Howard Ball, *The Vision and the Dream of Justice Hugo L. Black* (University, Ala., 1975) gives particular attention to Black's views on incorporation, due process and the First Amendment. The differences between Justices Black and Felix Frankfurter are discussed in Wallace Mendelson, *Justices Black and Frankfurter: Conflict in the Court*, 2d ed. (Chicago, 1966). The Justice's own statement of his views may be found in Hugo Black, *A Constitutional Faith* (New York, 1969); "The Bill of Rights," *New York University Law Review,* 35 (April, 1960), pp. 865-881; and "Justice Black and First Amendment 'Absolutes': A Public Interview," *New York University Law Review,* 37 (June, 1962), pp. 549-563. Hugo Black, *One Man's Stand for Freedom,* ed. Irving Dilliard (New York, 1963) presents a selection of Black's opinions on civil liberties issues from 1937 to 1961. An interesting and unusual volume is Daniel P. Meador, *Justice Black and His Books* (Charlottesville, 1974), which catalogues Black's personal library and has an introductory essay on the Justice's reading habits and on the books that most influenced him. There are multitudes of law review articles on Black; one useful collection is "Mr. Justice Black; Thirty Years in Retrospect," *UCLA Law Review,* 14 (1967), pp. 397-552, which presents topical articles on Black's role in developing different aspects of the law.

There are no good sources of information on Harry Blackmun. The Senate Judiciary Committe hearings on his nomination provide some hints of his judicial philosophy and include biographical information and a list of all the circuit court cases in which Blackmun participated. See U.S. Congress, Senate, Committee on the Judiciary, *Hearing on the Nomination of Harry A. Blackmun to be a Justice of the Supreme Court,* April 29, 1970, 91st Congress, 2d session (Washington, 1970). Blackmun has made a few speeches, but they are not very revealing of his constitutional views. See "Some Goals for Legal Education," *Ohio Northern Law Review,* 1 (1974), pp. 403-410, and "Thoughts About Ethics," *Emory Law Journal,* 24 (Winter, 1975), pp. 3-20.

Stephen J. Friedman, ed, *An Affair with Freedom: Justice William J. Brennan, Jr.* (New York, 1967) is a collection of opinions and speeches by Brennan during his first decade on the Court. Daniel M. Berman, "Mr. Justice Brennan: A Preliminary Appraisal," *Catholic University of America Law Review,* 7 (January, 1958), pp. 1-15, surveys Brennan's first term on the Court; "Mr. Justice William J. Brennan," *Catholic University of America Law Review,* 11 (January, 1962), pp. 1-39, is a collection of articles discussing Brennan's first five years on the Court with emphasis on his general approach to cases and his views on the Bill of Rights. John J. Regan, "Freedom of the Mind and Justice Brennan," *Catholic Lawyer,* 9 (Autumn, 1963), pp. 269-296 looks at Brennan's stance in cases on religion and on obscenity up to 1963. Several tributes to Brennan and an article on his first 10 years on the Court may be found in "Mr. Justice Brennan," *Harvard Law Review,* 80 (November, 1966), pp. 1-22; this collection is also reprinted in Friedman, ed., *An Affair with Freedom.* "Mr. Justice Brennan," *Rutgers-Camden Law Journal,* 4 (Fall, 1972), pp. 1-102 has essays discussing Brennan's position in several constitutional areas including the First Amendment and reapportionment. Until 1969 Brennan spoke fairly often in public. Speeches that give some insight into his constitutional views include, "The Bill of Rights and the States," *New York University Law Review,* 36 (April 1961), pp. 761-778; "Constitutional Adjudication," *Notre Dame Lawyer,* 40 (August, 1965), pp. 559-569; "The Supreme Court and the Meiklejohn Interpretation of the First Amendment," *Harvard Law Review,* 79 (November, 1965), pp.1-20. For a rare statement from Brennan after 1969, see "State Constitutions and the Protection of Individual Rights," *Harvard Law Review,* 90 (January, 1977), pp. 489-504.

Charles M. Lamb has written two useful articles examining Warren Burger's judicial philosophy and opinions while on the circuit court: "Warren Burger and the Insanity Defense—Judicial Philosophy and Voting Behavior on a U.S. Court of Appeals," *American University Law Review,* 24 (Fall, 1974), pp. 91-128, and "The Making of a Chief Justice: Warren Burger on Criminal

Procedure, 1956-1969," *Cornell Law Review*, 60 (June, 1975), pp. 743-788. Haig Bosmajian, "Chief Justice Warren Burger and Freedom of Speech," *Midwest Quarterly*, 15 (January 1974), pp. 121-140 is a critical survey of Burger's stance on various First Amendment issues through 1973. Nathan Lewin, "A Peculiar Sense of Justice," *Saturday Review*, 4 (May 28, 1977), pp. 15-20 offers a brief, very critical summary of Burger's views in several areas of law. Arthur R. Landever, "Chief Justice Burger and Extra-Case Activism," *Journal of Public Law*, 10 (1971), pp. 523-541 studies Burger's administrative work as Chief Justice and offers a preliminary assessment of it. A more recent article in this area is J.A. Gazell, "Chief Justice Burger's Quest for Judicial Administrative Efficiency," *Detroit College of Law Review*, (Fall, 1977), pp. 455-497. Chief Justice Burger's State of the Judiciary messages have been printed annually in the *American Bar Association Journal* beginning in 1970. Other statements by him recommending various reforms can be found in *American Bar Association Journal*, 56 (April, 1970), pp. 325-328; *American Bar Association Journal*, 57 (May, 1971), pp. 425-430; *Villanova Law Review*, 18 (December, 1972), pp. 165-172; *Fordham Law Review*, 42 (December, 1973), pp. 227-242; and, *American Bar Association Journal*, 62 (June 1976), pp. 727-729. Burger has also given several interviews as Chief Justice; see *U.S. News and World Report*, 69 (December 14, 1970), pp. 32–45; *U.S. News and World Report*, 73 (August 21, 1972), pp. 38-46; *U.S. News and World Report*, 78 (March 31, 1975), pp. 28-32; *The New York Times*, July 4, 1971; *American Bar Association Journal*, 61 (November 1975), pp. 1352-1353.

Harold Burton's views on questions of federal and state power in loyalty-security matters are examined by David N. Atkinson, "American Constitutionalism Under Stress: Mr. Justice Burton's Response to National Security Issues," *Houston Law Review*, 9 (November, 1971), pp. 271-288. *The Occasional Papers of Mr. Justice Burton* , ed. Edward G. Hudon (Brunswick, Me., 1969) is a collection of speeches by the Justice made while he was on the Court.

C.B. Dutton, "Mr. Justice Tom C. Clark," *Indiana Law Journal*, 26 (Winter, 1951), pp. 169-184 surveys Clark's first term on the Court. John P. Frank, "Justice Tom Clark and Judicial Administration," *Texas Law Review*, 46 (November, 1967), pp. 5-56 details Clark's work to improve the administration of justice at the state and federal levels over the decade from 1957 to 1967. During the 1960s and 1970s in particular, Clark was a frequent public speaker and contributor to law reviews in connection with his efforts to improve judicial administration. For a sampling of such statements, see "The Present State of Trial Advocacy," *DePaul Law Review*, 12 (Spring-Summer, 1963), pp. 185-196; "The Sixties—A Historic Decade in Judicial Improvement," *Brooklyn Law Review*, 36 (Spring, 1970), pp. 331-338; "Objectives for American Justice," *Journal of Public Law*, 19 (1970), pp. 169-178; 'The American Bar Association Standards for Criminal Justice," *Notre Dame Lawyer*, 47 (February 1972), pp. 429-441; and, "The Federal Judicial Center," *Arizona State Law Journal* (1974), pp. 537-547. Articles by Clark dealing with constitutional cases and issues include "Religion and the Law," *South Carolina Law Review*, 15 (1963), pp. 855-866; "Constitutional Responsibility, Concomitants," *University of Colorado Law Review*, 37 (Fall, 1964), pp. 1-10; "The First Amendment and Minority Rights," *University of Chicago Law Review*, 36 (Winter, 1969), pp. 257-267; "Gideon Revisited," *Arizona Law Review*, 15 (1973), pp. 343-353.

William O. Douglas, *Go East, Young Man* (New York, 1974) is an autobiography up through his appointment to the Supreme Court. John W. Hopkirk, "The Influence of Legal Realism on William O. Douglas," in Gottfried Dietze, ed., *Essays on the American Constitution* (Englewood Cliffs, 1964), pp. 59-76 discusses Douglas's career through his years on the Securities and Exchange Commission with emphasis on his involvement in the legal realist movement. Vern Countryman, who was law clerk to Douglas in 1942-43, has written *Douglas of the Supreme Court: A Selection of his Opinions* (Garden City, 1959) and *The Judicial Record of Justice William O. Douglas* (Cambridge, Mass., 1974). The latter is a topically organized survey of Douglas's views in various fields of law through the 1970 Court term. Countryman has also edited *The Douglas Opinions* (New York, 1977), which is also topically arranged.

There are a great many law review articles on Douglas. Several useful collections may be found in *Yale Law Journal,* 73 (May, 1964), pp. 915-998; *Washington Law Review* , 39 (Spring, 1964), pp. 1-73 and 40 (April, 1965), pp. 10-77; *UCLA Law Review,* 16 (June, 1969), pp. 699-838; *Columbia Law Review,* 74 (April, 1974), pp. 341-411; *Indiana Law Journal,* 51 (Fall, 1975), pp. 1-26; and, *Baylor Law Review,* 28 (Spring 1976), pp. 211-248. Among the more specialized articles, see Leon D. Epstein, "Justice Douglas and Civil Liberties," *Wisconsin Law Review* (January, 1951), pp. 125-157, which offers a useful review of Douglas's early stance in criminal rights and civil liberties cases; Vern Countryman, "Justice Douglas: Expositor of the Bankruptcy Law," *American Bankruptcy Law Journal,* 51 (Spring, 1971), pp. 127-194 and (Summer, 1971), pp. 247-275, on Douglas's bankruptcy opinions; and Tinsley E. Yarbrough, "Justices Black and Douglas: The Judicial Function and the Scope of Constitutional Liberties," *Duke Law Journal* (June, 1973), pp. 441-486, which examines the differences between these two Justices on civil liberties issues during Black's last years on the Court. Wallace Mendelson, "Mr. Justice Douglas and Government by Judiciary," *Journal of Politics,* 38 (November, 1976), pp. 918-937 discusses Douglas's views on jurisdictional questions. See also Bernard Wolfman et al., *Dissent Without Opinion* (Philadelphia, 1973), which analyzes Douglas's record in federal tax cases from 1939 to 1973 and has a useful bibliography.

Douglas himself has written over 25 books and dozens of articles on a variety of topics. See his *Beyond the High Himalayas* (Garden City, 1953) for an example of his travel writings; *A Wilderness Bill of Rights* (Boston, 1965) for an example of his work on conservation and the environment and *International Dissent: Six Steps toward World Peace* (New York, 1971) as an example of his writing on international affairs. For a sampling of some of his articles on legal topics, see "The Bill of Rights is Not Enough," *New York University Law Review,* 38 (April, 1963), pp. 207-242; "Vagrancy and Arrest on Suspicion," *Yale Law Journal,* 70 (November, 1960), pp. 1-14; "The Grand Design of the Constitution," *Gonzaga Law Review,* 7 (Spring, 1972), pp. 239-260; and "The Meaning of Due Process," *Columbia Journal of Law and Social Problems,* 10 (Fall, 1973), pp. 1-14.

Anthony Lewis, *Gideon's Trumpet,* (New York, 1964) tells of Abe Fortas's role in the celebrated case of *Gideon v. Wainwright.* Abe Fortas, *Concerning Dissent and Civil Disobedience* (New York, 1968) presents the Justice's views on questions raised by the civil rights and anti-war movements. Robert Shogan, *A Question of Judgment: The Fortas Case and the Struggle for the Supreme Court* (Indianapolis, 1972) offers a biography of Fortas along with detailed accounts of the flight over his nominations as Chief Justice and of the events surrounding his resignation from the Court.

Liva Baker, *Felix Frankfurter,* (New York, 1969) is the most recent complete biography of the Justice. Helen S. Thomas, *Felix Frankfurter: Scholar on the Bench* (Baltimore, 1960) is an older biography that emphasizes Frankfurter's years on the Court and analyzes his judicial views. Joseph P. Lash, ed., *From the Diaries of Felix Frankfurter* (New York, 1975) has a useful introductory essay by Lash with a good discussion of Frankfurter's career prior to joining the Court. Wallace Mendelson has edited two collections about Frankfurter; *Felix Frankfurter: A Tribute* (New York, 1964) is a set of remembrances and tributes from prominent figures in the law, academia, politics and journalism. The other volume, *Felix Frankfurter:The Judge* (New York, 1964) is a collection of essays on Frankfurter's views and contributions in several different areas of the law. Wallace Mendelson *Justices Black and Frankfurter: Conflict in the Court,* 2d ed (Chicago, 1966) analyzes the contrasting judicial views of the two men. Among the law review articles on Frankfurter, see Louis L. Jaffe, "The Judicial Universe of Mr. Justice Frankfurter," *Harvard Law Review* 62 (January, 1949), pp. 357-412; Wallace Mendelson, "Mr. Justice Frankfurter and the Process of Judicial Review," *University of Pennsylvania Law Review,* 103 (December, 1954), pp. 295-320; the collection of articles in "Mr. Justice Frankfurter,"*Yale Law Journal,* 67 (Secember, 1957), pp. 179-323; and Joseph L. Rauh, Jr., "Felix Frankfurter: Civil Libertarian," *Harvard Civil Rights-Civil Liberties Law Review,* 11 (Summer, 1976), pp. 496-520.

Felix Frankfurter Reminisces (New York, 1960) contains interviews with Frankfurter by Harlan B. Phillips, mostly concerning Frankfurter's career prior to his appointment to the Court. There are several collections of articles and addresses by Frankfurter. Philip Elman, ed., *Of Law and Men* (New York, 1956) covers the years from 1939 to 1956; Philip B. Kurland, ed., *Of Law and Life and Other Things That Matter* (Cambridge, Mass., 1965) covers 1956 to 1963. Kurland has also edited *Felix Frankfurter on the Supreme Court: Extrajudicial Essays on the Court and the Constitution* (Cambridge, Mass., 1970), a collection of papers and speeches by Frankfurter. In addition, he published *Mr. Justice Frankfurter and the Consitution* (Chicago, 1971) which contains topically organized selections from Frankfurter's Court opinions with commentary by Kurland.

On Arthur Goldberg's career as a labor attorney, see his *AFL-CIO: Labor United* (New York, 1956). Daniel P. Moynihan, ed., *The Defenses of Freedom: The Public Papers of Arthur J. Goldberg* (New York, 1966) includes speeches made by Goldberg while Secretary of Labor, Supreme Court justice and U.N. ambassador as well as a collection of his judicial opinions. John F. Marvin, "A Constitutional Prejudice for Liberty and Equality: Mr. Justice Arthur Goldberg," *University of Missouri at Kansas City Law Review,* 34 (Summer, 1966), pp. 289-324 offers a good survey of Goldberg's work on the Court. Ira H. Carmen, "One Civil Libertarian Among Many: The Case of Mr. Justice Goldberg," *Michigan Law Review,* 65 (December, 1966), pp. 301-336 analyzes Goldberg's libertarianism by comparing his views with those of other liberals on the Warren Court. For an expression of Goldberg's own views, see "Equality and Governmental Action," *New York University Law Review,* 39 (April, 1964), pp. 205-227, and his *Equal Justice: The Warren Era of the Supreme Court* (Evanston, Ill., 1971) which discusses and defends the Warren Court's criminal justice and civil liberties rulings. In the years after his resignation from the bench, Goldberg wrote several articles attacking the constitutionality of the death penalty; see "Declaring the Death Penalty Unconstitutional," *Harvard Law Review,* 83 (June, 1970), pp. 1773-1819 (with Alan M. Dershowitz), and "The Death Penalty and the Supreme Court," *Arizona Law Review,* 15 (1973), pp. 355-368.

On John Marshall Harlan, see Norman Dorsen, "The Second Mr. Justice Harlan," *New York University Law Review,* 44 (April, 1969), pp. 249-271, an adaptation of Dorsen's chapter on Harlan in Friedman and Israel, eds., *The*

Justices of the United States Supreme Court, noted above. Nathan Lewin, "Justice Harlan," *American Bar Association Journal,* 58 (June, 1972), pp. 579-583 is a brief summary of Harlan's career and judicial philosophy. "Mr. Justice Harlan," *Harvard Law Review,* 85 (December, 1971), pp. 369-391 contains a series of tributes and remembrances by friends and colleagues from the bench and the bar. J. Harvie Wilkinson III, "Justice John Marshall Harlan and the Values of Federalsim," *Virginia Law Review,* 57 (October, 1971), pp. 1185-1221 analyzes Harlan's views on federalism and separation of powers and the values underlying them. John M. Harlan, *The Evolution of a Judicial Philosophy,* ed. David L. Shapiro (Cambridge, Mass., 1969) is a selection of some of Harlan's opinions and off-the-bench statements. Other expressions of Harlan's legal views can be found in "Keeping the Judicial Function in Balance," *American Bar Association Journal,* 49 (October, 1963), pp. 943-945, and "The Bill of Rights and the Constitution," *American Bar Association Journal,* 50 (October, 1964); pp. 918-920.

Eugene C. Gerhart, *America's Advocate: Robert H. Jackson* (Indianapolis, 1958) is an admiring biography of Jackson with considerable emphasis on his non-judicial career. Gerhart supplemented the biography with *Lawyer's Judge: Supreme Court Justice Jackson* (Albany, 1961), a brief analysis of Jackson's Court opinions. G. Edward White has a chapter on Jackson's jurisprudence in *The American Judicial Tradition* (New York, 1976). Charles S. Desmond *et al, Mr. Justice Jackson* (New York, 1969) presents four lectures of varying quality on aspects of Jackson's life and legal views. Gordon Dean, "Mr. Justice Jackson: His Contribution at Nuremberg," *American Bar Association Journal,* 41 (October, 1955), pp. 912-915 discusses Jackson's role in the war crimes trials. Two good collections of essays on Jackson can be found in *Columbia Law Review,* 55 (April, 1955), pp. 435-525 and *Stanford Law Review,* 8 (December, 1955), pp. 1-76. Louis L. Jaffe, "Mr. Justice Jackson," *Harvard Law Review,* 68 (April, 1955), pp. 940-998 is a very good analysis of Jackson's opinions in economic and civil liberties cases and his judicial philosophy. Walter F. Murphy, "Mr. Justice Jackson, Free Speech and the Judicial Function," *Vanderbilt Law Review,* 12 (October, 1959), pp. 1019-1046 studies the Justice's First Amendment views in different contexts. Philip B. Kurland, "Justice Robert H. Jackson—Impact on Civil Rights and Civil Liberties," *University of Illinois Law Forum* (1977), pp. 551-576 discusses Jackson's views on various civil liberties questions. Robert H. Jackson, *Dispassionate Justice,* ed., Glendon Schubert (Indianapolis, 1969) offers a selection from Jackson's opinions with commentary. Jackson's own writings on the Court and the Constitution include *The Struggle for Judicial Supremacy* (New York, 1941); *Full Faith and Credit: The Lawyer's Clause of the Constitution* (New York, 1945); and, *The Supreme Court in the American System of Government* (Cambridge, Mass., 1955).

Randall W. Bland, *Private Pressure on Public Law: The Legal Career of Justice Thurgood Marshall* (Port Washington, N.Y., 1973) is the most complete biography of Marshall to date. Much of the chapter from this book on Marshall's Court career is also printed in "Justice Thurgood Marshall: An Analysis of His First Years on the Court, 1967-1971," *North Carolina Central Law Journal,* 4 (Spring, 1973), pp. 183-202. Richard Kluger, *Simple Justice* (New York, 1976) has much excellent material on Marshall up through the mid-1950s. Ronald R. Davenport, "The Second Justice Marshall," *Duquesne Law Review,* 7 (Fall, 1968), pp. 44-60 examines Marshall's first term on the Court. Justice Marshall has occasionally spoken out on the need for continuing enforcement of the 14th Amendment's guarantees and on the need for encouragement of group legal action and public interest law. For a sampling, see "The Continuing Challenge of the 14th Amendment," *Wisconsin Law Review* (1968), pp. 979-987; "Group Action in the Pursuit of Justice," *New York University Law Review*, 44 (October, 1969), pp. 661-672; and, "Financing Public Interest Law Practice," *American Bar Association Journal*, 61 (December, 1975), pp. 1487-1491.

George D. Braden, "Mr. Justice Minton and The Truman Bloc," *Indiana Law Journal*, 26 (Winter, 1951) pp. 153-168 analyzes Sherman Minton's first term on the Court and his position on civil liberties questions. Henry L. Wallace, "Mr. Justice Minton—Hoosier Justice on the Supreme Court," *Indiana Law Journal*, 34 (Winter, 1959), pp. 145-205 and (Spring, 1959), pp. 377-424, presents a detailed survey of Minton's views in all major areas of law while on the Court. Since 1974 David N. Atkinson has written a series of articles on Minton drawing on manuscript sources and interviews with Minton's law clerks and fellow justices. See "Justice Sherman Minton and the Balance of Liberty," *Indiana Law Journal*, 50 (Fall, 1974), pp. 34-59 on Minton's position in loyalty-security cases. "Justice Sherman Minton and Behavior Patterns Inside the Supreme Court," *Northwestern University Law Review*, 69 (November-December, 1974), pp. 716-738 discusses intra-Court relationships while Minton was on the bench and "Opinion-Writing on the Supreme Court, 1949-1956: The Views of Justice Sherman Minton," *Temple Law Quarterly*, 49 (Fall, 1975), pp. 105-118, deals with Minton's relationship with Chief Justices Vinson and Warren and his approach to the writing of opinions. "From New Deal Liberal to Supreme Court Conservative: The Metamorphosis of Justice Sherman Minton," *Washington University Law Quarterly* (1975), pp. 361-394 concentrates on Minton's views on the proper role of the Supreme Court, how this view developed and how it influenced the Justice's stance in various cases. "Justice Sherman Minton and the Protection of Minority Rights," *Washington and Lee Law Review*, 34 (Winter, 1977), pp. 97-117 details Minton's willingness to overturn discriminatory action by government, but not by private parties.

J. Woodford Howard, Jr., *Mr. Justice Murphy: A Political Biography* (Princeton, 1968) is now the primary biography of Frank Murphy, and it deals with his political and judicial careers. Sidney Fine, *Frank Murphy: The Detroit Years* (Ann Arbor, 1975) is a well-researched study of Murphy through 1933 and the first in a projected three volume series on Murphy which will include a volume on his Court years. Harold Norris, *Mr. Justice Murphy and the Bill of Rights* (Dobbs Ferry, 1965) presents selections from Murphy's speeches as Attorney General and from his opinions as a justice along with several articles on his Court career. Sidney Fine has written several articles on aspects of Murphy's judicial career; see "Mr. Justice Murphy and the Hirabayashi Case," *Pacific Historical Review*, 33 (May, 1964), pp. 195-209; "Frank Murphy, the Thornhill Decision and Picketing as Free Speech," *Labor History*, 6 (1965), pp. 99-120; and "Mr. Justice Murphy in World War II, " *Journal of American History, 53 (June, 1966), pp. 90-106. John P. Roche*, "Mr. Justice Murphy," in Allison Dunham and Philip B. Kurland, eds., *Mr. Justice*, rev. and enl. (Chicago, 1964), pp. 281-317 presents an overview of the Justice's career. There are a number of useful law review articles which also survey Murphy's judicial career. See Vincent M. Barnett, Jr., "Mr. Justice Murphy, Civil Liberties and the Holmes Tradition," *Cornell Law Quarterly*, 32 (November, 1946), pp. 177-221; John P. Frank, "Justice Murphy: The Goals Attempted," *Yale Law Journal*, 59 (December, 1949), pp. 1-26; Charles Fahy, "The Judicial Philosophy of Mr. Justice Murphy," *Yale Law Journal*, 60 (May, 1951), pp. 812-820; and, Eugene Gressman, "Mr. Justice Murphy—A Preliminary Appraisal," *Columbia Law*

Review, 50 (January, 1950), pp. 29-47. *The Michigan Law Review,* 48 (April, 1950), pp. 737-810 has several tributes to and remembrances of Frank Murphy as well as articles by Thurgood Marshall on Murphy and civil rights and by Archibald Cox on Murphy and labor law. Two later articles look at Murphy's career in light of the criticisms often made of him as a justice; see John P. Roche, "The Utopian Pilgrimage of Mr. Justice Murphy," *Vanderbilt Law Review,* 10 (February, 1957), pp. 369-394; and, Eugene Gressman, "The Controversial Image of Mr. Justice Murphy," *Georgetown Law Journal,* 47 (Summer, 1959), pp. 631-654.

A.E. Dick Howard, "Mr. Justice Powell and the Emerging Nixon Majority," *Michigan Law Review,* 70 (January, 1972), pp. 445-468, written when Powell was named to the Court, studies Powell's background for insights into the type of Justice he might become. Gerald Gunther, "In Search of Judicial Quality on a Changing Court: The Case of Justice Powell," *Stanford Law Review,* 24 (June, 1972), pp. 1001-1035 looks at Powell's first term on the Court and compares his approach to cases to that of Justice John M. Harlan. Larry W. Yackle, "Thoughts on *Rodriguez:* Mr. Justice Powell and the Demise of Equal Protection Analysis in the Supreme Court," *University of Richmond Law Review,* 9 (Winter 1975), pp. 181-247 is narrow in scope, focusing on Powell's approach to equal protection cases, but has some useful information on the Justice's views in other areas of law as well. "Honorable Lewis F. Powell, Jr.: Five Years on the Supreme Court," *University of Richmond Law Review,* 11 (Winter, 1977), pp. 259-430 offers the most complete survey of Powell's work on the Court to date and gives special attention in several articles to his views on jurisdictional matters. One chapter in J. Harvie Wilkinson III, *Serving Justice: A Supreme Court Clerk's View* (New York, 1974) contains a warm portrait of Powell by a former law clerk. The *New York Times,* August 11, 1976, has a revealing interview in which Powell discusses the changes in his life since becoming a Justice and some of the disadvantages as well as the benefits of joining the Court.

On Stanley Reed, see F. William O'Brien, *Justice Reed and the First Amendment* (Washington, 1958) which focuses on cases involving the free exercise of religion and establishment clauses but has useful information on other First Amendment issues and a general discussion of Reed's constitutional views. One portion of the book has been reprinted as "Mr. Justice Reed and Democratic Pluralism," *Georgetown Law Journal,* 45 (Spring, 1957), pp. 364-387.

David L. Shapiro, "Mr. Justice Rehnquist: A Preliminary View," *Harvard Law Review,* 90 (December, 1976), pp. 293-357, is a critical appraisal of William Rehnquist's jurisprudence and craftsmanship. John R. Rydell II, "Mr. Justice Rehnquist and Judicial Self-Restraint," *Hastings Law Journal,* 26 (February, 1975), pp. 875-915 surveys the Justice's votes and opinions in civil liberties and property cases. Warren Weaver, Jr., "Mr. Justice Rehnquist, Dissenting," *New York Times Magazine* (October 13, 1974, pp. 36+ examines the Justice's first two and a half years on the bench and the assessments of him as of that date. Since joining the Court, Rehnquist has given several lectures discussing the Court and constitutional issues. See "Sense and Nonsense About Judicial Ethics," *The Record of the Association of the Bar of the City of New York,* 28 (November, 1973), pp. 694-713; "Is an Expanded Right of Privacy Consistent with Fair and Effective Law Enforcement?" *University of Kansas Law Review,* 23 (Fall, 1974), pp. 1-22; "The Notion of a Living Constitution," *Texas Law Review,* 54 (May 1976), pp. 693-706; "Sunshine in the Third Branch," *Washburn Law Journal,* 16 (Spring, 1977), pp. 559-570; and, "The

First Amendment: Freedom, Philosophy and the Law," *Gonzaga Law Review,* 12 (Fall, 1976), pp. 1-18.

Fowler V. Harper, *Justice Rutledge and the Bright Constellation* (Indianapolis, 1965) is the only complete biography of Wiley Rutledge, and it focuses on his views regarding the Bill of Rights. John Paul Stevens, "Mr. Justice Rutledge," in Allison Dunham and Philip B. Kurland, eds., *Mr. Justice,* rev. and enl. (Chicago, 1964), pp. 319-344 emphasizes Rutledge's approach to cases and his decision-making and opinion-writing process. There are numerous law review articles on Rutledge. Among them, see the collection of essays on Rutledge's career and judicial views in *Iowa Law Review,* 35 (Summer, 1950), pp. 541-692, also printed in *Indiana Law Review,* 25 (Summer 1950), pp. 421-559. Landon G. Rockwell, "Justice Rutledge on Civil Liberties," *Yale Law Journal,* 59 (December, 1949), pp. 27-59 is a topically organized survey of Rutledge's stance in criminal rights and civil liberties cases. Lester E. Mosher studies several aspects of Rutledge's judicial views in "Mr. Justice Rutledge's Philosophy of Civil Rights," *New York University Law Review,* 24 (October, 1949), pp. 661-706; and "Mr. Justice Rutledge's Philosophy of the Commerce Clause," *New York University Law Review,* 27 (April, 1952), pp. 218-247. A brief statement by Rutledge can be found in his *A Declaration of Legal Faith* (Lawrence, Kans., 1947).

Three articles examine the opinions of John Paul Stevens as a circuit court judge in an attempt to determine how he will vote as a Supreme Court Justice. The most thorough is Kenneth Harmon et al., "The One Hundred and First Justice: An Analysis of the Opinions of Justice John Paul Stevens, Sitting as a Judge on the Seventh Circuit Court of Appeals," *Vanderbilt Law Review,* 29 (January, 1976), pp. 125-209. See also Francis X. Beytagh, Jr., "Mr. Justice Stevens and the Burger Court's Uncertain Trumpet," *Notre Dame Lawyer,* 51 (July, 1976), pp. 946-955, and Brandon Becker and Michael F. Walsh, "The Interpretation of Narrow Construction and Policy: Mr. Justice Stevens' Circuit Opinions," *San Diego Law Review,* 13 (July, 1976), pp. 899-930.

J. Francis Paschal, "Mr. Justice Stewart on the Court of Appeals," *Duke Law Journal* (Summer, 1959), pp. 325-340 reviews Potter Stewart's decisions while on the circuit bench. Daniel M. Berman, "Mr. Justice Stewart: A Preliminary Appraisal," *University of Cincinnati Law Review,* 28 (Fall, 1959), pp. 401-421 examines Stewart's first term on the Supreme Court. Helaine M. Barnett and Kenneth Levine, "Mr. Justice Potter Stewart," *New York University Law Review,* 40 (May, 1965), pp. 526-562 offers a good analysis of Stewart's views in the areas of First Amendment, procedural due process and federalism. Peter W. Lewis, "Justice Stewart and Fourth Amendment Probable Cause," *Loyola Law Review,* 22 (Summer, 1976), pp. 713-742 has a narrow focus, examining the Justice's stance in cases on probable cause for arrests and searches over the whole of his Court career. Stewart has given several speeches that provide some insight into his views on the role of the Court and on constitutional issues. See his "The Nine of Us: 'Guardians of the Constitution,'" *Florida Bar Journal,* 41 (October, 1967), pp. 1090-1097; "Robert H. Jackson's Influence on Federal-State Relationships," *Record of the Association of the Bar of the City of New York,* 23 (January, 1968), pp. 11-32; and, "'Or of the Press,'" *Hastings Law Journal,* 26 (January, 1975), pp. 631-637.

Alpheus T. Mason, *Harlan Fiske Stone: Pillar of the Law* (New York, 1956) is a complete biography of Stone and 20 years ago was a pathbreaking work in its use of Stone's personal papers to give a portrait of the inner workings of the Supreme Court. Samuel J. Konefsky, *Chief Justice Stone and the Supreme Court* (New York, 1945) is a topically organized discussion of Stone's work on the Court in several major areas of law. Noel T. Dowling et al., "Mr. Justice Stone and the Constitution," *Columbia Law Review,* 36 (March, 1936), pp. 351-381 surveys Stone's first 10 years on the Court and emphasizes economic issues. Noel T. Dowling "The Methods of Mr. Justice Stone in Constitutional Cases," *Columbia Law Review,* 41 (November, 1941), pp. 1160-1189 discusses Stone's view of the judicial function in constitutional cases. Allison Dunham, "Mr. Chief Justice Stone," in Dunham and Philip B Kurland, eds., *Mr. Justice,* rev. and enl. (Chicago, 1964), pp. 229-249 presents an overview of Stone's judicial career. The *Harvard Law Review,* 59 (October, 1946), pp. 1193-1236 contains several remembrances and tributes to the Justice and an article by Paul Freund on Stone and conflict of laws. A good collection of essays discussing Stone's views in several areas of law can be found in the *Columbia Law Review,* 46 (September, 1946), pp. 693-800. Stone's *Law and its Administration* (New York, 1915) is a collection of lectures given by Stone on various aspects of law. Among his writings and speeches while on the Court, see "Fifty Years' Work of the United States Supreme Court," *American Bar Association Journal,* 14 (August-September, 1928), pp. 428-436; "The Public Influence of the Bar," *Harvard Law Review,* 48 (November, 1934), pp. 1-14; and, "The Common Law in the United States," *Harvard Law Review,* 50 (November 1936), pp. 4-26.

"Fred M. Vinson," *Northwestern University Law Review,* 49 (March-April, 1954), pp. 1-75 presents a series of articles detailing Vinson's career before joining the Court and discussing his theory of constitutional government. John P. Frank, "Fred Vinson and the Chief Justiceship," *University of Chicago Law Review,* 21 (Winter, 1954), pp. 212-246 surveys Vinson's votes and opinions in different areas of law and evaluates the Chief Justice's overall performance on the Court. Irving F. Lefberg, "Chief Justice Vinson and the Politics of Desegregation," *Emory Law Journal,* 24 (Spring, 1975), pp. 243-312 seeks to explain the discrepancy between Vinson's liberal record in civil rights and his conservative stance on other issues.

On Earl Warren's career before his appointment to the Court, see Richard B. Harvey, *Earl Warren: Governor of California* (New York, 1969). There are two adequate biographies of Warren which include his years as Chief Justice; see John D. Weaver, *Warren: The Man, The Court, the Era* (London, 1968) and Leo Katcher, *Earl Warren: A Political Biography* (New York, 1967). *The Memoirs of Earl Warren* (Garden City, 1977) were published posthumuously. The book reviews all of Warren's life and, for the Supreme Court years, explains and defends some of the Warren Court's more controversial rulings. It also tells something of the Chief Justice's judicial philosophy and of life and work on the Court. Henry M. Christman, ed., *The Public Papers of Chief Justice Earl Warren* (New York, 1959) includes his speeches while governor and some early opinions and speeches while Chief Justice. There are tributes to and remembrances of Warren in *Harvard Law Review,* 83 (November, 1969), pp. 1-5; *California Law Review,* 58 (January, 1970), pp. 1-42; *American Bar Association Journal,* 60 (October, 1974), pp. 1228-1236; *Harvard Law Review,* 88 (November, 1974), pp. 1-12; *Yale Law Journal,* 84 (January 1975), pp. 405-412; and, *Hastings Constitutional Law Quarterly,* 2 (Winter, 1975), pp. 1-20. Writings by Warren include "The Bill of Rights and the Military," *New York University Law Review,* 37 (April 1962), pp. 181-203; "'All Men Are Created Equal,'" *The Record of the Association of the Bar of the City of New York,* 25 (June, 1970), pp. 351-364; "The Notre Dame Law School Civil Rights Lectures," *Notre Dame Lawyer,* 48 (October 1972), pp. 14-48; and, *A Republic, If You Can Keep It* (New York, 1972).

There are very few sources on Byron White. Dennis L. Thompson, "The Kennedy Court: Left and Right of Center," *Western Political Quarterly*, 26 (June, 1973), pp. 263-279 has information on White's votes and opinions in the 1961-1964 terms of the Court. Lance Liebman, "Swing Man on the Supreme Court," *New York Times Magazine* (October 8, 1972), pp. 16-17+, focuses on the 1971-72 term of the Court but contains a general discussion of White's approach to constitutional issues.

Daniel M. Berman, "Mr. Justice Whittaker: A Preliminary Appraisal," *Missouri Law Review*, 24 (January 1959), pp. 1-15 examines Charles Whittaker's record in several fields of law while a district court judge and during his first two terms on the Supreme Court. "Mr. Justice Whittaker," *Texas Law Review*, 40 (June, 1962), pp. 742-750 is a collection of tributes from fellow justices and others on Whittaker's retirement from the Court.

THE COURT

A good text on constitutional history is Alfred H. Kelly and Winfred A. Harbison, *The American Constitution: Its Origins and Development,* 4th ed. (New York, 1970). Useful general histories of the Supreme Court include Robert G. McCloskey, *The American Supreme Court* (Chicago, 1960); Leo Pfeffer, *This Honorable Court* (Boston, 1965); and Alpheus T. Mason and William M. Beaney, *The Supreme Court in a Free Society* (New York, 1968). Robert J. Steamer, *The Supreme Court in Crisis* (Amherst, 1971) is a history of the Court that focuses on its conflicts with Congress and the President. Paul L. Murphy, *The Constitution in Crisis Times, 1918-1969* (New York, 1972) is a good source on the Supreme Court in this century. Other studies focusing on recent Court history include Robert G. McCloskey, *The Modern Supreme Court* (Cambridge, Mass., 1972); Alpheus T. Mason, *The Supreme Court from Taft to Warren,* rev. and enl. (Baton Rouge, 1968); and, William F. Swindler, *Court and Constitution in the Twentieth Century: The New Legality, 1932-1968* (Indianapolis, 1970). Archibald Cox, *The Role of the Supreme Court in American Government* (New York, 1976) focuses on recent Court trends in the area of liberty and equality.

Since 1949 the *Harvard Law Review* has presented in every fall issue a discussion and analysis of the work of the preceding Court term. The *American Political Science Review* had a similar annual review of the Court's constitutional decisions up through the 1959-60 Court term. *The Supreme Court Review,* ed. Philip B. Kurland (Chicago, 1960-   ) is an excellent annual publication containing articles on recent Court decisions and trends. Law reviews are often the best source of material on constitutional history, current legal issues and Court cases. The *Index to Legal Periodicals* allows easy location of articles on a particular topic. Some of the best law review articles have been collected in Association of American Law Schools, *Selected Essays on Constitutional Law, 1938-1962* (St. Paul, 1963). Stephen M. Millett, *A Selected Bibliography of American Constitutional History* (Santa Barbara, 1975) is a useful starting point for locating sources on constitutional law and history.

C. Herman Pritchett, *Civil Liberties and the Vinson Court* (Chicago, 1954) is the best single source on the Vinson Court. Walter F. Murphy, *Congress and the Court (Chicago, 1962)* and C. Herman Pritchett, *Congress versus the Supreme Court, 1975-1960* (Minneapolis, 1961) have good discussions of the Warren Court's decisions in the 1950s. The best works on the Warren Court are Alexander M. Bickel, *The Supreme Court and the Idea of Progress* (New York,

1970); Archibald Cox, *The Warren Court* (Cambridge, Mass., 1968); Philip B. Kurland, *Politics, the Constitution and the Warren Court* (Chicago, 1970); and, Richard H. Sayler et al., eds., *The Warren Court* (New York, 1969). Also useful are Alexander M. Bickel, *Politics and the Warren Court* (New York, 1965) and G. Theodore Mitau, *Decade of Decision, 1954-1964* (New York, 1967). Adam C. Breckenridge, *Congress Against the Court* (Lincoln, Neb., 1970) studies the congressional response to the major Warren Court criminal justice decisions of the 1950s and 1960s. Clifford M. Lytle, *The Warren Court and Its Critics* (Tucson, 1968) examines various critics of the Court during the period from 1954 to 1961. Raoul Berger, *Government by Judiciary* (Cambridge, Mass., 1977) looks at the Court's recent use of the 14th Amendment in various fields and discusses both Warren and Burger Court rulings.

Richard Y. Funston, *Constitutional Counterrevoltion?* (New York, 1977) examines continuities and discontinuities between the Warren and Burger Courts. James F. Simon, *In His Own Image: The Supreme Court in Richard Nixon's America* (New York, 1973) is a balanced assesment of the Burger Court through the 1971-72 term. Philip B. Kurland analyzed the first three terms of the Burger Court in detail in articles in *The Supreme Court Review* for 1970, 1971 and 1972. Articles giving an overview and assessment of the Burger Court's work include William F. Swindler, "The Court, the Constitution and Chief Justice Burger," *Vanderbilt Law Review*, 27 (April, 1974), pp. 443-474; "The Burger Court: New Directions in Judicial Policy-Making," *Emory Law Journal*, 23 (Summer, 1974), pp. 643-779; "The Burger Court and the Constitution," *Columbia Journal of Law and Social Problems*, 11 (Fall 1974), pp. 35-71; and Henry J. Abraham, "Some Observations on the Burger Court's Record on Civil Rights and Liberties," *Notre Dame Lawyer*, 52 (October 1976), pp. 77-86 and, A.E. Dick Howard, "From Warren to Burger: Activism and Restraint," *Wilson Quarterly* (Spring 1977), pp. 109-120

Charles A. Miller, *The Supreme Court and the Uses of History* (Cambridge, Mass., 1969) and Paul L. Rosen, *The Supreme Court and Social Science* (Urbana, Ill., 1972) examine the Court's use of historical and social science materials in constitutional adjudication. For a discussion of the impact of Supreme Court decisions in practice, see Richard M. Johnson, *The Dynamics of Compliance* (Evanston, Ill., 1967); David H. Everson, ed., *The Supreme Court as Policy-Maker* (Carbondale, Ill., 1968); Theodore L. Becker, ed., *The Impact of Supreme Court Decisions* (New York, 1969); and, Stephen Wasby, *The Impact of the United States Supreme Court* (Homewood, Ill., 1970).

Some useful specialized studies that do not fall into the categories below include Paul R. Benson, *The Supreme Court and the Commerce Clause, 1937-1970* (New York, 1970); Robert G. Scigliano, *The Supreme Court and the Presidency,* (New York, 1971); and, Martin M. Shapiro, *The Supreme Court and Administrative Agencies* (New York, 1968). A. Frank Reel, *The Case of General Yamashita* (Chicago, 1949) offers a history and analysis of this case. Maeva Marcus, *Truman and the Steel Seizure Case* (New York, 1977) is the definitive history of the *Youngstown* case. Kent M. Weeks, *Adam Clayton Powell and the Supreme Court* (New York, 1971) discusses the events leading up to Powell's Supreme Court case and the Court's decision. Leon Friedman, ed., *United States v. Nixon* (New York, 1974) is a collection of documents from the celebrated Nixon tapes case.

Listed below are useful works in some of the more important areas of constitutional law for the modern Supreme Court.

Civil Liberties and Civil Rights

Abernathy, Glenn. *Civil Liberties under the Constitution* (New York, 1968).

Abraham, Henry J. *Freedom and the Court: Civil Rights and Liberties in the United States*, 3d ed. (New York, 1977).

Barker, Lucius J. and Twiley W. Barker. *Freedoms, Courts, Politics: Studies in Civil Liberties* (Englewood Cliffs, 1965).

Dorsen, Norman. *Frontiers of Civil Liberties* (New York, 1968).

———. et al. *Political and Civil Rights in the United States,* 4th ed. (Boston, 1976).

———, ed. *The Rights of Americans* (New York, 1971).

Kauper, Paul G. *Civil Liberties and the Constitution* (Ann Arbor, 1962).

Konvitz, Milton R. *Expanding Liberties* (New York, 1966).

———. *Fundamental Liberties of a Free People* (Ithaca, 1957).

O'Neil, Robert M. *The Price of Dependency: Civil Liberties in the Welfare State* (New York, 1970).

Pious, Richard M., ed. *Civil Rights and Liberties in the 1970s* (New York, 1973).

Wasby, Stephen L., ed. *Civil Liberties: Policy and Policy Making* (Lexington, Mass., 1976).

Wirt, Frederick M. and Willis D. Hawley, eds. *New Dimensions of Freedom in America* (San Francisco, 1969).

Free Expression and Association

Abernathy, Glenn. *The Right of Assembly and Association* (Columbia, S.C., 1961).

Berns, Walter. *Freedom, Virtue and the First Amendment* (Chicago, 1957).

Bosmajian, Haig A., ed. *The Principles and Practice of Freedom of Speech* (Boston, 1971).

Cord, Robert L. *Protest, Dissent and the Supreme Court* (Cambridge, Mass., 1971).

Emerson, Thomas I. *The System of Freedom of Expression* (New York, 1970).

Fellman, David. *The Constitutional Right of Association* (Chicago, 1963).

———. ed. *The Supreme Court and Education,* rev. and enl. (New York, 1969).

Horn, Robert A. *Groups and the Constitution* (Stanford, 1956).

Hudgins, H.C., Jr., *The Warren Court and the Public Schools* (Danville, Ill., 1970) includes a section on academic freedom.

Hudon, Edward G. *Freedom of Speech and Press in America* (Washington, 1963).

Kalven, Harry. *The Negro and the First Amendment* (Columbus, Ohio, 1965).

Krislov, Samuel. *The Supreme Court and Political Freedom* (New York, 1968).

Kurland, Philip B., ed. *Free Speech and Association: The Supreme Court and the First Amendment* (Chicago, 1975).

Rice, Charles E. *Freedom of Association* (New York, 1962).

Shapiro, Martin. *Freedom of Speech: The Supreme Court and Judicial Review* (Englewood Cliffs, 1966).

Wood, Virginia. *Due Process of Law, 1932-1949* (Baton Rouge, 1951) discusses due process in relation to free speech as well as criminal issues.

Loyalty-Security Issues

Barth, Alan. *Government by Investigation* (New York, 1955).

Beck, Carl. *Contempt of Congress* (New Orleans, 1957).

Bonsal, Dudley B. *The Federal Loyalty-Security Program* (New York, 1956).

Bontecou, Eleanor. *The Federal Loyalty-Security Program* (Ithaca, 1953).

Brown, Ralph S. *Loyalty and Security* (New Haven, 1958).

Carr, Robert K. *The House Committee on Un-American Activities, 1945-1950* (Ithaca, 1952).

Chase, Harold W. *Security and Liberty: The Problem of Native Communists, 1947-1955* (Garden City, 1955).

Fraenkel, Osmond K. *The Supreme Court and Civil Liberties*, 2d ed. (Dobbs Ferry, N.Y., 1963).

Gellhorn, Walter. *American Rights: The Constitution in Action* (New York 1960).

————. *Individual Freedom and Governmental Restraints* (New York, 1966).

————, ed. *The States and Subversion* (Ithaca, 1952).

Goodman, Walter. *The Committee* (New York, 1968) on the House Un-American Activities Committee.

Griswold, Erwin N. *The Fifth Amendment Today* (Cambridge, Mass., 1955).

Grodzins, Morton. *The Loyal and the Disloyal* (Chicago, 1956).

Hofstadter, Samuel H. *The Fifth Amendment and the Immunity Act of 1954* (New York, 1955).

Kelly, Alfred H., ed. *Foundations of Freedom* (New York, 1958).

Konvitz, Milton R. *Civil Rights in Immigration* (Ithaca, 1953).

Latham, Earl. *The Communist Controversy in Washington: From the New Deal to McCarthy* (Cambridge, Mass., 1966).

McGeary, M. Nelson. *The Development of Congressional Investigating Power* (New York, 1966).

Parrish, Michael E. "Cold War Justice: The Supreme Court and the Rosenbergs," *American Historical Review*, 82 (October, 1977), pp. 805-842.

Pritchett, C. Herman. *The Political Offender and the Warren Court* (Boston, 1958).

Rogge, O. John, *The First and the Fifth* (New York, 1960).

Schaar, John H. *Loyalty in America* (Berkeley, 1957).

Taylor, Telford. *The Grand Inquest: The Story of Congressional Investigations* (New York, 1955).

Freedom of the Press

Ashmore, Harry S. *Fear in the Air: Broadcasting and the First Amendment* (New York, 1973).

Barron, Jerome A. *Freedom of the Press for Whom?: The Right of Access to Mass Media* (Bloomington, 1973).

Clark, David G. and Earl R. Hutchison, eds. *Mass Media and the Law* (New York, 1970).

Devol, Kenneth S., ed. *Mass Media and the Supreme Court: The Legacy of the Warren Years* (New York, 1971).

Friendly, Alfred and Ronald L. Goldfarb. *Crime and Publicity: The Impact of News on the Administration of Justice* (New York, 1967).

Gillmor, Donald. *Free Press and Fair Trial* (Washington, 1966).

Grey, David L. *The Supreme Court and the News Media* (Evanston, Ill., 1968).

Hachten, William A. *The Supreme Court on Freedom of the Press* (Ames, Iowa, 1968).

Hudon, Edward G. *Freedom of Speech and Press in America* (Washington, 1963).

Lawhorne, Clifton O. *Defamation and Public Officials: The Evolving Law of Libel* (Carbondale, Ill., 1971).

Liston, Robert A. *The Right to Know: Censorship in America* (New York, 1973).

Lofton, John M. *Justice and the Press* (Boston, 1965).

Medina, Harold R. *Freedom of the Press and Fair Trial* (New York, 1967).

Nelson, Harold L., ed. *Freedom of the Press from Hamilton to the Warren Court* (Indianapolis, 1967).

Nelson, Harold L. and Dwight L. Teeter, Jr. *Law of Mass Communications: Freedom and Control of Print and Broadcast Media*, 5th ed. (Mineola, N.Y., 1969).

Pember, Don R. *Privacy and the Press: The Law, the Mass Media and the First Amendment* (Seattle, 1972).

Schmidt, Benno C., Jr. *Freedom of the Press vs. Public Access* (New York, 1976).

Twentieth Century Fund. Task Force on the Government and the Press. *Press Freedoms Under Pressure* (New York, 1972).

Ungar, Sanford J. *The Papers and the Papers: An Account of the Legal and Political Battle over the Pentagon Papers* (New York, 1972).

Obscenity and Censorship

Bosmajian, Haig A., ed. *Obscenity and Freedom of Expression* (New York, 1975).

Carmen, Ira H. *Movies, Censorship and the Law* (Ann Arbor, 1966).

Clor, Harry M. *Obscenity and Public Morality: Censorship in a Liberal Society* (Chicago, 1969).

DeGrazia, Edward. *Censorship Landmarks* (New York, 1969).

Ernst, Morris L. and Alan U. Schwartz. *Censorship: The Search for the Obscene* (New York, 1964).

Haney, Robert W. *Comstockery in America* (Boston, 1960).

Kuh, Richard H. *Foolish Figleaves? Pornography in—and Out of—Court* (New York, 1967).

Lewis, Felice F. *Literature, Obscenity and Law* (Carbondale, Ill., 1976).

Liston, Robert A. *The Right to Know: Censorship in America* (New York, 1973).

Paul, James C.N. and Murray L. Schwartz, *Federal Censorship: Obscenity in the Mail* (Glencoe, Ill., 1961).

Randall, Richard S. *Censorship of the Movies* (Madison, Wisc., 1968).

Rembar, Charles. *The End of Obscenity* (New York, 1968).

Schauer, Frederick F. *The Law of Obscenity* (Washington, 1976).

Sharp, Donald B., ed. *Commentaries on Obscenity* (Metuchen, N.J., 1970).

Sunderland, Lane V. *Obscenity: The Court, the Congress and the President's Commission* (Washington, 1974).

U.S. Commission on Obscenity and Pornography. *Report* (Washington, 1970).

Religion

Boles, Donald E. *The Bible, Religion and the Public Schools,* 3d ed. (Ames, Iowa, 1965).

Fellman, David. *Religion in American Public Law* (Boston, 1965).

Howe, Mark DeWolfe. *The Garden and the Wilderness: Religion and Government in American Constitutional History* (Chicago, 1965).

Hudgins, H.C. *The Warren Court and the Public Schools* (Danville, Ill., 1970).

Katz, Wilbur G. *Religion and American Constitutions* (Evanston, Ill., 1964).

Kauper, Paul G. *Religion and the Constitution* (Baton Rouge, 1964).

Konvitz, Milton R. *Religious Liberty and Conscience: A Constitutional Inquiry* (New York, 1968).

Kurland, Philip B. *Religion and the Law of Church and State and the Supreme Court* (Chicago, 1962).

Laubach, John H. *School Prayers* (Washington, 1969).

Morgan, Richard E. *The Supreme Court and Religion* (New York, 1972).

Muir, William K. *Prayer in the Public Schools* (Chicago, 1967).

Oaks, Dallin H., ed. *The Wall Between Church and State* (Chicago, 1963).

Pfeffer, Leo. *Church, State and Freedom,* rev. ed. (Boston, 1967).

———. *God, Caesar and the Constitution: The Court as Referee of Church-State Confrontations* (Boston, 1975).

Regan, Richard J. *Private Conscience and Public Law: The American Experience* (New York, 1972).

Sorauf, Francis J. *The Wall of Separation: The Constitutional Politics of Church and State* (Princeton, 1976).

Smith, Elwyn A. *Religious Liberty in the United States* (Philadelphia, 1972)

Reapportionment and the Electoral Process

Baker, Gordon E. *The Reapportionment Revolution* (New York, 1967).

Ball, Howard. *The Warren Court's Conceptions of Democracy* (Rutherford, N.J., 1971).

Claude, Richard. *The Supreme Court and the Electoral Process* (Baltimore, 1970).

Cortner, Richard. *The Apportionment Cases* (Knoxville, 1970).

Dixon, Robert G., Jr. *Democratic Representation: Reapportionment in Law and Politics* (New York, 1968).

Elliott, Ward E.Y. *The Rise of Guardian Democracy: The Supreme Court's Role in Voting Rights Disputes, 1845-1969* (Cambridge, Mass., 1974).

Goldwin, Robert A., ed. *Representation and Misrepresentation: Legislative Reapportionment in Theory and Practice* (Chicago, 1968).

Graham, Gene S. *One Man, One Vote: Baker v. Carr and the American Levellers* (Boston, 1972).

Hacker, Andrew. *Congressional Districting: The Issue of Equal Representation*, Rev. ed. (Washington, 1964).

Hanson, Royce. *The Political Thicket: Reapportionment and Constitutional Democracy* (Englewood Cliffs, N.J., 1966).

Lee, Calvin B.T. *One Man, One Vote: WMCA and the Struggle for Equal Representation* (New York, 1967).

McKay, Robert B. *Reapportionment: The Law and Politics of Equal Representation* (New York, 1965).

Polsby, Nelson W., ed. *Reapportionment in the 1970s* (Berkeley, 1971).

Schubert, Glendon A., ed. *Reapportionment* (New York, 1965).

Civil Rights

Aikin, Charles, ed. *The Negro Votes* (San Francisco, 1962).

Bardolph, Richard, ed. *The Civil Rights Record: Black Americans and the Law, 1849-1970* (New York, 1970).

Bartley, Numan V. *The Rise of Massive Resistance* (Baton Rouge, 1969).

Bell, Derrick A., Jr. *Race, Racism and American Law* (Boston, 1973).

Berger, Morroe. *Equality by Statute*, Rev. ed. (Garden City, 1967).

Blaustein, Albert P. and Robert L. Zangrando, eds. *Civil Rights and the American Negro: A Documentary History* (New York, 1968).

Blaustein, Albert P. and Clarence C. Ferguson, Jr. *Desegregation and the Law*, 2d ed. (New York, 1962).

Bolner, James and Robert Shanley. *Busing: The Political and Judicial Process* (New York, 1974).

Cox, Archibald, et al. *Civil Rights, the Constitution and the Courts* (Cambridge, Mass., 1967).

Dionisopoulos, P.A. *Rebellion, Racism and Representation: The Adam Clayton Powell Case and Its Antecedents* (DeKalb, Ill., 1971).

Dorsen, Norman, ed. *Discrimination and Civil Rights* (Boston, 1969).

Friedman, Leon, ed. *Argument: The Complete Oral Argument Before the Supreme Court in Brown v. Board of Education, 1952-1955* (New York, 1969).

Greenberg, Jack. *Race Relations and American Law* (New York, 1959).

Harris, Robert J. *The Quest for Equality: The Constitution, Congress, and the Supreme Court* (Baton Rouge, 1960).

Kalven, Harry, Jr. *The Negro and the First Amendment* (Columbus, Ohio, 1965).

King, Donald B. and Charles W. Quick, eds. *Legal Aspects of the Civil Rights Movement* (Detroit, 1965).

Kluger, Richard. *Simple Justice* (New York, 1975) is an excellent history of *Brown v. Board of Education*.

Konvitz, Milton R. *A Century of Civil Rights* (New York, 1961).

————. *The Constitution and Civil Rights* (New York, 1962).

Lawson, Stephen. *Black Ballots: Voting Rights in the South, 1944-1969* (New York, 1976).

Lewis, Anthony and the *New York Times*. *Portrait of a Decade* (New York, 1964).

McCord, John H., ed. *With All Deliberate Speed* (Urbana, Ill. 1969).

Miller, Loren. *The Petitioners* (Cleveland, 1966), is a history of Supreme Court rulings on the rights of blacks.

Muse, Benjamin. *The American Negro Revolution, 1963-1967* (Bloomington, Ind., 1968).

————. *Ten Years of Prelude: The Story of Integration Since the Supreme Court's 1954 Decision* (New York, 1964).

Paul, Arnold M., ed. *Black Americans and*

the Supreme Court Since Emancipation (New York, 1972).

Peltason, J.W. *Fifty-Eight Lonely Men* (Urbana, Ill., 1971) discusses Southern federal district judges and school desegregation.

Roche, John P. *The Quest for the Dream* (New York, 1963).

Schwartz, Bernard, ed. *The Fourteenth Amendment: Centennial Volume* (New York, 1970).

Sobel, Lester A., ed. *Civil Rights, 1960-1966* (New York, 1967).

Strong, Donald S. *Negroes, Ballots and Judges* (University, Ala., 1968).

Taper, Bernard. *Gomillion v. Lightfoot: The Tuskegee Gerrymander Case* (New York, 1963).

Tussman, Joseph, ed. *The Supreme Court on Racial Discrimination* (New York, 1963).

Vose, Clement E. *Caucasians Only* (Berkeley, 1959). a history of the restrictive covenant cases.

Wasby, Stephen L., et al. *Desegregation from Brown to Alexander: An Exploration of Supreme Court Strategies* (Carbondale, Ill., 1977).

Criminal Rights

Beaney, William M. *The Right to Counsel in American Courts* (Ann Arbor, 1955).

Casper, Jonathan D. *American Criminal Justice: The Defendant's Perspective* (Englewood Cliffs, 1972).

Chambliss, William J. *Crime and the Legal Process* (New York, 1969).

Clark, Leroy D. *The Grand Jury: The Use and Abuse of Political Power* (New York, 1975).

Dash, Samuel et al. *The Eavesdroppers* (New Brunswick, N.J., 1959).

Fellman, David. *The Defendant's Rights* (New York, 1958).

———. *The Defendant's Rights Today* (Madison, 1976).

Galloway, John, ed. *The Supreme Court and the Rights of the Accused* (New York, 1973).

Graham, Fred P. *The Due Process Revo-*

lution: *The Warren Court's Impact on Criminal Law* (New York, 1970).

———. *The Self-Inflicted Wound* (New York, 1970).

Griswold, Erwin N. *The Fifth Amendment Today* (Cambridge, Mass., 1955).

Harris, Richard. *The Fear of Crime* (New York, 1969).

Kamisar, Yale et al. *Criminal Justice in Our Time* (Charlottesville, 1965).

LaFave, Wayne R. *Arrest* (Boston, 1965).

Landynski, Jacob W. *Search and Seizure and the Supreme Court* (Baltimore, 1966).

Levy, Leonard W. *Against the Law: The Nixon Court and Criminal Justice* (New York, 1974).

Lewis, Anthony. *Gideon's Trumpet* (New York, 1964) is a history of *Gideon v. Wainwright.*

Long, Edward V. *The Intruders: The Invasion of Privacy by Government and Industry* (New York, 1966).

Medalie, Richard J. *From Escobedo to Miranda* (Washington, 1966).

Meltsner, Michael. *Cruel and Unusual: The Supreme Court and Capital Punishment* (New York, 1973).

Miller, Leonard G. *Double Jeopardy and the Federal System* (Chicago, 1968).

Milner, Neil. *The Court and Local Law Enforcement: The Impact of Miranda* (Beverly Hills, 1971).

Oaks, Dallin H. and Warren Lehman. *A Criminal Justice System and the Indigent: A Study of Chicago and Cook County* (Chicago, 1968).

Paulsen, Monrad G. and Charles H. Whitebread. *Juvenile Law and Procedure,* (Reno, 1974).

Pennock, J. Roland and John W. Chapman, eds. *Due Process* (New York, 1977).

Radzinowicz, Leon and Marvin E. Wolfgang, eds. *Crime and Justice,* 3 vols. (New York, 1971).

Rosenberg, Jerry M. *The Death of Privacy* (New York, 1969).

Schaefer, Walter V. *The Suspect and Society* (Evanston, Ill., 1967).

Sigler, Jay A. *Double Jeopardy: The Development of a Legal and Social Policy* (Ithaca, 1969).

Skolnick, Jerome H. *Justice without Trial: Law Enforcement in Democratic Society* (New York, 1966).

Stephens, Otis. *The Supreme Court and Confessions of Guilt* (Knoxville, 1973).

Taylor, Telford. *Two Studies in Constitutional Interpretation* (Columbus Ohio, 1968)—one section deals with search and seizure; the other, with fair trial and free press problems.

Trebach, Arnold S. *The Rationing of Justice: Constitutional Rights and the Criminal Process* (New Brunswick, N.J., 1964).

Westin, Alan F. *Privacy and Freedom* (New York, 1967).

Weston, Paul B. and Kenneth M. Wells. *The Administration of Justice* (Englewood Cliffs, N.J., 1967).

Wood, Virginia. *Due Process of Law, 1932-1949* (Baton Rouge, 1951).

Cases Cited

A

Abbate v. U.S.—40, 57, 140

Abington School District v. Schempp—58, 66, 95, 140, 158

Adams v. Williams—35, 68, 128, 143, 162

Adamson v. California—25, 64, 80, 115, 124, 131

Adderley v. Florida—29, 59, 67, 74, 142, 156

Adler v. Board of Education—56, 64, 111

Afroyim v. Rusk—67

Albertson v. Subversive Activities Control Board—66, 95

Alderman v. U.S.—163

Alexander v. Holmes County Board of Education—96, 107

Almeida-Sanchez. v. U.S.—108

Amalgamated Food Employees Union v. Logan Valley Plaza—108, 142

American Communications Association v. Douds—26, 51, 102, 123, 149

American Power & Light Co. v. Securities and Exchange Commission—116

American Tobacco Co. v. U.S.—52

Anderson v. Mt. Clemens Pottery Co.—52

Andreson v. Maryland—35

Apodaca v. Oregon—42, 47, 68, 108, 163

Aptheker v. Secretary of State—28, 66, 89, 95, 162

Argersinger v. Hamlin—47, 68, 108, 119

Arnett v. Kennedy—43, 69, 127

Ashcraft v. Tennessee—124

Ashe v. Swenson—35

Askew v. American Waterways Operators, Inc.—69

Avent v. North Carolina—156

Avery v. Midland County—96, 156, 162

B

Baggett v. Bullitt—57, 89, 157

Baird v. State Bar of Arizona—31, 164

Baker v. Carr—28, 40, 58, 66, 82, 96, 141, 157

Baldwin v. New York—68

Baltimore & Ohio Railroad Co. v. U.S.—74

Bantam Books, Inc. v. Sullivan—29, 40

Barenblatt v. U.S.—26, 40, 80, 94, 139, 155, 167

Barrows v. Jackson—52, 112, 150

Barsky v. Board of Regents—155

Bartkus v. Illinois—57, 81, 140, 168

Bates v. City of Little Rock—139

Beal v. Doe—37

Beauharnais v. Illinois—79, 112, 124

Beilan v. Board of Education—39, 51, 65, 80, 167

Bell v. Maryland—29, 88, 96

Bell v. Burson—43

Benton v. Maryland—28, 31, 96, 108, 158

Berger v. New York—30, 58

Betts v. Brady—25, 64, 73, 116

Bigelow v. Virginia—36

Bishop v. Wood—43, 136

Bivens v. Six Unknown Named Agents—47

Black v. U.S.—106

Blocker v. U.S.—47

Board of Education v. Allen—163

Bob-Lo Excursion Co. v. Michigan—103, 132, 150

Boddie v. Connecticut—43, 96

Bolling v. Sharpe—27, 52, 59, 81, 93, 103, 112, 124, 151, 154

Bond v. Floyd—157

Boynton v. Virginia—27, 106

Braden v. U.S.—57, 65, 140, 156, 167

205

Index

Index

A

B

C

D

E

F

G

H

MEN OF THE SUPREME COURT: Profiles of the Justices